THE

HAITIAN REVOLUTION

THE

HAITIAN

REVOLUTION

1789-1804

By Thomas O. Ott

THE UNIVERSITY OF TENNESSEE PRESS

Copyright © 1973 by The University of Tennessee Press, Knoxville. All Rights
Reserved. Manufactured in the United States of America. First Edition.

Library of Congress Cataloging in Publication Data

Ott, Thomas O.   1938–
   The Haitian revolution, 1789–1804.

   Bibliography: p.
   1. Haiti—Revolution, 1791–1804. 2. Haiti—
History—To 1791. I. Title.
F1923.O87   972.94'03   72–85085
ISBN 0–87049–143–1

FOR MY DAD

Acknowledgments

In my search for scattered materials for this study, the following institutions were both useful and cooperative: University of Florida, University of South Carolina, Library of Congress, National Archives, Peabody Institute, University of Tennessee, South Carolina Archives and Historical Society, Maryland Historical Society, Boston Public Library, New York Public Library, Essex Institute, Phillips Library, American Antiquarian Society, Pennsylvania Historical Society, Marine Historical Association, Henry E. Huntington Library, and The Institute of Jamaica. Of the many helpful librarians at those repositories, Laura Monti of the University of Florida Research Library went well beyond "the call of duty" in locating important manuscripts for me.

To three historians of the University of Tennessee—Dr. Roland E. Duncan, Dr. LeRoy P. Graf, and Dr. Ralph W. Haskins—I give special thanks for their advice, patience, and encouragement in the preparation of this study. I would also like to thank Dr. Jack D. Price of Florence State University, who read and criticized much of the manuscript. But to my wife, Margaret, I am especially indebted for aiding with the research, typing, and proofreading and for enduring my frustrations.

Preface

On the night of August 22, 1791, thousands of small illuminated specks, giving the appearance of a Milky Way, could be seen on the otherwise darkened Plaine du Nord. With a torch in one hand and a knife in the other, the slave of Saint-Domingue was destroying a society which had oppressed him for nearly one hundred years. From 1789 to 1791 whites and mulattoes in the colony had struggled to gain the guarantees of the French Revolution, while remaining oblivious to seething discontent among their slaves. But the agonies of the night of August 22 were only the beginning of a great socioeconomic explosion lasting almost thirteen years. During that period Saint-Domingue, the richest of the eighteenth-century Caribbean colonies, emerged as Haiti, the most impoverished nation in the Americas.

In tracing the course of that rather complex era, one notices a number of themes: the influence of the French Revolution, the abolition of slavery, the fear of spreading revolution among other slave societies, the intervention of foreign powers, and the rise of the first black republic in the Western Hemisphere. Yet the major theme of the period was not an event but a man—Toussaint Louverture (not L'Ouverture). Leaving a rather idyllic environment at Bréda Plantation on the Plaine du Nord, Toussaint joined the rebels and rose from obscurity to prominence within an astonishingly short time span. With the dexterity of a tightrope walker and the finesse of a fencer, Toussaint had outplayed all but one of his rivals for power by mid-1800. The one who remained, however, was Napoleon Bonaparte. In the final contest between these two men, Toussaint, dying a tragic death in a dank French prison, would see his vision of Haitian independence near oblivion.

ix

But the fading dream was rescued by Jean Jacques Dessalines, Toussaint's fierce lieutenant, and by the Haitian people themselves.

Within the Haitian Revolution, one can find the essentials of other great upheavals: political cycles, brutalities, rivalries, and lost hopes. Yet unlike the other upheavals the Haitian Revolution had the distinction of proving that the Negro was, after all, a man—an animal noted for his stupidity and intelligence, his fiendishness and humanity, his cowardice and bravery.

T. O. O.

Florence, Alabama
December 5, 1972

Contents

Acknowledgments   *page* vii

Preface   *page* ix

One.   Before the Revolution: Saint-Domingue to 1789   *page* 3

Two.   The Road to Revolution, 1789–1791   *page* 28

Three. Explosion and Confusion, 1791–1792   *page* 47

Four.   The White Collapse, 1792–1793   *page* 65

Five.   Toussaint and the British Invasion, 1793–1798   *page* 76

Six.   The Consolidation of Power, 1798–1801   *page* 100

Seven. Toussaint's New Order, 1797–1801   *page* 127

Eight. The French Invasion, 1801–1802   *page* 139

Nine.   The French Defeat, 1802–1804   *page* 170

Ten.   Conclusions and Legacy of Revolution   *page* 188

Bibliography   *page* 204

Index   *page* 225

Illustrations

Toussaint Louverture. The Bettmann Archive.
Frontispiece

Toussaint as commander in chief, *following page* 50

Toussaint requests English officers to leave the island

Battle of Ravin-à-Couleuvre, *following page* 82

Capture of Toussaint

MAPS 1. The West Indies and its Neighbors, *page* 8

2. Saint-Domingue in 1789, *page* 34

3. Spanish and British Offensives, 1793–94, *page* 88

4. Toussaint's Spring Offensive, 1798, *page* 102

5. The "War of Knives": Rigaud's Invasion, 1799, *page* 113

6. Invasion Routes of Leclerc, 1802, *page* 156

THE

HAITIAN REVOLUTION

CHAPTER ONE

Before the Revolution:
Saint-Domingue to 1789

Leaving Cuba after failing in his search for riches, Columbus set sail for Great Inagua (Barbeque) early in December 1492. There, if his Indian guides were correct, he would find wealth.[1] But on the way Columbus sighted the shoreline of a strange island; that island was Hispaniola, which the natives called Haiti, a term meaning mountainous.[2] Disembarking at the future location of Port-de-Paix on Hispaniola's northwestern coast, Columbus beheld a beautiful river valley lined with green wooded mountains and swaying palms; he called it Paradise Valley.[3] He was not the only traveler dazzled by the beauty of western Hispaniola. François Alexandre Stanislaus, Baron de Wimpffen, landing at Jacmel nearly three hundred years later, exclaimed, "What a country!"[4]

There are three major geographical and administrative divisions of Haiti. North Province (Nord), separated from West Province by an east-west mountain chain, is the most isolated and prosperous of the three. Le Cap-Haitien, known as Le Cap François in colonial times, is its urban center and one of the best natural ports in Haiti. In the interior of North Province the Plaine du Nord forms a rich agricultural area. The trade winds blow across the northern slopes of the mountains and deposit their moisture on the plain, while much of the remainder of Haiti is semiarid. West Province (Ouest), the largest of the three divisions, has Port-au-Prince as its chief port, and the Artibonite Valley and Plaine du Cul-de-Sac are its most important agricultural centers. Mountains, however, border West Province to the north and west and prevent an adequate rainfall. Thus the colonial prosperity of this province depended on irrigation, which is still essential. South Province

3

(Sud) is much like West Province and has its main port at Les Cayes.[5]

Besides mountains, the three provinces share two other natural characteristics—climate and earthquakes. Earthquakes occurred frequently enough to force the inhabitants to build mostly one-story houses.[6] The torrid heat and humidity cause extreme human hardship, as Baron de Wimpffen pointed out: "Europeans have . . . no small difficulty to accustom themselves to the climate: severe labour would infallibly destroy them."[7] Malaria and yellow fever are common in this type of climate, and the mosquito, their carrier, seems to single out the newcomer for attack. "This distinction, whatever the motive may be," according to Baron de Wimpffen, "is extremely troublesome to those who are honoured with it, and who cannot, with all their efforts, escape from the sting of the perfidious animal."[8] April to September, the mosquito's most active period in Haiti, was recognized as the malarial season during colonial times.

After Columbus' discovery of Hispaniola, *conquistadores* arrived in search of riches, and the island became Spain's earliest center of empire. Interest in the colony waned, however, as the *conquistadores* depleted the mineral resources and found New Spain and Peru more lucrative areas of conquest. The Spanish therefore deserted most of the western part of Hispaniola for the eastern section, where a few sparse mineral deposits remained. Another inducement to retreat occurred in 1553 when François Le Clerc, a French pirate, destroyed the little hamlet of Yaguana, later to become Port-au-Prince. By the end of the sixteenth century the only inhabitants on the western part of the island were the roving herds of cattle and swine, which had escaped the Spanish.[9]

Not everyone lost interest in western Hispaniola. Interlopers from the neighboring island of Tortuga (Tortue) came in search of a meat supply. These were the famous *boucaniers*, a name derived from the French *boucaner* ("to smoke"). The *boucaniers*, or buccaneers, were a cosmopolitan group with the French in predominance. France only gradually established control over the area, largely through the work of one man, Bertrand d'Ogeron, who became governor of Tortuga in 1665.[10]

Upon his arrival in western Hispaniola, Ogeron found the buccaneers living like savages and immediately set himself the task of organizing a colony. He was able to control such terrible buccaneers as Jean David Nau, forced some of the more disorderly inhabitants to move to Tortuga, encouraged families to settle in western Hispaniola, and developed several towns.[11] One of Ogeron's shrewdest moves was to import women from Paris to domesticate his buccaneers. Baron de Wimpffen claimed that they were "prostitutes from the hospitals, abandoned wretches raked up from the mud of the capital."[12] By 1675, the year of Ogeron's death, the buccaneers were rapidly becoming planters, and western Hispaniola had clearly become the French colony of Saint-Domingue. By the end of the century Ogeron's work was confirmed and completed when Spain officially recognized French Saint-Domingue in the Treaty of Ryswick (1697) and when Louis XIV forced the remaining buccaneers to accept slaves rather than booty as payment for a raid on Cartagena.[13]

By the eighteenth century France had fully developed an administrative system for Saint-Domingue. The most important official was the minister of marine in France, who represented the crown and appointed colonial officials and whose decrees had the force of law. Next in line came the governor, who commanded the military and represented the crown in the colony. He and the intendant, who had mostly civil functions, especially the administration of public finance, presided jointly over the courts of law, and both had some powers of appointment.[14] Potentially the two administrators could have acted tyrannically, but often they were at cross purposes, and their tenure was usually short. According to one observer, "Scarcely has a governor . . . time to acquire the local knowledge which ought to form the basis of his administration, ere he sees himself replaced by a successor still more a novice than himself."[15]

Despite their short tenure and cross purposes, the governor and the intendant monopolized political and economic power in Saint-Domingue. The planter had no real political strength, although in 1787 the crown established two superior councils in the colony and permitted more local control. But even the superior councils were only "rubber stamps" of the governor and the intendant, and local control applied mainly to criminal court decisions involving slaves. The economy was more difficult to control, but enterprising governors and intendants could always find a way. Typical were the Marquis de Vaudreuil and Jean-Baptiste Laporte-Lalanne, governor and intendant respectively in the late 1750s, who, for a price of course, favored two rings of merchants to the exclusion of others.[16] As in the *peninsular*-creole quarrel in the Spanish colonies, bureaucratic discrimination against white colonials constituted a source of tension and struggle.

The real importance of Saint-Domingue, both for France and for other nations, was economic. Yet in the seventeenth century there were very few indications of Saint-Domingue's future economic worth. Martinique was considerably more valuable. During that century the small proprietorship represented the characteristic economic unit, while the labor supply mainly consisted of white indentured servants and some Negro slaves. But the eighteenth century brought change, partly because of the economic decline of the British West Indies after 1763, a similar decline in Martinique and Guadeloupe, and the importation of large numbers of slaves.[17] The plantation and slave labor became basic to the economy of Saint-Domingue, which reached its "golden age" from 1763 to 1791. On the eve of the Haitian Revolution, Saint-Domingue had 655 sugar plantations, 1,962 coffee plantations, and 398 cotton and indigo plantations.[18] There were other indications of prosperity: by 1787 the colony was producing 131,000,000 pounds of sugar and 70,000 pounds of indigo, and in 1788 it legally imported 29,506 slaves. Ludwell Lee Montague estimated that even as early as 1783 Saint-Domingue was contributing two-thirds of the French tropical produce, and, of greater importance, the French colony comprised one-third of the foreign trade of France. Another evaluation, made in 1787, placed the annual value of this legal commerce, which employed 471 French ships (157 from Bordeaux), at 300,000,000 livres.[19] No one knows the total value of the illicit commerce for this or any year, but it was undoubtedly large.

Economic prosperity was also evident in various scenes. At Le Cap François, Samuel Perkins, an American observer, noted that the harbor for "three quarters of a mile was filled with merchandise being shipped; all was bustle, noise, and cheerful labor."[20] Even the overall appearance of Le Cap François itself reflected prosperity. Bryan Edwards, the British observer-historian, stated that it "would have ranked among the cities of the second class in any part of Europe for beauty and regularity."[21] By 1791 the city had a population of about fifty thousand people, three-fourths of them slaves.[22] On the surrounding Plaine du Nord, economic activity was as intense as in Le Cap François. As one French creole noted, "the many buildings and the blazing furnaces, the variety of crops and their wise supervision, the dutiful slaves working in cadence, the rustic wagon creaking beneath the heavy load, all attest to abundance and peace."[23]

But Saint-Domingue's great prosperity belonged primarily to the mother country, at least according to Jean-Baptiste Colbert's economic theories, collectively known as the Exclusive. In the theory of the Exclusive, the colonies should be a source of profit only for France, and their products should not compete with home industry. Thus France's exclusion of rum and molasses to protect her wine industry, the activities of profiteering middlemen, the inability of the French market to absorb colonial products, and various other commercial disabilities often galled the Saint-Domingue colonist.[24]

There was, however, a wide gulf between the theory of the Exclusive and actual practice. As the eighteenth century progressed, the Saint-Domingue colonist began to expand his trade relations, often illegally, to make up for deficiencies in French commerce. In this endeavor he primarily depended upon the British continental colonies, an arrangement which continued after America's independence. And the United States, especially New England, continued to use Saint-Domingue as a source of cheap molasses and as a market for refuse fish—a food needed for the slaves, but one which the French could not adequately supply. Other products came from the United States, such as iron, flour, cattle, and house frames.[25] According to Baron de Wimpffen, "the number of foreign ships, principally American, which in 1788 assisted in furnishing Saint-Domingo with provisions, was considerable."[26] The desire of the United States to maintain this rich trade was a primary consideration in its policy toward the Haitian Revolution. But America was not the only country interested in Saint-Domingue. "Spanish barks would put into the little bays and creeks near Cape

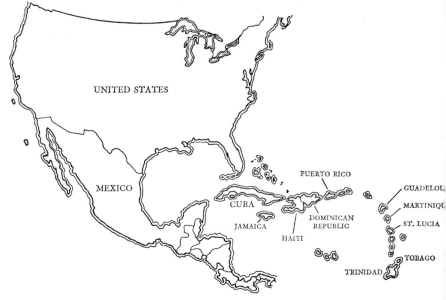

UNITED STATES

MEXICO

PUERTO RICO

CUBA

JAMAICA

DOMINICAN
REPUBLIC

HAITI

GUADELOU

MARTINIQU

ST. LUCIA

TOBAGO

TRINIDAD

THE WEST INDIES AND ITS NEIGHBORS

François, and carry on their clandestine commerce."[27] Even in the purchase of slaves, the colonist by the mid-eighteenth century, as demand exceeded supply, looked beyond France. Great Britain, the leader of the slave trade, the United States, and perhaps others met this need.[28]

The French government could not ignore the economic realities of Saint-Domingue and of the other French West Indian colonies. Consequently the Exclusive underwent liberal modifications, much like the Bourbon Reforms of the Spanish Empire. Between 1763 and 1767, France, in hopes of meeting the planters' needs, established free ports at Martinique, Guadeloupe, Saint Lucia, and at Saint-Domingue's Môle Saint Nicolas. In 1783–84 foreign ships could enter additional ports in Saint-Domingue and in the French Windward Islands. The "lion's share" of this trade went to the United States. Le Comte Duchillau, governor of Saint-Domingue until early 1790, wanted to remove all restraints on American shipping, but the French merchants successfully opposed him.[29]

Thus on the eve of the French Revolution, the creole merchants and planters, much like the *porteños* and other groups in Spanish America twenty years later, had a taste of free trade but wanted more.

The social structure of Saint-Domingue was characterized by a caste system of three divisions: the whites, the *gens de couleur*, and the slaves. In 1787 there was a great statistical imbalance among the three castes. The white population stood at 24,000, the *gens de couleur* at 20,000, and the rapidly increasing slaves at 408,-000.[30] It was this caste system which made Saint-Domingue especially explosive at the time of the French Revolution.

At the apex of the white caste was the European-born bureaucrat. He, like the Spanish *peninsular*, monopolized the best administrative positions and seemed primarily intent upon amassing a quick fortune and returning to France. His arrogance was particularly upsetting to the white planter, or *grand blanc*.[31] Often the competition between bureaucrat and *grand blanc* was strongest among their wives, and while the ladies engaged in wars of vanity, their husbands frequently deserted them for the more sensuous mulattresses. According to Baron de Wimpffen:

> The European ladies seldom see the creoles but to ridicule them, especially when they have not been educated in France; and these, in their turn, see little in the others but creatures of affectation and folly; while the men, who seldom find, and above all in the former, the degree of sensibility on which the mulatto ladies pique themselves, leave both to lament . . . the depravity of the tastes of our sex.[32]

The *grands blancs*, socially and economically resembling the affluent Spanish American creoles, were the planters, great merchants, and wealthy maritime agents. Many were descendants of the early buccaneers, but others represented the old French noble families of Chateauneuf, Boucicaut, de Vaudreils, and others. A typical *grand blanc* was Jean Pebarte, who owned a large coffee plantation near Port-au-Prince which employed a thousand slaves and could produce eighty thousand pounds of coffee annually. Often, as in the case of Augustin Du Bois Martin, he would have a town house in one of the larger cities, such as Port-au-Prince or Le Cap François.[33]

9

The overriding desire of this class was to make a fortune as fast as possible and then lavish it in the cultured ease of a Parisian life. This practice resulted in a high incidence of absentee ownership, which frequently meant rougher treatment for the slave because there was no one to protect him from the overseer.[34] Lieutenant Howard, a British observer, noticed that even when the *grands blancs* were present on their plantations:

> These men, almost always, made bad masters to their slaves and dependents; for it is from their labour that they must acquire their former degree of splendor, and every year that is spent accomplishing this is a year lost in the calculation of their happiness, the poor slaves belonging to their estates have no respite from work, no indulgence.[35]

The *grands blancs* were an indolent and indulgent class. The men liked their mulattresses, who made love not only a profession but an art. This preference is partly explained by the lack of white women in the colony, although marriage to a mulatto was out of the question.[36] According to Bryan Edwards, "No white man, who had the smallest pretension to character, would ever think of marriage with a Negro or mulatto woman: such a step would immediately have terminated in his disgrace and ruin."[37] The wives of the *grands blancs* were equally indulgent. One of their amusements was to be stretched out on a mat, "where their supreme delight is to have the soles of their feet tickled by a female slave."[38] At times, indulgence might evolve into extreme cruelty, as in a case pointed out by an American observer: a white woman caught her husband casting admiring glances at one of the household slaves, and when he left "she ordered one of her slaves to cut off the head of the unfortunate victim, which was immediately done."[39] Despite author C. L. R. James's assertions, however, there is no substantial proof that either the master or mistress made a normal practice of killing their slaves.[40]

Regardless of their shortcomings, the *grands blancs* had many charming qualities—one being their hospitality. Jean-Bernard Bossu, a French traveler in Saint-Domingue, related the story of a planter who visited the docks to invite wayfarers to his estate. Once this planter took two young men "to his home where they found a table set for twenty people with as many Negro servants to wait on them. One of the newcomers asked if they had been invited to a wedding reception and was astonished to learn that this was just an ordinary meal."[41]

White cultural development, imitative of France, was mainly the result of the efforts of the *grands blancs*. In Le Cap François, for example, there was a playhouse which could seat two thousand people; any mulattoes present sat in the third tier, segregated from the white audience. At Port-au-Prince the theater of M. Acquaire seated eight hundred persons. These theaters usually presented current French hits, such as the plays of Molière, Corneille, Racine, and Voltaire. Besides the theater, Le Cap François, the cultural center, had a Royal Society of the Arts and Sciences, headed by M. Gauché, a museum and botanical gardens, an Academy of Agriculture, several newspapers, and lodges of Freemasons. On the other hand, education was deficient in the colony, despite a few finishing academies, for one was expected to be educated in France. Furthermore, it might be noted that the culture of the *grands blancs*, closely attuned to France, acted as a vehicle for the transmission of revolutionary ideas to Saint-Domingue.[42]

The white middle and lower classes—plantation overseers, artisans, grocers, and city rabble—formed the *petits blancs*, the last group within the white caste. They disliked the *grands blancs*, whose affluence and position irritated them, and often allied themselves with the bureaucrats against them.[43] Both the *grands blancs* and the *petits blancs* probably would have agreed that "the black is here to the white, what the stupid brute is to the angel of light."[44] Yet the *petits blancs* carried white superiority much further, especially since the *gens de couleur* were frequently their superiors in every respect except skin color. They intensely hated both the mulatto and the Negro, which earned them the title "Aristocrats of the Skin."[45] Howard pointed out that the *petits blancs* "often bragged about the numbers of poor unfortunate blacks whom they have shot, merely perhaps for having trespassed on their lands, the same in Europe as you would speak of having killed a dog."[46]

The white caste in Saint-Domingue, comprised of European bureaucrats, *grands blancs*, and *petits blancs*, found that they had little in common except the color of their skin, and their antipathies not only speeded the coming of the revolution but contributed to their inability to cope with it. The *gens de couleur*—mulattoes and free blacks—formed the second caste. According to Louis XIV's Code Noir of 1685, the members of this caste were to have full French citizenship.[47] But the *gens de couleur* were really an appendage of slavery, and their disabilities increased as that institution expanded. By the mid-eighteenth century they could not "hold any public office, trust, or employment, however insignificant; they were not even allowed to exercise any of those professions, to which some sort of liberal education is supposed to be necessary."[48] Even the law perpetuated this unequal justice. A *personne de couleur*, for example, could have his right arm removed for striking a white, while the white was only subject to a minor fine for doing the same to him.[49] Despite the contention of some observers that this law was rarely enforced, its psychological oppression must have been great. Perkins called it "a never ceasing canker in the minds of the free colored people."[50] There were many other discriminatory laws, such as the one passed in 1765 which forbade the *gens de couleur* to assemble—a second offense bringing loss of freedom. Finally, the *gens de couleur* had to face social discrimination, even in their friendships with the whites. A mulatto might invite a white to dinner, but he could not sit at the same table with him.[51]

Compared with the mixed bloods of other West Indian colonies, the *gens de couleur* of Saint-Domingue suffered a lower general status. In Spanish Santo Domingo there were laws against the mulattoes, but they were generally disregarded. Moreau de Saint-Méry observed "that prejudice with respect to color, so powerful with other nations . . . is almost unknown in the Spanish Part of Saint-Domingo."[52] Even in Jamaica, which had a very large slave population, the condition of the mulatto was better—but still oppressive. He had no legal civil rights, such as the right to testify against whites, and he was supposed to wear a blue cross on his right side to indicate his racial mixture. But there was a wide gulf between law and practice in Jamaica. In reality the mulatto could vote and sit in the local assembly and was considered white if he was three generations removed from his last Negro ancestor. In

Saint-Domingue one drop of Negro blood permanently confined one to the *gens de couleur* caste.[53]

The *gens de couleur* of Saint-Domingue, however, did have some advantages. By far the greatest was the fact that they could amass large amounts of capital and real estate. Many mulattoes imitated the *grands blancs* by sending their children to France for an education, by acquiring large numbers of slaves, and by adopting other white cultural habits.[54] In fact, the mulatto slaveholders, especially the females, often outdid the *grands blancs* in mistreating their slaves.[55] Military service was another advantage of the *gens de couleur*, even though they composed only the "rank and file." They were forced to join a *maréchausée*, a local police organization, for general law enforcement and for capturing fugitive slaves, and after three years of service they graduated to the militia. By 1789 the militia was made up of 156 companies, the *gens de couleur* forming 104 of them, and was expected to supplement the King's Troops of about two thousand regulars.[56] Thus the mulattoes were physically sharpened for the coming conflict, for as Perkins stated, "the mulattoes . . . were in general very fine troops; handsome, tall, straight, and beautiful men."[57]

The great desire of the *gens de couleur* was to obtain equal status with the whites, especially the *grands blancs*, and to blot out their Negro past.[58] In fact, there were grounds for an alliance between the *grands blancs* and the *gens de couleur*: both were often large property holders, both disliked the *petits blancs*, and both desired French acculturation. On the other hand, their greatest divisive factor was skin color; the *grands blancs* could never quite overcome their prejudice.[59] One of the greatest tragedies of the revolution was that the mulattoes and big whites never made this potential alliance, for it might have prevented some of the bloodier and more destructive aspects of that upheaval.

Slavery formed the third caste. As early as 1510 Portuguese slavers began to bring their black cargoes, mostly from Senegal, to Hispaniola, but the slave trade did not flourish in Hispaniola until Saint-Domingue began to mature in the eighteenth century. Most of the slaves were drawn from West Africa and represented such tribal groups as the Ibos, Senegalese, Bambaras, Aradas, Congolese, and Dambas. Each tribe usually had a different dominant characteristic; for example, the Aradas were good agriculturalists and the Congolese excellent fishermen. The latter group, actually drawn from Angola as well as the Congo, was the most common among the slaves of Saint-Domingue.[60] As the colony's demand for blacks exceeded the supply, the price per slave became inflated. As Baron de Wimpffen observed, "a picked Negro, who costs at present [1790] near three thousand livres, might have been sold a century ago for three hundred."[61]

The African background of these slaves is the subject of controversy, but that they lived an unrestrained existence in Africa is a popular myth. They were frequently regimented by kings, priests, and large landowners; moreover, historian-sociologist Melville Herskovits demonstrated that slavery and *dokpwe*, the cooperative work gang system, were common to West Africa. Basil Davidson in his *History of West Africa*, however, maintained that slavery in West Africa was much milder than that of the Europeans because a slave could buy his freedom, marry his master's daughters, and even become a king. But Daniel Mannix and Malcolm Cowley have pointed out that this humane treatment applied only to household slaves, not to prisoners of war, who were unprotected by law and often treated harshly.[62] There is no conclusive evidence at present to prove that the slave's African background made him either restive toward or adaptable to slavery.

From the time slaves first left Africa until the destruction of slavery as an institution, the burden of the black was rigorous at best and cruel at worst, particularly in Saint-Domingue. Just surviving his induction into slavery was something of an accomplishment for the black. There was the horrible Middle Passage, which sometimes caused one out of six of his number to perish. Once the black reached his Caribbean destination, he had to undergo a still more rigorous "seasoning period" lasting several months, during which up to one-third of the Negroes died.[63] A British historian estimated that "for every African who became a 'seasoned slave' at least one other African was killed."[64]

Besides his much-needed brawn, the black brought his cultural baggage with him, much of it destined to leave a permanent imprint on Saint-Domingue. Black folkways left the deepest impression, despite the slave's role as an artisan or skilled tropical farmer. This was particularly true of *vodou*, better known as voodoo, an animistic religion with a pantheon of gods and goddesses, referred to as *loas*. The *loas* are personal spirits who are peevish and who possess their worshipers in ritualistic ceremonies; moreover, there is no moral significance attached to the acts of the *loas*.[65] A priesthood developed in connection with this religion, and, according to Moreau de Saint-Méry, the priests "had the right to the unlimited respect of those who composed it [the cult]."[66] Voodoo was perhaps one of the most cohesive forces among the slaves and one which the whites tried to suppress.[67] Dancing was a favorite folkway also, especially the *chica*, the talent for which "is in the perfection with which one can move his haunches and the lower part of his back, while keeping the rest of his body in a kind of immobility."[68]

The black man was brought to Saint-Domingue to work, and work he did. According to Baron de Wimpffen, the plantation day began with "the cracking of whips, the smothered cries, and the indistinct groans of the Negroes, who never see the day break but to curse it; who are never recalled to a feeling of their existence but by sufferings—this, Sir, is what takes place on the crowing of the early cock."[69] The daily schedule of the slave began at 5:30 A.M. and ended at 6 P.M., a half-hour break for breakfast and an hour for lunch. This was the usual routine, but during the harvest of the sugar cane, popularly known as "crop," the slave frequently worked to the point of exhaustion. Yet not all was work, for often the planter allowed the stealing of rum, the chewing of sugar cane, and a harvest feast. The slave also was allowed to plant his own garden to supplement his sparse rations, and on Sunday, his day off, he could sell any surplus at the local markets. Market day was his main social gathering of the week and is still important in Haiti today.[70]

What about the treatment of the slave? Was it cruel? On the surface, the Code Noir (1685) was designed to give minimum protection to the slave: he could make complaints to the crown's *procureur-général* in cases involving maltreatment by his master; he was to be raised in the Catholic faith; no restriction was placed on his emancipation; and slave families were to remain intact when sold. Yet even legally the slave was exposed to mistreatment:

he could be tortured in official investigations and sentenced to a grotesque death, and he could not expect equal justice for equal crimes—"blind justice" peeked in the case of the white man.[71] The greatest flaw in the legal system, however, was that it usually proved to be inoperative in the small protection that it might have afforded the slave.[72] The famous Le Jeune case of 1788 made this painfully clear.

The Le Jeune case began when fourteen slaves complained to the *procureur-général* of Le Cap François that their master was unmercifully torturing two black women suspected of poisoning one-fourth of his work gang. An investigation confirmed the slaves' accusations and Le Jeune was brought to trial. The whites were enraged and flooded the tribunal with their petitions for Le Jeune's acquittal. Some whites wanted the informers to receive fifty lashes for betraying their master, and Le Jeune's father even wanted Couet de Montarand, one of the prosecution officers, banished from the colony.[73] With such pressure on them, the judges acquitted Le Jeune, and, as Pierre de Vaissière stated, "it affirmed once again the solidarity which must unite the whites before their slaves."[74]

Another institution which might have been useful in protecting the slave was the Church, but it offered him even less protection than the legal system. According to the Code Noir, the Church was to give the slaves religious instruction. In reality the clergy, mostly defrocked monks, had little zeal, and their influence over master and slave was slight. The only sacrament that the master allowed regularly was baptism, and he herded his slaves to church for that purpose. And in spite of the baptized slave's claim to superiority over his unbaptized brother, baptism itself had little moral significance for either master or slave. Perhaps one reason for the laxness of the Church and the master to give the slave religious instructions is that they both feared the suggestion of equality. Another possible reason is that the master simply did not want any outside interference in the control of his slaves.[75]

Stanley Elkins has asserted that nowhere in Latin America did the master enjoy "powers of life and death over the slave's body."[76] Elkins is incorrect, for this was exactly what the Saint-Domingue master enjoyed, especially with no institutions to shield the slave from abuse. Matbon de la Cour, an eighteenth-century writer, up-held this view when he said that the French slave system "allowed all to the master and nothing to the slave."[77] But it is not easy to declare that the master was either humane or inhumane. Pierre de Vaissière, in his monumental social history of Saint-Domingue, gave only an evasive answer: "There were some good masters and there were some bad masters. I have the impression that the former have been more numerous than the latter; but it is only an impression!"[78]

Obviously there were some good masters in Saint-Domingue. Perkins observed the kindness of the *grand blanc* Chevalier Du-perier, who cared for his slaves' physical needs and saw to it that they were humanely treated, even making it a point to visit his hospital several times a day and to provide the sick with food from his own table.[79] Furthermore, during the revolution there were many faithful slaves, including Toussaint Louverture himself, who gratefully defended their masters. Finally, there was an economic factor: why would a master make a practice of the immediate destruction of his capital investment?

Evidence shows, however, that the Saint-Domingue master was cruel, especially in the economic factor of gradual human destruction. That is, the master found it more economical to work his slaves to death and replace them than to encourage their reproduction; slaveholders in many of the West Indian colonies, except perhaps those of Spain, shared this practice. After all, they wanted quick wealth and a fast return to Europe. In addition, the West Indies shared the common statistic of a higher death rate than birth rate.[80] Of course, one should use this statistic with reservation because Saint-Domingue imported over two males for every female and because health standards were low—Moreau de Saint-Méry observed a pregnant Negress carrying a large stone on her back, "persuaded that without this compression the moment of childbirth will not arrive."[81] After Saint-Domingue gained its independence, this statistic was reversed. There were a number of other widespread practices which indicate cruelty, such as the branding of slaves to prevent escapes and the use of mutilation as a disciplinary device.[82] To be fair, the historian must view these cruelties within the historical context of a generally harsh eighteenth century, for, as Howard asked, "If a poor devil took the value of a penny in England, do you not tie him to the cart . . . and flog him . . . unmercifully?"[83] Nevertheless, this does not make what happened to the slave in Saint-Domingue more palatable. Slaves also suffered the psychological scar of bondage. How deep it ran the historian may never know, but its presence cannot be denied. Even if a master was humane, his slaves could observe the cruelty of other slaveholders and knew that the same might befall them. It is possible that such an observation contributed to Toussaint's determination to free the blacks.[84]

The black openly resisted his enslavement and poor treatment. As early as 1700, three hundred slaves near Le Cap François revolted and were suppressed, their leader fleeing into exile in Spanish Santo Domingo. There were also a number of other futile uprisings during the eighteenth century, the major one led by François Macandal. A maroon (fugitive slave) and an expert in the use of poison, Macandal organized a widespread network of poisoners who were to assassinate the whites in a coordinated conspiracy. The plot was discovered and Macandal was burned at the stake in March 1758.[85]

Open rebellion had little chance of success until the social earthquake of the French Revolution, and so the slaves turned to more subtle forms of resistance. Moreau de Saint-Méry seemed to sense this when he stated that "the Negroes, such as they are in the colony, generally demonstrate courage in their resignation."[86] A vengeful slave might poison his fellow blacks to injure his master where it hurt the most—"in the pocketbook."[87] Or he might find some solace in the antiwhite orientation of voodoo, especially in one chant: "We swear to destroy the whites and all that they possess; let us die rather than fail to keep this vow."[88]

Fugitive slaves, known as maroons, lived in isolated settlements throughout the West Indies. Although they seldom challenged white authority directly, except for occasional raids on plantations for food and women, the maroons were feared by the whites, who believed that the infection of freedom might spread. Yet there is no evidence that when the revolution erupted, these maroons came to the aid of their fellow blacks. In fact, the historian T. Lothrop Stoddard maintained that they played a reactionary role. It is possible that they viewed the general freedom of the slaves as a threat to their own position.[89]

The white conscience was also an ally to slave resistance, as the abolition movements gained momentum in late-eighteenth-century Europe. The British movement relied heavily upon evangelical Protestantism and economic change, while that of France gained much of its inspiration from the Enlightenment. Both movements were closely associated, and each drew a number of thoughts from the other.

There are certain ideas in evangelical Protestantism which supported the British abolition movement. One of these is millennialism, the belief that man's sinful nature can be changed and that the world can be transformed into "heaven on earth." Millennialism stood for progress, and those who embraced it frequently equated sin with slavery and virtue with reform. As early as 1676 the Quaker William Edmundson came close to this position when he stated that "Negroes were slaves to sin because they were slaves of men." [90] Two other important concepts, both Arminian in nature, are the freedom of the will and the belief that all men are children of God. Both were damaging to slavery and both are essential to another important concept—the conversional experience. An act of free will, the conversional experience emphasizes personal commitment. This is seen in the case of William Wilberforce, destined to become a major leader of the British abolitionists. A member of Parliament and an amiable socialite, Wilberforce was not dedicated to any particular cause. In 1784, however, John Wesley converted him to evangelicalism, and shortly thereafter Wilberforce committed himself to the antislavery crusade. John Newton and other abolitionists repeated this pattern.[91]

Many Enlightenment thinkers provided the abolitionists with additional ideas. There was Charles de Secondat Montesquieu, who emphasized environment and social utility as bases for local institutions. Montesquieu even upheld slavery if it could be proved to be useful. On the other hand, the abolitionists used the idea of social utility to support the uselessness of slavery; Thomas Clarkson, the famous British abolitionist, won an essay contest at Cambridge on this subject in 1785. There was also Jean Jacques Rousseau, who attacked slavery not as an end in itself, but to prove the general injustice of society once it departed from natural equality. Chevalier de Jaucourt and the other Encyclopedists increasingly concerned themselves with antislavery thought after 1765, but perhaps Abbé Raynal's *Histoire des deux Indies* had the greatest Enlightenment impact on abolition. Diderot rather than Raynal probably wrote most of this work, which contains three basic ideas: the invalidity of slavery, the freedom of the will, and sympathy toward violent emancipation. Translated into a number of foreign languages and read by Toussaint prior to the revolution, the *Histoire* had a wide intellectual appeal.[92]

Yet it took economic change and public opinion to transform antislavery ideas into active abolition movements. The decline of the British West Indies after the Seven Years' War had the greatest economic impact. High sugar prices in England, shifting British commercial interests, and land exhaustion in the Anglo Lesser Antilles combined to accelerate this decline. A favorable public opinion toward antislavery accompanied this economic change: the Quakers were definitely committed to the antislavery movement after 1761, there were sugar boycotts, and Wedgwood cameos depicting the slave's plight became fashionable. Even Dr. Johnson, the famous Tory writer, toasted the next West Indian slave insurrection![93]

Once ideas, economics, and public opinion laid the foundation of abolition, political action followed. First came the Somerset Case of 1772, which freed all slaves in England. Then there was the strongly religious Clapham Sect, an abolitionist community near Westminster which involved itself in various antislavery activities, one being the establishment of Sierra Leone in 1787 as a home for freed slaves. The antislavery movement did not coalesce, however, until the Committee for the Abolition of the Slave Trade was founded on May 22, 1787, providing the abolitionists with a powerful vehicle for political action. Granville Sharp was the chairman and William Wilberforce and Thomas Clarkson the most active members; moreover, William Pitt the Younger, who became prime minister in 1783, closely associated himself with this group through Wilberforce, his good friend. The organization had important Quaker antecedents, which may partly explain its gradualist approach toward abolition. The committee's official view was that stopping the slave trade would soon lead to better treatment of the blacks and eventually to emancipation itself.[94] The group spawned a more radical French counterpart, *Amis des Noirs*. Even though France refused to back Pitt's efforts to end the slave trade, the British committee sent abolitionist literature to interested Frenchmen and generally encouraged the formation of a sister society. On February 19, 1788, a handful of men met at Numéro Trois, rue Française in Paris and established the *Amis des Noirs*. Its membership included Brissot de Warville (chairman), Mirabeau, Valady, Clavière, Condorcet, and others.[95] At first the *Amis des Noirs* was gradualist in nature, emphasizing mulatto equality even more than the abolition of the slave trade as the initial step toward the eventual emancipation of the slaves.[96] However, the French society was more radical from the first than its English associate.[97] When the French Revolution swung to radicalism, the *Amis des Noirs* went with it, and gradualism became immediatism.

By 1789 Saint-Domingue was on the verge of a social upheaval. White disunity, exploitation of the *gens de couleur*, maltreatment of the slave, and the abolition movements all contributed to the explosive situation. Yet violence might never have erupted had it not been for the social shock waves of the French Revolution. Even then the whites might have survived had they not followed the road to revolution during the crucial years of 1789 to 1791.

NOTES FOR CHAPTER ONE

1. Samuel Eliot Morison, *Admiral of the Ocean Sea: A Life of Christopher Columbus* (Boston: Little, 1942), 277.

2. Medéric-Louis-Élie Moreau de Saint-Méry, *A Topographical and Political Description of the Spanish Part of Saint-Domingue*, 2 vols. (Philadelphia: Moreau de Saint-Méry, 1796), I, 1.

3. Morison, *Admiral of the Ocean Sea*, 285; Samuel Eliot Morison, trans. and ed., *Journals and Other Documents of the Life and Voyages of Christopher Columbus* (New York: Heritage, 1963), 121.

4. *A Voyage to Saint-Domingo, In the Years 1788, 1789, and 1790*, trans. J. Wright (London: T. Codell and W. Davies, 1797), 22.

5. Ludwell Lee Montague, *Haiti and the United States, 1714-1938* (Dur-

ham, N.C.: Duke Univ. Press, 1940), 9–10; T. Lothrop Stoddard, *The French Revolution in San Domingo* (Boston: Houghton, 1914), 7.

6. Baron de Wimpffen, *Voyage to Saint-Domingo*, 101.

7. *Ibid.*, 47.

8. *Ibid.*, 107.

9. W. Adolphe Roberts, *The French in the West Indies* (Indianapolis: Bobbs-Merrill, 1942), 17.

10. Nellis Crouse, *The French Struggle for the West Indies, 1665–1713* (New York: Octagon Books, 1966), 128.

11. Pierre de Vaissière, *Saint-Domingue: La société et la vie créole sous L'Ancien Régime (1629–1789)* (Paris: Perrin et Cie, 1909), 18–19; Roberts, *French West Indies*, 60–63.

12. *Voyage to Saint-Domingo*, 82.

13. Roberts, *French West Indies*, 86–87; Elizabeth Donnan, ed., *Documents Illustrative of the History of the Slave Trade to America*, 4 vols. (New York: Octagon Books, 1965), I, 431.

14. Bryan Edwards, *An Historical Survey of the French Colony in the Island of San Domingo* (London: John Stockdale, 1797), 2–4.

15. Baron de Wimpffen, *Voyage to Saint-Domingo*, 211.

16. Richard Pares, *War and Trade in the West Indies, 1739–1763* (Oxford: Clarendon, 1936), 177–78; Edwards, *San Domingo*, 4–5; *Almanach de Saint-Domingue* (Port-au-Prince: De L'Imprimerie de Mozard, 1790), 71–72.

17. Shelby T. McCloy, *The Negro in the French West Indies* (Lexington: Univ. of Kentucky Press, 1966), 3, 11; J. H. Parry and P. M. Sherlock, *A Short History of the West Indies* (London: Macmillan, 1956), 117–18; Donnan, *Slave Trade*, II, 449–50; Roberts, *French West Indies*, 74.

18. France, Ministère de Finance, *État Détaillé des Liquidations par la Commission chargée de répartir l'Indemnité attribuée aux ancien Colons de Saint-Domingue, en exécution de la loi du 30 avril, 1826, et conformément aux dispositions de l'Ordonnance du mai suivant* (Paris: De L'Imprimerie Royale, 1831), 511–17. Lowell Ragatz and an article published in *The Times* of London made more generous assessments. Lowell Ragatz, *The Fall of the Planter Class in the British Caribbean, 1763–1833* (New York: Octagon Books, 1963), 204; *The Times* (London), Jan. 7, 1792.

19. *The Times* (London), Jan. 7, 1792; *Almanach*, v; Philip D. Curtin, *The Atlantic Slave Trade: A Census* (Madison: Univ. of Wisconsin Press, 1969), 77; Montague, *Haiti and the United States*, 5.

20. *Reminiscences of the Insurrection in St. Domingo* (Cambridge, Mass.: Harvard Univ. Press, 1886), 61.

21. *San Domingo*, 130.

22. Baltimore *Daily Repository*, Nov. 19, 1791.

23. Althéa de Puech Parham, trans. and ed., *My Odyssey: Experiences of a Young Refugee from Two Revolutions, By a Creole of Saint-Domingue* (Baton Rouge: Louisiana State Univ. Press, 1959), 23.

24. Roberts, *French West Indies*, 68, 132; Ralph Korngold, *Citizen Toussaint*, 2d ed. (New York: Hill, 1965), 15–16; Baron de Wimpffen, *Voyage to Saint-Domingo*, 85–86.

25. Baron de Wimpffen, *Voyage to Saint-Domingo*, 251–54.

26. *Ibid.*, 254.

27. Thomas Jeffreys, *The Natural and Civil History of the French Dominions in North and South America* (London: Charing-Gros, 1760), 69.

28. Here the historian must rely on logic because accurate figures are not available for those slaves the French did not report. But by the 1780s Saint-Domingue could easily have absorbed France's annual trade of from 20,000 to 30,000 slaves. Thus Saint-Domingue especially relied on Great Britain's annual trade of 38,000 slaves. Furthermore, the British West Indies, Jamaica in particular, were deeply involved in the re-exportation of slaves. After Great Britain, the U.S. and Portugal were the most active. Reginald Coupland, *The British Anti-Slavery Movement*, 2d ed. (New York: Barnes and Noble, 1964), 22; Ragatz, *The British Caribbean*, 30; Donnan, *Documents*, II, lii, xli, xlviii–ix; *Almanach*, v.

29. Parry and Sherlock, *West Indies*, 133, 140; Baron de Wimpffen, *Voyage to Saint-Domingo*, 212–13.

30. *The Times* (London), Jan. 7, 1792.

31. Parham, *My Odyssey*, 38; Baron de Wimpffen, *Voyage to Saint-Domingo*, 55.

32. *Voyage to Saint-Domingo*, 109.

33. Vaissière, *Saint-Domingue*, 216; "A Description of Jean Pebarte's Plantation in St. Domingo, n.d.," The Barbot-Chartrand Papers (South Carolina Historical Society); Record of Services, May 25, 1819, The DuBois Martin Papers (Maryland Historical Society).

34. Parry and Sherlock, *West Indies*, 153; Roberts, *French West Indies*, 69; Lieutenant Howard, "Journal of the Army of Occupation in Haiti from February 8, 1796, to January, 1798," 3 vols. (Boston Public Library), III, 4.

35. Howard, "Journal of Occupation," 3.

36. Medéric-Louis-Élie Moreau de Saint-Méry, *Description topographique, physique, civile, politique, et historique de la Partie française de l'île de Saint-Domingue*, 2 vols. (Philadelphia: Chez l'auteur, 1798), I, 95.

37. *San Domingo*, 9.

38. Baron de Wimpffen, *Voyage to Saint-Domingo*, 295.

39. Mary Hassal, *Secret History of the Horrors of St. Domingo in a Series of Letters, Written by a Lady at Cape François to Colonel Burr, Late Vice-President of the United States* (Philadelphia: Bradford and Inskeep, 1808), 18–19.

40. *The Black Jacobins*, 2d ed. (New York: Vintage Books, 1963), *passim*.

41. *Travels in North America, 1751–1762*, trans. and ed. Seymour Feiler (Norman: Univ. of Oklahoma Press, 1962), 17–18.

42. Parham, *My Odyssey*, 37; *Almanach*, xxiii; Baron de Wimpffen, *Voyage to Saint-Domingo*, 170; Germán Arciniegas, *Latin America: A Cultural*

History, trans. Joan MacLean (New York: Knopf, 1967), 445; Moreau de Saint-Méry, *La Partie française*, I, 15; Baltimore *Daily Repository*, Nov. 19, 1791.

43. James, *Black Jacobins*, 36.

44. Baron de Wimpffen, *Voyage to Saint-Domingo*, 58.

45. Vaissière, *Saint-Domingue*, 229; Howard, "Journal of Occupation," III, 9.

46. "Journal of Occupation," 7.

47. Selden Rodman, *Haiti: The Black Republic* (New York: Devin-Adair, 1961), 7.

48. Edwards, *San Domingo*, 8.

49. *Ibid.*, 9.

50. *Ibid.*, 10; Perkins, *Reminiscences*, 8.

51. McCloy, *West Indies*, 37; Baron de Wimpffen, *Voyage to Saint-Domingo*, 62. The *gens de couleur* were partly to blame for the discrimination against them because they prided themselves on their white blood. Thus the nearer one progressed toward whiteness, the higher one's intracaste recognition. Moreau de Saint-Méry, *La Partie française*, I, 86–87, 93, 98.

52. *Spanish Saint-Domingo*, I, 56.

53. Perkins, *Reminiscences*, 8; Bryan Edwards, "Legal Capacities Annexed to a Mulatto in Jamaica and in St. Domingo, May 16, 1793," Public Record Office, Colonial Office 137/50, Jamaica Correspondence (hereafter cited as C. O. 137/50); Baron de Wimpffen, *Voyage to Saint-Domingo*, 42; Edwards, *San Domingo*, 8.

54. Edwards, *San Domingo*, 10; Howard, "Journal of Occupation," III, 13; McCloy, *West Indies*, 57; "Mémoire historique et politique sur la Situation actuelle de la colonie," Donatien Rochambeau Documents (Univ. of Florida Library), 7.

55. Howard even pointed out that many of the mulattoes, the women in particular, had slaves "to wait on them, and are proud, disdainful, and cruel; unfortunate is the poor wretch who is doomed to be their property." "Journal of Occupation," III, 12.

56. Moreau de Saint-Méry, *La Partie française*, I, 451; McCloy, *West Indies*, 66–67; Perkins, *Reminiscences*, 8.

57. *Reminiscences*, 7.

58. Moreau de Saint-Méry, *La Partie française*, I, 98; Baltimore *Daily Repository*, Aug. 18, 1792.

59. One of the more interesting aspects of this problem of skin color involved an interview Thomas Clarkson, the British abolitionist, had with six representatives of the *gens de couleur* caste in France. According to these representatives, who officially spoke for the propertied *gens de couleur*, their caste would be willing to emancipate the slaves to gain mulatto-white equality. Thus the *gens de couleur* themselves recognized that their condition was closely connected to slavery. Thomas Clarkson, *The History of*

the Rise, Progress, and Accomplishment of the Abolition of the African Slave-Trade by the British Parliament (Philadelphia: Brown and Merritt, 1808), 107–108.

60. Melville J. Herskovits, *Life in a Haitian Valley* (New York: Octagon Books, 1964), 18, 20; Howard, "Journal of Occupation," III, 15; Matbon de la Cour, "Sur la Traite et l'Esclavage des Nègres," 72 (Bibliothèque de l'Académie, Lyons and the Library of Congress); McCloy, *West Indies*, I, 4; Coupland, *British Anti-Slavery*, 18; Curtin, *Slave Trade*, 194–95.

61. *Voyage to Saint-Domingo*, 72.

62. Herskovits, *Haitian Valley*, 25–26; Davidson, *A History of West Africa to the Nineteenth Century* (Garden City, N.Y.: Anchor Books, 1966), 180–81; Mannix and Cowley, *Black Cargoes: A History of the Atlantic Slave Trade, 1518–1865* (New York: Viking, 1962), 44–45.

63. Coupland, *British Anti-Slavery*, 24–26.

64. *Ibid.*, 26.

65. McCloy, *West Indies*, 250–52.

66. *La Partie française*, I, 46.

67. Boukmann, one of the early leaders of the Revolution, was a voodoo priest. James, *Black Jacobins*, 18.

68. Moreau de Saint-Méry, *La Partie française*, I, 45.

69. *Voyage to Saint-Domingo*, 98.

70. Howard, "Journal of Occupation," III, 17; Parry and Sherlock, *West Indies*, 145; Perkins, *Reminiscences*, 11–12; Baron de Wimpffen, *Voyage to Saint-Domingo*, 233.

71. David B. Davis, *The Problem of Slavery in Western Culture* (Ithaca: Cornell Univ. Press, 1966), 263; Elsa V. Goveia, "The West Indian Slave Laws of the Eighteenth Century," *Revista de ciencias sociales*, IV (March 1960), 95–97, 99.

72. The word *usually* is used here because one can sometimes find an exception. Such was the case in 1790 of Sieur Mainguy who was convicted for having tortured his slaves by hacking them with knives and scissors, by applying hot coals and irons to their bodies, and by committing other mutilations. Mainguy was sentenced to a fine of 10,000 livres, a nine-year banishment, and prohibited from ever owning a slave again. *The Times* (London), Dec. 29, 1790.

73. Vaissière, *Saint-Domingue*, 186–88.

74. *Ibid.*, 188.

75. Baron de Wimpffen, *Voyage to Saint-Domingo*, 132, 281; Moreau de Saint-Méry, *La Partie française*, I, 39; Korngold, *Citizen Toussaint*, 39.

76. *Slavery: A Problem in American Institutional and Intellectual Life* (Chicago: Univ. of Chicago Press, 1959), 74.

77. "La Traite et l'Esclavage des Negres," 80.

78. *Saint-Domingue*, 205.

79. *Reminiscences*, 11.

80. David A. G. Waddell, *The West Indies and the Guianas* (Englewood Cliffs, N. J.: Prentice-Hall, 1967), 52–53; Parry and Sherlock, *West Indies*, 95; Davis, *Slavery in Western Culture*, 233; Coupland, *British Anti-Slavery*, 33–34; Baron de Wimpffen, *Voyage to Saint-Domingo*, 255.

81. *La Partie française*, I, 41; *Almanach*, v. Saint-Domingue's slave importation patterns were not peculiar to the West Indies, for in 1789 even Spain demanded that black cargoes brought to Spanish colonies consist of one-third women. Donnan, *Documents*, IV, 47.

82. Robert West and John Augelli, *Middle America: Its Lands and Peoples* (Englewood Cliffs, N. J.: Prentice-Hall, 1966), 152, 159; Vaissière, *Saint-Domingue*, 192–93.

83. "Journal of Occupation," III, 19.

84. Stephen Alexis, *Black Liberator: The Life of Toussaint Louverture*, trans. William Sterling (New York: Macmillan, 1949), 13.

85. Jeffreys, *French Dominions*, 54; Korngold, *Citizen Toussaint*, 44–45; McCloy, *West Indies*, 39–40.

86. *La Partie française*, I, 61.

87. Baron de Wimpffen, *Voyage to Saint-Domingo*, 301; McCloy, *West Indies*, 43.

88. James, *Black Jacobins*, 18. This is James's translation, and in the original text it is "*Eh! Eh! Bomba hen! Hen! Canga bafio té. Canga mourné de lé. Canga do ki la. Canga li.*" Moreau de Saint-Méry, *La Partie française*, I, 49.

89. Stoddard, *San Domingo*, 63–64; Baron de Wimpffen, *Voyage to Saint-Domingo*, 228.

90. Davis, *Slavery in Western Culture*, 295–97, 307.

91. *Ibid.*, 363, 367, 389; Parry and Sherlock, *West Indies*, 176, 178; Coupland, *British Anti-Slavery*, 72–73.

92. Coupland, *British Anti-Slavery*, 67; James, *Black Jacobins*, 24–25; Davis, *Slavery in Western Culture*, 394, 406–408, 413–21.

93. Waddell, *West Indies and the Guianas*, 71; Parry and Sherlock, *West Indies*, 117–18, 178; Davis, *Slavery in Western Culture*, 330; Coupland, *British Anti-Slavery*, 59.

94. Coupland, *British Anti-Slavery*, 74–77, 83–84; Parry and Sherlock, *West Indies*, 68, 71, 81, 177–78; McCloy, *West Indies*, 72; David B. Davis, "The Emergence of Immediatism in British and American Anti-Slavery Thought," *Mississippi Valley Historical Review* 46 (Sept. 1962), *passim*; Eloise Ellery, *Brissot de Warville: A Study in the History of the French Revolution* (Boston: Houghton, 1915), 185; J. P. Brissot de Warville, *Oration upon the Necessity of Establishing at Paris, A Society to Promote the Abolition of the Trade and Slavery of the Negroes* (Philadelphia: Francis Bailey, 1788), 135, 154.

95. Brissot de Warville, *Oration*, 152; Coupland, *British Anti-Slavery*, 62–63; Ellery, *Brissot de Warville*, 184, 186; Clarkson, *Abolition of the African Slave-Trade, passim*.

96. The reason for the emphasis of the *Amis des Noirs* on mulatto equality

as the route to emancipation cannot be conclusively answered; however, there are some distinct possibilities. One is that the mulattoes in Paris were well organized as a pressure group under Julien Raimond, Vincent Ogé, and others. Another possibility is that the *Amis des Noirs* felt too weak to challenge the powerful slavers of Nantes, Bordeaux, and elsewhere; thus the society's emphasis on mulatto equality was a tactical maneuver to outflank this opposition. Clarkson, *Abolition of the African Slave-Trade*, 103, 109, 113.

97. Ellery, *Brissot de Warville*, 185; Brissot de Warville, *Oration*, 142.

CHAPTER TWO

The Road to Revolution, 1789-1791

Saint-Domingue experienced its first tremor of revolution in mid-1787, after financially troubled Louis XVI dismissed the Assembly of Notables and attempted to subvert noble privileges with an attack on the *parlements*. The "aristocratic revolt" had begun. The *grands blancs* watched this struggle with interest because the aristocrats were fighting monarchial centralization; a crown defeat might mean more colonial home rule and economic self-direction, limited to the *grands blancs*, of course. By August 1788 the aristocrats won a temporary victory. Controller-General Loménie de Brienne resigned, and the Estates-General was to convene in May 1789. Many *grands blancs* were elated and prepared to join the scheduled assembly, but they erred by becoming embroiled in the turmoil of France. Even though the early leaders of the French Revolution had no intention of exporting that upheaval, it spread to the colonies, especially to Saint-Domingue.[1]

Not all *grands blancs* were optimistic about getting involved in the turmoil of France, for they sensed a potential threat to their status. They felt that reticence was the best policy under the circumstances, at least until the direction of events in France was clarified. This faction, perhaps composing a majority, did not form soon enough to prevent the participation of Saint-Domingue in the Estates-General. Instead, a faction that called itself the Colonial Committee was able to impose its policy of active participation because of its militancy and better organization.[2]

The Colonial Committee drafted a *cahiers des doléances*, in which they voiced their demands for more home rule and economic freedom, and selected thirty-one (later thirty-seven) delegates to the Estates-General. Comte de Peynier, the governor of Saint-Domingue, did all he could to block the sending of these representatives, and when he failed, his authority declined.[3] Events were soon to prove, however, that the Colonial Committee should have had "nothing to do with the French Revolution."[4]

Upon their arrival in France, the Saint-Domingue delegates had difficulty gaining admission to the Estates-General, but were allowed to sit provisionally with the Third Estate. The colonial delegates seemed to be strategically situated when on June 17 the Third Estate constituted itself as the National Assembly, empowered to represent the nation. Three days later, when Gouy d'Arcy led the colonial delegates in support of the Tennis Court Oath, Saint-Domingue and some of the other colonies gained even more favorable recognition. When Louis XVI accepted the *fait accompli* of a national assembly by ordering the other two estates to join it on June 20, the hopes of the *grand blanc* delegates reached new heights. But soon the colonials would have their first skirmish with a formidable adversary, the *Amis des Noirs*.[5]

The task of the *Amis des Noirs* was large indeed, for the National Assembly was bourgeois and not inclined to cut off a great source of its wealth—slavery and the slave trade. Even Mirabeau, one of the most enthusiastic members of the *Amis des Noirs*, realized that there was little chance of abolishing the slave trade, since only one-fourth of the members of the National Assembly would support such a motion.[6] Furthermore, many members of the *Amis des Noirs* feared that an attack on the slave trade would alienate Bordeaux, Marseilles, Le Havre, Nantes, and other important ports which were quite favorable to the French Revolution. Besides, the planters were already hypersensitive to the *Amis des Noirs*, and they formed committees to watch the society's every move.[7] Faced with strong opposition and its own reservations, the *Amis des Noirs* retreated from an earlier plan of direct assault on the slave trade and turned to another possible means of accomplishing its program—the Mulatto Question. Campaigning for mulatto rights was less likely to offend the bourgeois leaders of the French Revolution, for Parisian mulattoes were respected and often were large property owners. Also, the mulattoes were militant and had organized into a pressure group known as the *Colons*

Américains, led by Julien Raimond and Vincent Ogé. Consequently the mulatto became the wedge that the abolitionists used to pry into slavery itself. The assault in this new direction began when the *Amis des Noirs* successfully contested Saint-Domingue's right to thirty-seven delegates in the National Assembly, maintaining that the colony's deputies represented only the *grand blanc* portion of the population; as a result, Saint-Domingue was awarded only six seats early in July. The debate on the rights of the *gens de couleur* had just begun and would not end until Saint-Domingue was in ashes.[8]

Other events followed with such rapidity that the Saint-Domingue delegates began to lose their composure. On July 14 the Bastille fell and, for all practical purposes, so did much of the crown's authority. Then the peasants attacked the châteaux and destroyed the manorial registers during July and August. The nobles surrendered many, but not all, of their rights and fiscal immunities in the decrees of August 5 and 11, and the Declaration of Rights of Man and Citizen was adopted on August 26.[9] Now the Colonial Committee temporarily understood that its fortunes were tied to the old regime and that the National Assembly was not only an uncertain ally, but a potential enemy. One delegate from Saint-Domingue observed that the Assembly "is truly of a nature to cause the most horrible apprehension; we see it and we are forced to keep quiet: *they are drunk with liberty.*"[10]

Of the various events, the Declaration of Rights caused the most fear among the Saint-Domingue delegates. It was, according to George Rudé, a statement of the revolutionary bourgeoisie and its allies.[11] Although the declaration stated that law is the expression of the general will and that "men are born and remain free and equal in rights," both of these important social-leveling concepts were linked to property as a "sacred and inviolable right."[12] Slavery could not be touched as long as slaves were recognized as property. But the propertied *gens de couleur* seemed to meet every specification under the Declaration of Rights for what was known as "active" citizenship; how long this would go unnoticed by the National Assembly was an uncertainty the colonial delegates had to endure. It is also significant that on September 20, 1789, a delegation of *gens de couleur* appeared before the Assembly and demanded full citizenship under Article Fifty-nine of the Code Noir. Although the Assembly evaded the problem by referring it to the colonies for decision, the Mulatto Question was once more intensified.[13]

In Paris the *grand blanc* reaction to the succession of events took various forms. On August 20 the *grands blancs* opposing active participation in the French Revolution finally united as the Club Massiac. Then early in September it closed ranks with the Colonial Committee in sending a request for colonial autonomy to La Luzerne, the minister of marine. This unity was only temporary, for the Colonial Committee abandoned the plan on September 27 and continued to fight for *grand blanc* interests in the Assembly. Even more extreme was the reaction of the white colonials in Saint-Domingue. Ferrand de Beaudierre, a *grand blanc* who had married a mulatto, called for the application of the Declaration of Rights to the *gens de couleur*. Viewed as a traitor to his own caste, he was literally torn to pieces by a white mob.[14] One delegate from Saint-Domingue, M. Gerard, did have the foresight to advise his constituency to unite with the mulattoes: "Win over the *gens de couleur* class to your cause. They surely could not ask for more than conforming their interests with yours, and of employing themselves with zeal for common security. It is therefore only a question of being just to them and of treating them better and better."[15] Unfortunately the *grands blancs* ignored Gerard's advice.

For the next few months it seemed as if the Colonial Committee might achieve a *grand blanc* victory in the National Assembly after all. On March 2, 1790, the colonial delegates outmaneuvered the *Amis des Noirs* by having questions of empire referred to an Assembly committee of twelve members, officially known as the Colonial Committee (not to be confused with that of Saint-Domingue). Of course, the *grands blancs* thought that only planters should be committee members, and they vehemently but futilely opposed an at-large selection from the Assembly. No doubt they were greatly relieved that Antoine Pierre Joseph Marie Barnave, one of the Triumvirate and related to a Saint-Domingue planter, was selected chairman of the Colonial Committee and that no one with *Amis des Noirs* connections was selected as a member. On March 8 the *grands blancs* seemed to have achieved their objectives; a decree was passed which allowed the colonies to form their own local systems of government and to present plans for their internal control to the Assembly for approval. Yet before the *grands blancs* could savor their victory, it was soured by an amendment.[16]

The *Amis des Noirs* and the mulattoes were angry over their setback, and they pressed the Assembly to amend the March 8 Decree with the instructions which were to accompany it. Barnave and the Assembly found themselves faced once again with arguments in favor of the propertied *gens de couleur*. Obviously they were swayed by men like the Marquis de Nicolas, Robert de Cocherel, who maintained that "all the proprietors . . . ought to be active citizens."[17] Cocherel, however, opposed giving active citizenship to the *petits blancs*, who often lacked an economic stake in society. Attempting to establish some sort of compromise, the Assembly issued the Instructions of March 28, which gave all taxpayers and proprietors over twenty-five years of age the right to participate in local colonial assemblies. But the Assembly failed actually to name the propertied *gens de couleur* in the instructions. Obviously the bourgeois-dominated Assembly intended this to be a compromise in word only, for this was all the *grand blanc* needed to ignore the mulatto once more. Yet the mulatto would no longer be ignored, as events all through the French West Indies would soon prove.[18]

While the Assembly decided Saint-Domingue's future in theory, its inhabitants were deciding it in fact. As the news of events in France reached Saint-Domingue, the whites became even more factional. An observer noted that "the French Revolution . . . necessarily produced among the inhabitants of that colony, a diversity of opinion with respect to its effects on their political rights."[19] At first the *grands* and *petits blancs* did stand together against the bureaucrats, an alliance that lasted roughly from September 1789 to June 1790. The *petits blancs* were particularly aggressive, causing fear among the *grands blancs* and, in turn, the eventual breakdown of the alliance.

The revolt of the colonial whites against bureaucratic authority began with the interception of Governor Peynier's dispatches and the adoption of the revolutionary cockade, which "everybody who had a white face, and whether they liked it or not . . . were forced to wear." [20] Furthermore, national guards, in imitation of those in France, were formed. Those in North Province were gathered by Bacon de la Chevalerie, who led his mob-army to Port-au-Prince in order to seize François Barbé-Marbois, the intendant who had opposed a more liberal economic policy. Fortunately, the intendant fled to France before Chevalerie could seize him. [21] Each province established its own assembly and made plans for a general colonial assembly at Léogane which had the sanction of the crown on the condition that Saint-Domingue await instructions (the March 8 Decree and the Instructions of March 28). [22] But the bureaucracy, symbolic of crown authority, was not yet defeated. [23]

On April 16, 1790, a general colonial assembly met at Saint Marc rather than at Léogane. Colonel Antoine Mauduit, commander of a regiment of regulars at Port-au-Prince, led the bureaucracy in opposing the meeting. His strategy was to preserve bureaucratic authority by supporting the mulattoes against the whites. The Saint Marc Colonial Assembly did make some attempt at a mulatto alliance by equalizing white–*personne de couleur* military obligations, but the whites refused to include the mulattoes in the Instructions of March 28. Thus Mauduit was able to outplay the Colonial Assembly for mulatto support. As a result, the colonial whites were faced with two failures: the lack of mulatto support and the inability to confine the turmoil to the white caste. The latter failure was one major reason that the *gens de couleur* and eventually the slaves themselves would be drawn into the ever widening conflict. In the meantime, the Saint Marc Colonial Assembly settled down to the problem of developing a constitution. [24]

The development of the constitution made it clear to the *grands blancs* that the Patriots (*petits blancs*) were attempting to seize control of the colony; the *grands blancs* saw the safety of their position in allegiance to France and feared the gravitation of the Patriots toward independence. The Constitution of May 28 seemed to confirm their fears: the crown was the only recognized superior authority, and "the National Assembly cannot decree laws concerning the internal regime of Saint-Domingue." [25] What really alarmed the *grands blancs* was that the Patriot-controlled Saint Marc Colonial Assembly became the only valid lawmaking body

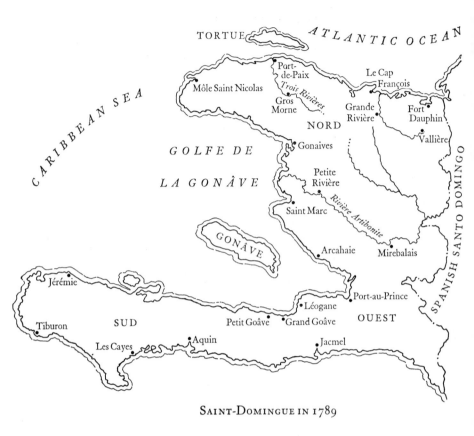

SAINT-DOMINGUE IN 1789

for internal affairs. Accordingly, the *grands blancs* of North Province seceded and returned to their provincial assembly. North Province refused all overtures from the Saint Marc Assembly to return, even threatening to deport two emissaries to France if they did not leave Le Cap François before sundown. Mauduit saw his chance and restored bureaucratic authority with a *grand blanc* alliance. Saint-Domingue was on the brink of civil war.[26]

On July 29, 1790, the Patriots of Port-au-Prince captured a government patrol with a force of about four hundred men. Mauduit reacted with energy and dispersed the Patriot band, but Saint Marc was ready to retaliate. Thomas Millet, president of the Colonial Assembly, proclaimed that "all the parishes are invited to assemble immediately to revenge the murders committed at Port-au-Prince. The horrible conspiracy is at length declared; the execrable Peynier, Mauduit, Corirtard, de la Salle, etc., bathe themselves in blood." [27] Just when civil war seemed imminent, the Saint Marc Colonial Assembly voted to adjourn and send eighty-five of its delegates to France to present its case to the National Assembly. The delegates fled Saint-Domingue on board the *Léopard* and arrived at Brest on September 21. Civil war was averted, at least temporarily. [28]

Why did the Patriots make this daring decision? Evidently they were worried about the appearance of their actions to the National Assembly. As early as May they had asked persons in Nantes to represent them before the king and the Assembly, believing themselves to be the victims of misrepresentation. By early October, however, the Patriots' gamble failed, for the National Assembly was obviously on the side of the *grands blancs*. Barnave, seeing the danger of a *petit blanc*–controlled Saint-Domingue, successfully led the opposition, which censured a Patriot address on October 5 and annulled the Saint Marc Assembly itself on October 12. Even though the *petits blancs* suffered a major setback, they were still a powerful faction in Saint-Domingue. While the whites continued to fight among themselves, another storm was brewing on the colonial horizon—the mulattoes. [29]

All over the French West Indies the mulatto was ready to break out of the confines of his caste. He was frustrated by the failure of the National Assembly to grant him full citizenship, aroused by pamphlets from the *Amis des Noirs*, and angered by white brutality. Although the mulatto had no intention of taking the slave with him in his drive for equality with the whites, except perhaps as a last resort, he could not restrict the upheaval to his caste; soon it would filter down to the slaves themselves. [30]

The first incident occurred outside Port-au-Prince on April 22, 1790, when several mulattoes killed three whites near the city. Although many whites thought this was the beginning of a general mulatto rebellion, it was not. [31] Martinique, rather than Saint-Domingue, experienced the first serious mulatto upheavals. On June 8 the whites in Martinique discovered plans for a widespread *personne de couleur* rebellion. As a result, the whites residing at Fort Royal were determined to exterminate all *gens de couleur* within the city. One observer noted "twenty-five [mulattoes] hang-ing together, and . . . the whites determined to kill everyone in the town, and never permit any to live there again."[32] Before order could be restored, two hundred mulattoes were executed without even the semblance of a trial.[33] In early October riot-torn Martinique experienced another uprising, which involved the white citizenry and about ten thousand Negroes and mulattoes. Hundreds of soldiers arrived from Basse-Terre, Guadeloupe, to help suppress the rebellion, but conflict continued to rage. Even Guadeloupe felt several serious mulatto disturbances, which hin-dered the sending of more reinforcements to Martinique. These revolts were only of local significance, however, mainly because the mulattoes lacked the leadership necessary to attract the at-tention of the National Assembly. This changed with the arrival of Vincent Ogé in Saint-Domingue.[34]

Ogé was particularly angered by the failure of the National As-sembly to seat mulatto delegates or even to listen to their com-plaints; moreover, the refusal of the white colonials to include the *gens de couleur* in the Instructions of March 28, as well as white brutality toward the mulatto, convinced him that the only recourse was force.[35] In a conversation with Clarkson in Paris, Vincent Ogé unleashed his frustrations: "I begin not to care whether the Na-tional Assembly will admit us or not. But let it beware of the consequences. We will no longer be held in a degraded light. Dis-patches shall go directly to St. Domingo; and we will soon follow them. . . . Our arms shall make us independent and respectable."[36] Ogé left France early in July 1790, stopping in England and at Charleston, South Carolina, before finally landing near Le Cap François in mid-October. The details of his trip are obscure, but he did communicate with Petrie, the French consul at Charleston, and perhaps won his support. Ogé, however, made his plans too public, for news of his plot preceded him to Saint-Domingue.[37]

Landing in North Province, Ogé made his headquarters at Grande Rivière, fifteen miles from Le Cap François, and ap-pointed his two brothers and Marc Chavannes as his chief lieu-tenants.[38] After gathering a small force of about seven hundred mulattoes, Ogé sent a letter on October 29 to the Provincial Assembly of the North, making it clear that he wanted the *gens de couleur* included in the Instructions of March 28 and that he did not "include . . . the Negro in slavery."[39] Yet Ogé did secretly plan to lead the slaves in a general insurrection to gain mulatto-white equality. He seemed to have the naïve belief that he could control the unleashed power of the blacks for the benefit of mulattoes only. Ogé lacked the genius of organization, and the whites under the command of Mauduit quickly drove the mulatto conspirators in the vicinity of Le Cap François into the nearby mountains. Those mulattoes conspiring with Ogé near Les Cayes in South Province fared no better; about seven hundred of them held out stubbornly against the whites in mountain positions until their resistance was broken. Seeing that their plot had failed, Ogé and Chavannes fled to St. Jago in Spanish Santo Domingo.[40]

Besides obviously intensifying mulatto-white hatreds, the Ogé rebellion seriously injured the bureaucracy. Many whites feared that Mauduit had convinced the mulattoes to disperse with the promise that their hopes would be fulfilled, since Mauduit had used the mulattoes earlier to preserve bureaucratic authority. To dispel this fear, Blanchelande, who replaced Peynier as governor in November, made strenuous efforts to have Ogé and Chavannes extradited from Spanish Santo Domingo. Early in 1791 Captain-General Joaquín García y Moreno returned the two men, and they stood trial before Blanchelande and two other magistrates. After receiving the death penalty, Ogé and Chavannes were broken on the wheel and hanged on March 9. Eventually the purge resulted in some two hundred executions. But the whites were still suspicious of Governor Blanchelande, believing that he had suppressed the details of Ogé's confession during interrogation and that the governor might even be a member of the *Amis des Noirs*. Although these beliefs were erroneous, they were nevertheless widely accepted as fact. Yet the major blow to bureaucratic authority had already occurred: the assassination of Mauduit.[41]

Early in March, two French regiments arrived at Port-au-Prince to reinforce the bureaucracy. The troops, however, mutinied and aligned themselves with the *petit blanc*–infiltrated National Guard, swearing to avenge the defeat Mauduit had inflicted on the *petits blancs* a year earlier.[42] Mauduit saw that the situation in Port-au-Prince was verging on civil war and sent Blanchelande to the safety of Le Cap François. But Mauduit lacked any real authority because his own regiment had joined the mutineers, tearing the white feathers of the old regime from their caps. Mauduit offered to return the captured colors of the *petits blancs* as a gesture of good will, hoping that this would satisfy his opponents and perhaps save what was left of bureaucratic authority. The return of the colors on March 4 was tense; the mutineers and *petits blancs* were assembled on the parade grounds for the ceremony. Just when Mauduit appeared to have the situation in hand, "one of his own grenadiers shouted for his head. Mauduit was hacked to pieces and they fixed his head on a bayonet."[43] With the death of Mauduit, the bureaucracy was through, even though Blanchelande was allowed to remain as governor. It is also significant that Mauduit was killed just five days before the execution of Ogé. Obviously the whites, especially the *petits blancs*, connected both men with the Mulatto Question.[44]

Yet it was in death, rather than in life, that Ogé accomplished one of his major objectives—the popularization of the Mulatto Question in France. Of course Brissot de Warville approved of the mulatto insurrection, and he said so in his *Patriote françois*; however, there is no proof that the *Amis des Noirs* was directly involved in the Ogé plot.[45] Many Frenchmen now agreed with the *Amis des Noirs* that something needed to be done for the mulatto, because "the blood of those martyrs, Ogé and Chavannes, ignominously shed upon the scaffold, cried aloud for vengeance."[46] Ogé became a popular hero, just as John Brown did in the northern United States almost seventy years later, and "the planters . . . for a time . . . dared not to appear in the streets of Paris."[47] As popular feeling rose, so did agitation for the National Assembly to take action on the Mulatto Question. The Jacobin Club of Angers began the movement with a circular letter which called for full citizenship for propertied mulattoes. Soon the demands of the French public moved the Assembly to pass the May Decree (1791).[48]

Even though the *Amis des Noirs* now had unprecedented support, it still had to face a difficult struggle within the bourgeois-dominated National Assembly. The resulting May Degree did not appear to be much of an abolitionist victory. Philippe Roume, a colonial observer, warned the Assembly that "the colonies would collapse if the Declaration of Rights was applied to the slaves, and it would hurt France commercially."[49] The Assembly did not need the reminder, for the arguments of Robespierre, Abbé Grégoire, and Brissot against slavery and the slave trade made no headway; the dreams of the *Amis des Noirs* would not be accomplished until after the establishment of Jacobin control. Seeing its frontal attack on slavery fail, the *Amis des Noirs* returned to its traditional tactic of approaching slavery through the mulatto. On May 15 Rawbell, a radical Jacobin, recommended the enfranchisement of all mulattoes who both met necessary property qualifications and were born of free parents. Only a very small percentage of the *gens de couleur*—perhaps no more than a few hundred—would be included. The motion passed, and it seemed to be only a slight setback for Barnave and the Colonial Committee. After all, the Assembly saw no harm in enfranchising a group that shared many of its own characteristics. But underneath the surface of tranquility was a strong undertow: Robespierre clearly broke with the Triumvirate, and Abbé Grégoire instructed the mulattoes to lead the slave "progressively to liberty."[50] The most unforeseen result of the May Decree was the violent reaction in the French West Indies, especially Saint-Domingue. The Assembly soon saw the error of the decree, but by then it was too late.[51]

The colonial deputies of Saint-Domingue, Martinique, and Guadeloupe bolted the Assembly with the passage of the May Decree, a move which was minimal compared to the reaction of Saint-Domingue itself when news of the legislation reached there on July 1.[52] The whites, believing that the decree included all mulattoes, were outraged. One observer noted that "you have no idea of the violent propositions made, and not contradicted, both against the mulattoes and France: nothing less than to cut the throats of the former, desert the latter, and call in the English."[53] The observer was right, especially about the English, for now many whites saw the preservation of their society in a British protectorate, at least until the Assembly returned to its senses. Captain

Davidson of the *Charming Sally* reported that as soldiers landed in the French West Indies to enforce the May Decree, the *grands* and *petits blancs* resisted:

> The white inhabitants . . . resented it in the most violent manner, particularly at Cape-François, where they immediately secured a ship of war . . . to prevent her falling under the faction of the National Assembly. They then plucked the national cockades from their hats, mounted black British ribbons, and in less than an hour, dispatched two packets, one to England, the other to Jamaica, soliciting their protection.[54]

After this initial shock, the May Decree brought both unity and polarization among the colonists. For the first time since the beginning of the French Revolution, the whites seemed in agreement —the mulattoes must be stopped. Even Blanchelande was determined that the May Decree should not be enforced, and he approved the call for a new colonial assembly to meet at Léogane. After convening on August 9, the Léogane Assembly adjourned, with its next session scheduled for the more centrally located Le Cap François. This was an obvious concession to the *grands blancs*, designed to reduce the chances of another secession. With their new-found unity, the whites had second thoughts about an English protectorate. They agreed to the ultimate authority of the National Assembly in all external matters, and the colonial deputies in Paris returned to the Assembly to work for the repeal of the May Decree. The mulattoes were furious at the white tactics; it seemed as if two years of struggle had netted them nothing. They armed themselves and prepared to follow the example of Ogé *en masse*. Yet neither white nor mulatto appeared to be aware that the sparks of their various conflicts had been smoldering in the veritable "powder keg" of slavery. Soon, even before the new general assembly could reconvene, an explosion occurred which completely shattered Saint-Domingue. From the rubble modern Haiti emerged.[55]

Why were the slaves about to join the Haitian Revolution? One influence was the ideology of the French Revolution, which reached Saint-Domingue in various ways. The *Amis des Noirs* bombarded the colony with pamphlets, and the whites themselves transmitted ideas to the slaves through indiscreet conversation. Several of Abbé Grégoire's pamphlets had particularly wide circulation among the mulattoes and eventually filtered down to the slaves themselves. His basic theme was the emancipation of all slaves in the French West Indies. Of course the slaves often construed the idea of emancipation to fit their own frame of reference, defining freedom from slavery as meaning freedom from work, a problem which would continually plague Toussaint Louverture.[56] The boundless nature of ideas also made the principles of the French Revolution dangerous in a slave society: how were the slaves to know that they were not included? It is significant that one Negro chief, after the slaves revolted, asked the whites in beseiged Le Cap François, "Have you not sworn to maintain the French Constitution? . . . Have you forgotten that you have formally sworn to the Declaration of Rights . . . which says that men are born free and equal?"[57]

There were other influences at work besides ideology. One was the hatred some slaves felt toward their masters, as indicated by the antiwhite orientation of voodoo. Closely connected with this hatred was the desire of many slaves to destroy the institution of slavery itself. One proof is the case of a planter who bought nine slaves at Le Cap François during August 1791. Before he could return home, all had committed suicide. Other slaves wished only to alter the routine of slavery, proposing three days off as the price necessary for the cessation of their rebellion.[58] The reverence the slaves had for the king of France, who represented a sort of great father image to them, caused many to take even a reactionary position. James Delaire stated that "the slaves revolted in the name of Louis XVI, in order (said they) to reinstate him on his throne and restore to the clergy and nobility their rights, properties, and privileges."[59] Jean François, the most important early slave leader, proudly wore a captured Cross of St. Louis. Eventually he and Biassou, another early leader, became completely reactionary and fought on the side of the Spanish. Then there was the *caudillo*-type influence which compelled a large number of slaves to follow their leader blindly and to force others to do the same, regardless of what he advocated (much like the *llaneros* who later followed Boves and Páez in Venezuela).[60]

Because there were so many active influences, it is inaccurate to state simply, as Basil Davidson did, that the "slaves demanded their freedom" or to take James's view that "the slaves worked on the land, and, like revolutionary peasants everywhere, they aimed at the extermination of their oppressors."[61] There was no monolithic cause of the slave rebellion. The destruction of slavery was a major goal of the Haitian Revolution, but it was not firmly established until mid-1793. It was the two years of anarchy and turmoil during 1789–91, rather than any single reason for rebellion, which allowed slaves of various persuasions to revolt simultaneously.

Georges Lefebvre in his classic *History of the French Revolution* maintained that "the Revolution reduced Louis XVI to impotence, but until 1793 it had no government."[62] This was also true in the French West Indies, where France especially "neglected Saint-Domingue, abandoning the factions to themselves."[63] As early as February 2, 1791, the National Assembly decided to send three commissioners to Saint-Domingue to restore order through firm rule, but the Assembly was so engrossed in its own problems that none came until after the slaves revolted in late August.[64]

Nor was Saint-Domingue adequately garrisoned to maintain order. Troops that were sent to the French West Indies met resistance from the white colonials, who believed them to be agents of propaganda—"hence the new soldiery cannot be trusted."[65] Furthermore, the bureaucracy's control steadily declined after the beginning of the French Revolution, and none of the other factions —*grands blancs*, *petits blancs*, or mulattoes—was strong enough to dominate the others and fill the power vacuum. While the factions struggled, "the slave, completely astonished, searched to know the causes of this restlessness and each day became more avid in his astonishment. The moment was favorable in order to throw off the chains of barbarity."[66] That moment came on the night of August 22, 1791, when thousands of slaves, motivated by different reasons, revolted. The whites and mulattoes had handed them the colony by default.[67]

NOTES FOR CHAPTER TWO

1. Georges Lefebvre, *The French Revolution*, 2 vols. (New York: Columbia Univ. Press, 1962), I, 99–101; M. J. Sydenham, *The French Revolution* (New York: Capricorn Books, 1966), 27–29; Mitchell Garrett, *The French Colonial Question, 1789–1791* (Ann Arbor: George Wahr Publishers, 1916), 6; Clarkson, *Abolition of the African Slave Trade*, 131; *Gazette Nationale, ou Le Moniteur Universel* (Paris), Aug. 31, 1789 (hereafter cited as *Le Moniteur*).

2. France, *Lettre du Comité Colonial de France, au Comité Colonial de Saint-Domingue* (Paris: n.n., 1788), 110–12.

3. *Le Moniteur*, July 6 and Aug. 31, 1789; Garrett, *Colonial Question*, 10; Blanche Maurel, ed., *Cahiers des doléances de la colonie de Saint-Domingue* (Paris: Libraire Ernest Leroux, 1933), 263–67; Edwards, *San Domingo*, 14.

4. Observations of James Delaire to Timothy Pickering, Secretary of State, Aug. 10, 1798, U.S., Dept. of State, Consular Dispatches, Cap-Haitien, vol. 1 (National Archives).

5. Garrett, *Colonial Question*, 10–11; Sydenham, *French Revolution*, 42–45; Leo Gershoy, *The French Revolution and Napoleon* (New York: Appleton, 1933), 109–13.

6. Clarkson, *Abolition of the African Slave-Trade*, 131.

7. *Ibid.*, 103–105, 113–14. The planters demonstrated their fear of the *Amis des Noirs* in many ways. One was when the entire society was threatened with assassination. Another was the belief that the *Amis des Noirs* was collecting an arsenal of weapons with which to arm the slaves. This rumor gained such wide acceptance that soldiers searched the society's committee room, where they found "two or three books and some waste paper."

8. *Ibid.*, 101, 107; Perkins, *Reminiscences*, 7; *Le Moniteur*, July 6, 1789.

9. George Rudé, *Revolutionary Europe, 1783–1815* (New York: Harper, 1964), 97–100, 106–108; Lefebvre, *French Revolution*, I, 130.

10. *Correspondance secrète des Députés de Saint-Domingue avec les Comités de cette île* (Paris: n.n., 1790), 7.

11. *Revolutionary Europe*, 108.

12. Frank M. Anderson, ed., *The Constitution and Other Select Documents Illustrative of the History of France, 1789–1907*, 2d ed. (New York: Russell and Russell, 1908), 59, 61.

13. *Correspondance secrète*, 13.

14. Garrett, *Colonial Question*, 16–18; Edwards, *San Domingo*, 21.

15. *Correspondance secrète*, 10.

16. Lefebvre, *French Revolution*, I, 172; *Le Moniteur*, March 4, 1790; Carl L. Lokke, *France and the Colonial Question, 1763–1801* (New York: Columbia Univ. Press, 1932), 128; Delaire to Pickering, Aug. 10, 1798, Consular Dispatches, Cap-Haitien, vol. 1.

17. *Réclamations de Marquis de Nicolas, Robert de Cocherel, Relative au travail du Comité des Douze sur le mode de convocation des Assemblées des Colonies* (Paris: n.n., 1790), 18.

18. *Ibid.*; *Le Patriote françois* (Paris), March 29, 1790.

19. Peter Chazotte, *Historical Sketches of the Revolution, and the Foreign and Civil War in the Island of St. Domingo, with a Narrative of the Entire Massacre of the White Population of the Island: Eyewitness Report* (New York: William Applegate Co., 1840), 9.

20. Perkins, *Reminiscences*, 12–13.

21. Baron de Wimpffen, *Voyage to Saint-Domingo*, 285–86; *Le Moniteur*, Jan. 12, 1790.

22. Edwards, *San Domingo*, 22.

23. Martinique was experiencing similar difficulties as the commanding general and his officers, symbolic of royalty and aristocracy, fought the colonial militia for control. The militia won and made Comte Damask, one of their supporters, commandant of the island. Letter Extract from St. Pierre, Martinique, March 27, 1790, in *State Gazette of South Carolina* (Charleston), May 17, 1790.

24. Letter Extract from Les Cayes, Saint-Domingue, Nov. 23, 1790, in Boston *Independent Chronicle*, Jan. 6, 1791; Edwards, *San Domingo*, 25–26.

25. *Le Moniteur*, Oct. 11, 1790.

26. *Ibid.*, Aug. 14, 1790; Perkins, *Reminiscences*, 7.

27. *The Times* (London), Sept. 25, 1790.

28. *Ibid.*, Sept. 28, 1790; Delaire to Pickering, Aug. 10, 1798, Consular Dispatches, Cap-Haitien, vol. 1.

29. *Le Moniteur*, June 23 and Oct. 13, 1790; *The Times* (London), Oct. 12, 1790.

30. Roume to National Assembly, May, 1791, Philippe Roume Papers (Library of Congress); Perkins, *Reminiscences*, 16; "Mémoire historique," Rochambeau Documents, 7; M. Gros, *Récit historique sur les qui se succédes dans les camps de la Grande-Rivière, du Dondon, de Ste.-Suzanne et autres, depuis le 26 Octobre jusqu'au 24 Decembre de la même année* (Baltimore: S. and J. Adams, 1793), 20; Clarkson, *Abolition of the African Slave-Trade*, 107–108.

31. Letter Extract from Jacmel, Saint-Domingue, May 10, 1790, in St. George's *Chronicle and Grenada Gazette*, July 2, 1790.

32. Letter Extract from St. Eustatius, June 8, 1790, in *State Gazette of South Carolina*, July 22, 1790.

33. Boston *Independent Chronicle*, July 1, 1790.

34. Letter Extracts from Basse-Terre, Guadeloupe, Sept. 30 and Oct. 1, 1790, in *ibid.*, Nov. 4, 1790; *The Times* (London), July 24, 1790.

35. Vincent Ogé to the Provincial Assembly of the North, Oct. 29, 1790, in *Le Moniteur*, Dec. 29, 1790; Clarkson, *Abolition of the African Slave-Trade*, 120–21.

36. Clarkson, *Abolition of the Slave-Trade*, 120–21.

37. Delaire to Pickering, Aug. 10, 1798, Consular Dispatches, Cap-Haitien, vol. 1; *Le Moniteur*, Dec. 25, 1790.

38. *Le Moniteur*, Dec. 25, 1790; Perkins, *Reminiscences*, 14.

39. Ogé to Provincial Assembly of the North, Oct. 29, 1790, in *Le Moniteur*, Dec. 29, 1790.

40. Letter Extract from Le Cap François, Nov. 8, 1790, in *Maryland Journal and Baltimore Advertiser*, Dec. 24, 1790; Letter Extract from Les Cayes, Saint-Domingue, Nov. 23, 1790, in Boston *Independent Chronicle*, Jan. 6, 1791.

41. Letter Extract from Le Cap François, Nov. 8, 1790, in *Maryland Journal and Baltimore Advertiser*, Dec. 24, 1790; Edwards, *San Domingo*, 46; *State Gazette of South Carolina*, April 28, 1791; Delaire to Pickering, Aug. 10, 1798, Consular Dispatches, Cap-Haitien, vol. 1; Perkins, *Reminiscences*, 14.

42. The reasons for this mutiny are not clear, but perhaps the regulars associated the bureaucracy and *grands blancs* with royalty and aristocracy; thus they may have identified the *petits blancs* with themselves. This would not be unusual since there were several examples in France of enlisted men rebelling against their aristocratic officers. There was at least one clear case of this in Saint-Domingue: the commandant of Le Cap François was murdered by his own corps because he wore a yellow jacket—"a mark of aristocracy as it was the color of the regiment of d'Artois, the famous French counterrevolutionary." Perkins, *Reminiscences*, 25–26.

43. Letter Extract from Port-au-Prince, March 5, 1791, in Boston *Independent Chronicle*, April 22, 1791.

44. *Ibid.*; Perkins, *Reminiscences*, 7; Edwards, *San Domingo*, 55–57.

45. *Le Patriote françois*, Jan. 5, 1791.

46. Baron de Vastey, *An Essay on the Causes of the Revolution and Civil Wars of Hayti* (London: Western Luminary Office, 1823), 19.

47. Edwards, *San Domingo*, 61.

48. *Le Moniteur*, May 22, 1791.

49. Roume to National Assembly, May, 1791, Roume Papers.

50. "Abbé Grégoire's Address to the Mulattoes concerning the May Decree, June 8, 1791," in Edwards, *San Domingo*, 100.

51. James M. Thompson, *Robespierre*, 2 vols. (New York: Appleton, 1936), I, 132–34; Garrett, *Colonial Question*, 104, 120.

52. *State Gazette of South Carolina*, Aug. 18, 1791.

53. Attorney General of Le Cap François to Charles de Chabanon, July 9, 1791, in *The Times* (London), Aug. 31, 1791.

54. *State Gazette of South Carolina*, Aug. 8, 1791.

55. Extract of Register of General Assembly of the French of St. Domingo in Session at Léogane, Aug. 9, 1791, San Domingo File (South Carolina Archives); Edwards, *San Domingo*, 66–67; Baron de Wimpffen, *Voyage to Saint-Domingo*, 335–36; *Le Moniteur*, June 23, 1791.

56. *Le Moniteur*, Jan. 12, 1790; Perkins, *Reminiscences*, 8–9, 16; Parham,

My Odyssey, 34; Gros, *Récit historique*, 20; Major General Adam William-son to Secretary Dundas, Sept. 1791, C. O. 137/50; Roume to National As-sembly, May 1791, Roume Papers; "Mémoire historique," Rochambeau Documents, 12; Letter Extract, n.d., in Philadelphia *Aurora*, Feb. 17, 1795.

57. France, Convention Nationale, *Précis de la justification de Joseph-Paul-Augustin Cambefort, Colonel du Régiment du Cap, et des autres Mili-taires déportés de Saint-Domingue Rigoureusement demontrée par les seules Pieces deposées au Comité Colonial de la Convention Nationale* (Paris: N. H. Nyon, 1793), 4–5.

58. Newport *Mercury*, Oct. 15 and 22, 1791; Boston *Independent Chroni-cle*, Oct. 13, 1791.

59. Delaire to Pickering, Aug. 10, 1798, Consular Dispatches, Cap-Haitien, vol. 1. Gros, in another valuable eyewitness account, stated that the slaves knew of the king's confinement, a situation intensified by his futile flight on June 20, 1791. Moreover, the slaves believed that the king had ordered them to arm themselves to free him. Gros, *Récit historique*, 23.

60. Gros, *Récit historique*, 45; *Maryland Journal and Baltimore Adver-tiser*, Oct. 21, 1791; *The Times* (London), Oct. 14, 1794; Laplace to Don García, Captain-General of Santo Domingo, April 4, 1794, Etienne Laveaux Papers (Library of Congress and Bibliothèque Nationale).

61. Davidson, *West Africa*, 229; James, *Black Jacobins*, 85.

62. *French Revolution*, I, 135.

63. *Courrier Français* (Philadelphia), Oct. 21, 1797.

64. *Le Moniteur*, Feb. 3, 1791.

65. Fulwar Skipwithe to Thomas Jefferson, Secretary of State, May 1, 1791, U.S., Dept. of State, Consular Dispatches, Martinique, vol. I (National Archives).

66. François Joseph Pamphile Lacroix, *Mémoires pour servir à l'histoire de la révolution de Saint-Domingue*, 2 vols. (Paris: Pillet Aine, 1820), I, 88–89.

67. Unrest among the slaves was widespread in the West Indies but usually was met with suppression. On the British island of Dominica a slave rebel-lion erupted under the leadership of Paulinaire during Jan. 1791. It was basically the result of a dispute over the number of days off the slaves were to have. The blacks wanted three days for themselves, but the planters re-fused. The rebellion, however, failed both because the white caste was united and because the island was adequately garrisoned. It was only in the French West Indies that slave unrest succeeded in toppling the collapsing and ill-protected white castes from power. Of the French Caribbean colonies, Guadeloupe and Saint-Domingue had the closest related experiences until their reconquest in 1802. Martinique was the only French West Indian colony which escaped serious collapse, and this was due only to the British, who captured and held the island from 1794 to 1801. *Supplement to the Cornwall Chronicle* (Montego Bay, Jamaica), Aug. 6, 1791.

CHAPTER THREE

Explosion and
Confusion, 1791-1792

Even though the whites and the mulattoes had struggled among themselves for two years, they were not oblivious to the possibility of a slave uprising. As early as November 1789 the whites suspected a widespread rebellion around Le Cap François. Some believed that as many as twenty thousand slaves were involved, but their suspicions never materialized because of a general white alert. Of the other indications of unrest, the most serious occurred on August 16, 1791—just six days before the masses of slaves revolted. A slave driver who was arrested and interrogated for burning a trash house confessed a plot to destroy many plantation owners and even named some of the other conspirators. The whites treated the plot as a local problem and seemed unaware of its general nature. Little did they know that colonial Saint-Domingue, the "Pearl of the Antilles," was about to be engulfed in a tide of black humanity.[1]

The particulars surrounding the planning of the slave rebellion are obscure, but Boukmann's role was certainly important. A huge, muscular man and a fugitive slave from Jamaica, Boukmann was a voodoo priest who despised whites. He used the deep roots of voodoo among the slaves as a communications system to organize rebellion. Others besides Boukmann were involved, among them Gilles and John Baptiste, both killed in the early phase of fighting, as was Boukmann. Another early leader may have been Jean François, who had been well treated as a slave but who had spent the last few years prior to 1791 as a maroon. Most of François' power and leadership, however, came after the slaves rebelled.[2]

Late on the night of August 22, Boukmann gathered the slaves of the Turpin, Flaville, Clement, Trémes, and Noé plantations on the Plaine du Nord. One of their first victims was a refiner's apprentice on the Noé plantation whom they dragged to "the front of the dwelling house, and there hewed him into pieces with their cutlasses: his screams brought out the overseer, whom they instantly shot."[3] The slaves had joined the Haitian Revolution.

The rebellion "spread like wildfire." Perhaps as many as 100,000 slaves were involved in North Province alone, where masses of blacks threatened the safety of Le Cap François. According to Lacroix, an eyewitness, the slaves had become enraged, like angry tigers on the prowl.[4] One anonymous observer saw blacks dragging their victims along the roads, and "young children transfixed upon the points of bayonets were the bleeding flags which followed the troop of cannibals."[5] Another onlooker noted that the slaves "massacred a great number of the whites, and have taken as prisoners some females of that complexion, whom they force to do the duties of servants."[6] Many of the dead whites were even found spiked to the ground with wooden stakes.[7]

Human destruction was not the only object of the slaves; some vented their wrath against the plantation, symbol of Negro oppression. One dismayed *grand blanc* observed that rebel blacks destroyed "the aqueduct which conducted the river water to the great wheel of the mill; and they drained the pond by numerous irrigation trenches, that picturesque lake which carried such coolness to the habitation."[8] As the whites of the Plaine du Nord made their way to the protection of Le Cap François, over three hundred plantations were destroyed amid roaring "fires and the explosions and whistling of cannon."[9]

Not all slaves were "tigers," however; some did not even want to join the rebellion. Influenced by humanity and loyalty, many slaves protected their masters' estates until the black rebels, ceaselessly attacking the plantations, forced them into the mountains and Le Cap François. One kind master who benefited from slave loyalty was Chevalier Duperier. When he was informed of the rebellion, Duperier decided to flee to Le Cap François. Learning of their master's plan, Duperier's slaves asked permission to give him an armed escort to his destination.[10] Unsatisfied with this demonstration of their affection, they loaded the household furnishings of their master upon mule-drawn carts and, "surrounding him in a body, armed with clubs, brought him safely to the city."[11]

Loyal slaves did not have the organization, however, to withstand the swarming black hordes of rebels. Often they faced capture, indoctrination, and death by those in revolt. The expanding conflict, like a tidal wave, swept faithful blacks along in its currents, disregarding their feelings.[12]

The whites in Northern Province were stunned when ten thousand *grands* and *petits blancs* were cornered in Le Cap François by forty thousand slaves. Moreover, the whites continued to be divided, with both groups trying to control Governor Blanchelande; the governor himself was confused to the point of indecision. Yet most were agreed on one program: the black rebels, often known as Insurgents, must be exterminated.[13] As one English eyewitness noted, the whites "have six gallows erected in one of their squares, together with a wheel, to put the poor devils to the torture, as they are brought in."[14] Captain Bickford of Salem, Massachusetts, reported that "the white troops, who now take no prisoners, but kill everything black or yellow, leave the Negroes dead upon the fields."[15] Despite these measures, the Insurgents continued their siege. Furthermore, the majority of the inhabitants of Le Cap François were slaves, forcing the whites into a position of defense because "they could only keep the rebellion out and keep the blacks inside from uniting with those outside."[16] Still the whites felt confident in their supposed military superiority.

At first this belief seemed to be justified. Many *gens de couleur* of Le Cap François unexpectedly came to the aid of the whites, took firearms from the king's store, and killed many Insurgents. After all, equality with whites might be their reward. In the meantime, Blanchelande firmly secured the defenses of the city, which withstood heavy black onslaughts. Hundreds of Insurgents and their leaders fell in battle: Gilles was killed, beheaded, and exposed on the gallows for four days; Boukmann and John Baptiste shared similar fates. The whites now felt secure enough to make sallies against enemy positions near Le Cap François. On September 20, 1791, whites and *gens de couleur* under the command of Colonel Louis Touzard made a major assault against Insurgents at the Galifauit plantation, a few miles from the city. After furious fighting and slaughter, the black rebels retreated to Red Bank, about thirty miles from Le Cap François.[17]

Subsequently many whites became contemptuous toward their black adversaries. A French general and his junior officers were dining together, an eyewitness reported, when the alarm for approaching Insurgents was sounded. Quite unconcerned, the general and his subordinates continued their meal until

> A cannon ball passed through the window and carried away, right under our beards, the table and all the plates. The general, infuriated by this mishap, mounted his horse with food still in his mouth, and left camp with six hundred men and four pieces of artillery. Two hours later one could not find a living Negro within a circle of two and a half miles, and the roads were strewn with their bloody remains.[18]

White military superiority was an illusion, despite the disorganized and quixotic appearance of the Insurgents. Often some black rebels were "nude, some in tatters, and some grotesquely decked in rich apparel taken from . . . [white] wardrobes. They were armed with guns, knives, and all the sharp utensils of kitchen and farm."[19] Disorganization, however, soon began to disappear in the black armies. One amazed participant noted that "they now come in regular bodies, and a considerable part of them are well armed."[20] Moreover, the Insurgent forces showed considerable resolve as they marched into battle to African martial music and with unfurled banners inscribed with "death to all whites."[21]

Nor did the black man lack ingenuity. On one occasion a group of unarmed Insurgents withstood a white assault by using improvised cotton mattresses as shields against the musket balls.[22] The blacks, furthermore, were excellent guerrilla fighters. Advancing white armies often encountered poisoned water holes, booby traps, and ambuscades. As one frustrated *grand blanc* put it, "each tree, each hole, each piece of rock, hid from our unseeing eyes a cowardly assassin."[23] In guerrilla fighting the Insurgent sometimes used a subtle tactic, best described as playing "Old Sambo." That is, when captured he attempted to portray the white man's image of the good slave: a childlike being who was both

TOUSSAINT AS COMMANDER IN CHIEF OF THE ARMY OF HAITI. *The Bettmann Archive.*

TOUSSAINT REQUESTS ENGLISH OFFICERS TO LEAVE THE ISLAND, 1798. *The Bettmann Archive.*

faithful and stupid. If his ruse was discovered, the Insurgent often faced his fate stoically; in one case "when he saw that his fate was sealed, he began to laugh, sing, and joke."[24]

With growing Insurgent strength and France's neglect of proper reinforcements for Saint-Domingue, any white resurgence was destined to be only temporary. Colonel Touzard led another expedition against four thousand blacks who were massed at the Latour plantation. This time he was repulsed and forced into full retreat. Had the blacks pursued him, Le Cap François itself might have fallen. Even more disastrous was Blanchelande's attempt to confine the rebellion to North Province with a military cordon along its mountainous southern border. This line of defense was ineffective because both the governor and the Colonial Assembly were slow to put it into operation and because it was undermanned. Besides, even if the cordon had been successful, indigenous rebellion was already brewing in South and West provinces.[25]

The situation in these provinces involved a three-way civil war among whites, mulattoes, and blacks, especially in West Province, where the *gens de couleur* revolted late in August in the parish of Mirebalais. They were quickly joined by thousands of slaves and even by a band of maroons known as "The Swiss," in imitation of Louis XVI's bodyguard. Together they went on a rampage of destruction and completely defeated a white detachment sent against them from Port-au-Prince. The coffee plantations adjacent to the Cul-de-Sac suffered particularly severe damage, and the excesses against humanity were as terrible as those in North Province.[26] Three mulattoes led the rebellion: André Rigaud, Louis Beauvais, and Pierre Pinchinat.[27]

On September 13, four thousand mulattoes laid siege to Port-au-Prince, last major stronghold of the whites in West Province. But the *gens de couleur* found it distasteful that the slaves, their comrades in arms, might gain equality with them. They wanted to join the *grands blancs*, not destroy them. Therefore the mulattoes offered Humus de Jumecourt and Coutard, leaders of the white planters, their assistance in suppressing the slaves.[28] With this agreement, "the mulattoes turned on all the Negroes who had come to their aid."[29] Among the whites, the *petits blancs* found the new alliance most objectionable. Yet with the black man

51

storming the walls of Port-au-Prince, even they saw its immediate necessity. On September 14 the *gens de couleur* gave a large public dinner for the whites, and afterward they went arm in arm to Mass and sang the Te Deum. The bargain became official for all Saint-Domingue on September 20 when the Colonial Assembly not only recognized the May Decree, but applied it to all mulattoes, regardless of their parentage.[30]

In the meantime the Insurgents were putting great pressure on Port-au-Prince. Incensed by the desertion of the mulattoes, they demanded surrender of all the *gens de couleur* within the city or else they would attack.[31] The whites refused and braced for the onslaught. "Every house," said one observer, "has a cask of water and lights before the door, for fear of the Negroes in town setting fire to them."[32] In a fierce attack the Insurgents took heavy losses and retreated. Part white had saved white. As quickly as fear disappeared, however, so did the promise of mulatto equality.[33]

Once again the mulattoes of West Province revolted and joined the blacks in the mountainous backlands. Soon fifteen hundred mulattoes seized Léogane and pressed on toward Port-au-Prince; an army of twenty thousand slaves was headed in the same direction. Faced with destruction, the whites of Port-au-Prince resurrected their promises to the mulattoes; by the end of October, there was a new alliance between them. Brimming with new hope, the *gens de couleur* entered Port-au-Prince on November 7. But the new agreement was not without dishonor for the mulattoes; they had consented to the deportation of "The Swiss," their faithful allies. On November 3, "The Swiss" embarked upon a voyage which would end in their mass execution.[34]

While fighting raged within Saint-Domingue, nations with Caribbean interests began to react. Understandably, England's response resulted mainly from fear for its West Indian colonies. When news of the slave rebellion reached Jamaica, Lord Effingham, the governor, sent arms and ammunition to the besieged French planters. At about the same time he ordered the Mountain Blues, a tough group of Negro soldiers, to embark and sail for Saint-Domingue. Moreover, Effingham attempted to suppress the ideology of the Haitian Revolution by keeping French planters and their slaves out of Jamaica. In Parliament the events in Saint-

Domingue worked against the movement to abolish the slave trade. One reason was that British West Indian commerce suddenly became more valuable because of the economic devastation of Saint-Domingue. The main reason for the reactionary mood in Parliament, however, was fear—fear that any move toward suppression of the slave trade might touch off slave revolts in the British Caribbean, especially Jamaica. In 1792, therefore, the House of Commons agreed only to the principle of gradual liquidation of the slave trade; abolition did not come until 1808.[35]

Spain looked on the slave rebellion as an opportunity to regain the western end of Hispaniola. From the beginning, the Spanish gave aid and encouragement to the Insurgents. Gros, an eyewitness, overheard a Spaniard speak to a group of Insurgents, claiming France "had lost her best men, no longer remembered the king, lost all of her religious sense, covered herself in crime, and deserved the greatest punishment."[36] Such lines of reasoning drew most of the black leaders to the side of the Spanish. By mid-1793 this policy was on the point of success, as Spain, like England, invaded Saint-Domingue. In the long run, however, Spain was the loser because its policy of aggression contributed to the eventual loss of Spanish Santo Domingo to the black armies of Toussaint Louverture.[37]

The policy of the United States toward the Haitian Revolution followed two lines, sometimes coordinated, sometimes at loggerheads. The first was the defense of Southern slave society. As the Saint-Domingue Insurgents gained momentum, the South's fear of a slave revolt intensified. In a message to Saint-Domingue's Colonial Assembly, Governor Charles Pinckney of South Carolina expressed this feeling: "When we recollect how nearly similar the situation of the Southern States and St. Domingo are in the profusion of slaves—that a day may arrive when they may be exposed to the same insurrections—we cannot but sensibly feel for your situation."[38]

Many Southerners believed that the day had already arrived, for at every turn they saw the influence of Saint-Domingue at work. Thomas Newton wrote to James Wood, lieutenant governor of Virginia, about a suspected slave uprising involving a Negro preacher named Garwin. The slaves from Saint-Domingue, he added, "would be ready to operate against us with the others."[39] Peter Gram of Richmond pointed out that the suspected rebellion would even include South Carolina as well as Virginia and that the method of destruction was to be fire because "the Negroes of Cape François have obtained their liberties by this method and they will proceed here in the same manner."[40] Alexander Garden of South Carolina saw the importation of blacks from Saint-Domingue as a gigantic conspiracy to undermine the authority of the master, even claiming that Charleston had a chapter of the *Amis des Noirs*. He advocated that all Saint-Domingue blacks be expelled as a solution.[41] Some Southern states took Garden's advice, and Georgia and South Carolina went beyond it by temporarily suspending the foreign slave trade itself.[42]

The other line of American foreign policy, of particular interest to New England, called for the maintenance of Saint-Domingue as a trade base. This usually meant support of the government in power. As long as the white colonials maintained their grip, the two American policy lines coincided. In fact, there are several examples of Yankee ship captains and their crews standing "shoulder to shoulder" with the embattled whites of Saint-Domingue. Moreover, the United States loaned France 1.5 million livres ($300,000) for white relief in the colony. Yet once the whites fell from power, the blacks under Toussaint received much official and unofficial American aid and support. The "business-as-usual" philosophy of many American traders prevailed over the fears of the Southern planters. This triumph of the commercial interest may well have stemmed from the political control of the Federalists during the 1790s.[43]

The nation most appalled by the Saint-Domingue slave rebellion was France. A few abolitionists like Brissot saw it as material for propaganda against the planter; he especially emphasized English aid to the *grands* and *petits blancs* as an example of treachery. The bourgeois National Assembly, now in its last days, saw the error of the May Decree, reasoning that anything endangering Saint-Domingue was a mistake.[44] Furthermore, the chambers of commerce of Le Havre, Bordeaux, Marseilles, and Nantes put great pressure on the Assembly to revoke the decree. Within the Assembly itself, Barnave led the opposition to mulatto equality, stating his fear that the slaves were on the brink of freedom and advocating colonial self-determination in internal matters. On September 23 he moved for the repeal of the May Decree; the motion was carried on the next day. The Assembly went further. Mirbeck, Saint-Léger, and Roume were appointed as peace commissioners to Saint-Domingue, and an expedition of eighteen thousand soldiers was to accompany them. Little did the National Assembly know that its actions would injure rather than help France's most valued and beleaguered colony.[45]

Even though news of the repeal of the May Decree reached Saint-Domingue late in October, it did not mean the automatic loss of mulatto rights. That was left to the discretion of the Colonial Assembly. Gripped by a quiet tenseness, mulattoes and whites awaited a decision. Early in November the Colonial Assembly rejected its pledges of mulatto-white equality. The mulattoes were infuriated. Any incident involving a mulatto might set off a rebellion.[46]

That event occurred at Port-au-Prince on November 21. Whites had sentenced a mulatto to death and were about to execute him when many *gens de couleur* began to riot.[47] Much of Port-au-Prince was destroyed, but the mulattoes abandoned the city and retreated to Croix-des-Bouquets, a short distance away. Many whites, *grands blancs* in particular, who were tired of shabby mulatto treatment and fearful about their position, joined the *gens de couleur*. Among the white defectors were Coutard and Jumecourt, the two most prominent *grands blancs* in West Province.[48] One observer noted that "the mulattoes . . . look up to M. Coutard as their God, and all their maneuvers are directed by him."[49] Essentially the *grands blancs* and mulattoes of West Province, masters of the countryside, were fighting the *petits blancs*, masters of Port-au-Prince. In South Province the pattern was much the same, except the whites did not split.[50]

By the end of the year white power was largely broken in West and South provinces; only Port-au-Prince, Léogane, and Les Cayes remained in their possession. In the areas of mulatto occupation the whites were disarmed and obviously at the mercy of their *gens de couleur* conquerors. In the meantime the black Insurgents were still quite active.[51] Adding to the already great loss of life and material destruction, "the Negroes," noted one eyewitness, "go on destroying the country."[52] Everywhere "flames were perceived as far as the sight could reach."[53]

In North Province the situation was no better, for the whites and Insurgents still could not reach an agreement.[54] Moreover, the Colonial Assembly, located at Le Cap François, had no effective control outside North Province; West Province had even seceded. At the end of the year the *gens de couleur* sent a delegation to the Colonial Assembly, making clear their demands that white military power be curtailed and that the *petits blancs* be deported from the colony. Once again the Colonial Assembly was plunged into a dilemma, for the *petit blanc* was a bulwark against the Insurgents in North Province. This was the situation in Saint-Domingue when Saint-Léger, Mirbeck, and Roume arrived early in December.[55]

Although the peace commissioners came with a strong determination to pacify Saint-Domingue, their position was weak from the beginning. The French government had not backed them with adequate military force; eighteen thousand soldiers had been promised, but only six thousand arrived, and most of these succumbed to tropical diseases. Despite their weak position, the commissioners nearly succeeded in making peace.[56]

The primary aim of the mission was to reach an agreement with the Insurgent chiefs of North Province, Jean François and Biassou. Once these rebels were neutralized, dealing with the mulattoes would be easier. Accordingly, the first step of the commissioners was to declare a general amnesty for all those who would cease fighting. The Insurgents responded.[57]

Jean François, believing that a large French army would arrive soon and that his unconditional surrender might result, was especially anxious for peace. Perhaps he reasoned that any white concessions were better than none. To demonstrate his good faith, he ordered his army to cease devastating the Plaine du Nord and arranged to meet Biassou at the plantation of Madame du Fahy. At the conference Biassou expressed skepticism about a peace with the whites, but the war weariness of his troops led him to follow François. They then agreed to make their demands minimal. They asked for freedom for themselves and fifty high-ranking black leaders; in exchange their followers would return to the plantations of their former masters.[58] Both men, however, soon realized that the commissioners were too weak militarily to guarantee a settlement; therefore they decided to approach the Colonial Assembly. All was now up to the whites.[59]

On December 8 two Insurgent emissaries with a letter from Jean François arrived before the Colonial Assembly. The Assembly, lost in its own bigotry, refused to receive them, for it would be undignified for white to parley with black. Moreover, equality was implied. No, let the Insurgents surrender first and then the blacks would be shown "the known clemency of their proprietors."[60] Perhaps it was "the known clemency" of the whites which convinced François and Biassou of the insincerity of the Colonial Assembly. Yet they decided to pursue their policy of peace. This time, however, their only chance for success was to deal directly with the commissioners. A meeting was set for December 22 at the Saint-Michel plantation.[61]

By the end of 1791 peace no longer appeared elusive. At the meeting François brought white prisoners with him and released them as a token of his good will. He even threw himself on his knees before the commissioners, begged their forgiveness, and praised their humanity. The final arrangements for peace included amnesty for the Insurgents and the surrender of their weapons, the freeing of all white prisoners, and the return of black "rank and file" to the plantations.[62]

Bent on revenge, the Colonial Assembly refused to abide by the agreements and planned to massacre the Insurgents once they had given up their weapons. Biassou and François learned of the plot just as the white prisoners were being released. How they found out is not clear. La Roque, a high-ranking French officer at Le Cap François, may have warned them, or the blacks themselves may have uncovered the plot with their own agents.[63] "After this moment," reported one eyewitness, "not a single day would pass which would be unlighted by flames."[64] The last chance of the whites had collapsed under the weight of their own vengeance.

A black both discouraged and angered by the failure to achieve peace was Toussaint Louverture. Toussaint, now forty-eight years old, had been a slave on the Bréda plantation, where Comte de

Noé and Bayon de Libertad, owner and factor respectively, favored him with especially good treatment. He had even been made steward of Bréda, and his life with his wife, Suzanne Simone Baptiste, was rather peaceful. Toussaint was a born leader, a characteristic reinforced by his knowledge of herbs, which gave him the image of a medicine man among many slaves. Some believed that he even communicated with the gods. When the black insurrection erupted, however, Toussaint remained aloof. He wanted to be sure of its permanence before committing himself to it; meanwhile he aided the escape of Bayon de Libertad and his family to America. Late in September 1791, after this act of fidelity, Toussaint left Bréda and made his way to the camp of the Insurgents.[65]

When he got there, he was attached to the command of Jean François and received the rank of "Physician-in-Chief to the Armies of the King of France." Soon Toussaint began to demonstrate his superior organizational and fighting abilities in combat near Morne Pélé, not far from Le Cap François. Furthermore, Toussaint surrounded himself with such excellent subordinate officers as Jean Jacques Dessalines, Charles Bélair, Moyse, and others. Thus his command, only of secondary importance at first, became the core of a new, slowly emerging black army—eventually a good match for even French regulars. Along with his ability, Toussaint began to demonstrate his complicated Machiavellian-humanitarian character. For example, he seemed not only firmly committed to the freedom of the slaves but also equally devoted to his own personal power. Although these goals usually coalesced, they finally conflicted, forcing Toussaint to choose between them. That choice, fortunately, did not come until 1802.[66]

While Toussaint rose in power, the whites splintered and declined. The commissioners—Mirbeck, Saint-Léger, and Roume—had tried to halt white disunity but failed because of their inability to control the very group that they were attempting to rescue. Moreover, the whites suspected the commissioners of coming to free the slaves, especially after they failed to make peace with Jean François and Biassou. The commissioners, in turn, suspected the whites of counterrevolution, a fear well founded since many whites continued to negotiate with Pitt for a British protectorate. Nor was

Governor Blanchelande spared. The Colonial Assembly blamed him for not bringing the Insurgents to terms and believed him guilty of treason. In April 1792 Blanchelande had an ugly confrontation with the Colonial Assembly, while an angry crowd shouted for his head. Obviously the governor had no power; now all he could do was to await his recall.[67]

Constant conflict reigned between civil and military powers, contributing further to white disintegration. One participant pointed out that the military was "vexed at the encroachments which the civil power has lately attempted, and at its interference in cases which fundamentally affect the discipline of armies."[68] Even the Colonial Assembly itself was divided. Late in May 1792, according to Captain Elias Porter of the *Greyhound*, the delegates "actually drew their swords on each other, and the House would have been drenched in blood had not the interposition of some less turbulent spirits subsided the dreadful ferment."[69] With the failure of the whites to bring peace to Saint-Domingue and to maintain their unity, the civil war intensified. All sides seemed decided on a fight to the finish.

Mulattoes in South and West provinces seized the military initiative. General Blake, commanding a force of *gens de couleur*, laid siege to Les Cayes. The siege, however, collapsed after the arrival of a small white military expedition, and Blake himself was caught and executed. But the mulattoes received reinforcements and once again returned to the offensive.[70] In West Province, a strange alliance of mulattoes, *grands blancs*, and Insurgents besieged Port-au-Prince. On March 23, 1792, fifteen hundred soldiers, mostly *petits blancs*, attempted to lift the siege but were badly beaten.[71] At Léogane, not far from Port-au-Prince, the Insurgents struck on their own. On March 12 thousands of them attacked, some with nothing more than sharpened sticks, against whites and mulattoes armed with rifles and bayonets. Two thousand blacks fell and many of the surrounding plantations were destroyed.[72]

In North Province the Insurgents were equally active; they besieged Fort Dauphin and constantly attacked Le Cap François.[73] On the Plaine du Nord "the noise of firing is heard every night. All the plantations, except one or two, are destroyed by Negroes and on these they are constantly making . . . attempts."[74] The climate also took its toll among the whites, who were "dying by hundreds on the burning plains without even the consolation of having signalized themselves by one deed of daring."[75]

Under such circumstances, Mirbeck and Saint-Léger gave up in despair and prepared to return to France; Roume remained but would be ineffective. With the departing commissioners went the last chance of the whites to regain their former power.

NOTES FOR CHAPTER THREE

1. *Le Moniteur*, Jan. 12, 1790; Santo Domingo, Assemblée Générale, *A Particular Account of the Insurrection of the Negroes in St. Domingo, begun in August, 1791* (London: J. Sewell, 1792), 2.

2. Lacroix, *Mémoires*, I, 90; *Maryland Journal and Baltimore Advertiser*, Oct. 14 and Nov. 4, 1791.

3. Edwards, *San Domingo*, 68.

4. *Mémoires*, I, 70–91.

5. Parham, *My Odyssey*, 28.

6. Letter Extract from Le Cap François, Sept. 7, 1791, in *Maryland Journal and Baltimore Advertiser*, Oct. 7, 1791.

7. Boston *Independent Chronicle*, Nov. 3, 1791.

8. Parham, *My Odyssey*, 60.

9. *Ibid.*, 29.

10. *Maryland Journal and Baltimore Advertiser*, Oct. 21, 1791; Perkins, *Reminiscences*, 21–22.

11. Perkins, *Reminiscences*, 21–22.

12. Gros, *Récit historique*, 13; *Maryland Journal and Baltimore Advertiser*, Oct. 21, 1791.

13. Boston *Independent Chronicle*, Sept. 22, 1791; *The Times* (London), Nov. 1, 1791.

14. *The Times* (London), Nov. 1, 1791.

15. Boston *Independent Chronicle*, Nov. 3, 1791.

16. Santo Domingo, Assemblée Générale, *Particular Account*, 6.

17. *Maryland Journal and Baltimore Advertiser*, Nov. 4, 1791; Boston *Independent Chronicle*, Sept. 29, Oct. 3, and Nov. 3, 1791; Newport *Mercury*, Oct. 1 and 15, 1791.

18. Parham, *My Odyssey*, 32.

19. *Ibid.*, 31.

20. Boston *Independent Chronicle*, Nov. 3, 1791.

21. *Ibid.*

22. *Ibid.*, Sept. 29, 1791.

23. Parham, *My Odyssey*, 31.

24. *Ibid.*, 33.

25. *The Times* (London), Nov. 1, 1794; Perkins, *Reminiscences*, 20; Gros, *Récit historique*, 45; Edwards, *San Domingo*, 72.

26. Edwards, *San Domingo*, 78–79; Baltimore *Daily Repository*, Oct. 24, 1791; Alexis, *Black Liberator*, 30–31.

27. André Rigaud was born in Les Cayes and received an education in Bordeaux, France. He served with the French at Savannah, Ga., during the American Revolution. Afterward he returned to Saint-Domingue, where he practiced his goldsmith trade until the outbreak of the Haitian Revolution. The other two mulatto leaders, Beauvais and Pinchinat, were also important. Beauvais, like Rigaud, served during the Revolution at Savannah. After his service in America, Beauvais returned to Saint-Domingue and taught until the beginning of the Haitian Revolution. As for Pinchinat, he had the benefits of a French education, but could never overcome his special hatred for whites. Unlike Rigaud and Beauvais, both good military commanders, Pinchinat was more of a politician and negotiator than a field general. Korngold, *Citizen Toussaint*, 117; James, *Black Jacobins*, 97.

28. Letter Extract from Port-au-Prince, Sept. 17, 1791, in *Maryland Journal and Baltimore Advertiser*, Oct. 21, 1791; Letter Extract from Port-au-Prince, Sept. 18, 1791, in Boston *Independent Chronicle*, Oct. 27, 1791.

29. Baltimore *Daily Repository*, Nov. 2, 1791.

30. Jean Philippe Garran de Coulon, *Rapport sur les troubles de Saint-Domingue, fait au nom de la Commission des Colonies, des Comités de Salut Public, de Législation et de Marine réunis*, 6 vols. (Paris: De L'Imprimerie Nationale, 1799), II, 284–85; Letter Extract from Port-au-Prince, Sept. 18, 1791, in Boston *Independent Chronicle*, Oct. 27, 1791.

31. *Maryland Journal and Baltimore Advertiser*, Oct. 28, 1791.

32. Boston *Independent Chronicle*, Oct. 27, 1791.

33. *Ibid.*, Dec. 1, 1791.

34. *Ibid.*, Dec. 15, 1791; Alexis, *Black Liberator*, 31; Letter Extract from Le Cap François, Oct. 22, 1791, in *Maryland Journal and Baltimore Advertiser*, Nov. 15, 1791.

35. Letter Extract from Le Cap François, Oct. 4, 1791, in *Maryland Journal and Baltimore Advertiser*, Nov. 8, 1791; General Assembly of Le Cap François to William Pitt, Sept. 25, 1791, in Newport *Mercury*, Nov. 12, 1791; *The Times* (London), May 19, 1797; *Le Moniteur*, Nov. 6, 1791; Coupland, *British Anti-Slavery*, 99–100; Major General Adam Williamson to Secretary Dundas, Sept. 1791, C. O. 137/50; Parry and Sherlock, *West Indies*, 172; Philadelphia *Aurora*, Jan. 3, 1795.

36. Gros, *Récit historique*, 23.

37. *Ibid.*, 34; Howard, "Journal of Occupation," III, 35; *The Times* (London), Oct. 28, 1791.

38. Governor Pinckney to the Colonial Assembly of St. Domingo, Sept. 1791, San Domingo File.

39. Newton to Wood, n.d., *ibid.*

40. Gram to A. Vanderhorst, Aug. 16, 1793, *ibid.*

41. "Rusticus" [Alexander Garden] to "Gentlemen," Miscellaneous Papers (South Carolina Historical Society).

42. Even when South Carolina resumed the slave trade in 1803, West Indian slaves were still barred. All other imported slaves over 15 years old had to prove, according to law, that they were not rebels. Coupland, *British Anti-Slavery*, 152; Winthrop Jordan, *White over Black: American Attitudes toward the Negro, 1550–1812* (Chapel Hill: Univ. of North Carolina Press, 1968), 382.

43. Boston *Independent Chronicle*, Oct. 13, 1791; Ternard to Edmond Genêt, March 26, 1791, Edmond Genêt Papers (Library of Congress).

44. One example of the National Assembly's attitude toward the colonies can be found in Title VII of the Constitution of 1791: "The French colonies and possessions in Asia, Africa, and America, which are part of the French Empire, are not comprised in the present Constitution." Obviously the great merchants of Bordeaux, Nantes, Le Havre, and elsewhere intended to leave the colonies untouched by the French Revolution. The Legislative Assembly, which convened on Oct. 1, 1791, maintained the same attitude. J. M. Roberts and R. C. Cobb, eds., *French Revolution Documents*, 1 vol. (New York: Barnes and Noble, 1966–), I, 364.

45. *Le Patriote français*, Sept. 23 and Nov. 8, 1791; Garrett, *Colonial Question*, 131; Boston *Independent Chronicle*, March 15, 1792.

46. Boston *Independent Chronicle*, Dec. 15, 1791; Letter Extract from Le Cap François, Nov. 16, 1791, in Baltimore *Daily Repository*, Dec. 27, 1791.

47. The reason for the mulatto's execution is not certain. One eyewitness believed him to be a convicted murderer, but another maintained him to be an innocent victim of a lynch mob. Letter Extract from Port-au-Prince, Nov. 29, 1791, in *Maryland Journal and Baltimore Advertiser*, Jan. 3, 1792; Boston *Independent Chronicle*, Jan. 5, 1792.

48. Boston *Independent Chronicle*, Jan. 5, 1792; Providence *Gazette and Country Journal*, Feb. 4, 1792; Edwards, *San Domingo*, 91.

49. Letter Extract from Le Cap François, Dec. 28, 1791, in *Maryland Journal and Baltimore Advertiser*, Feb. 14, 1792.

50. Boston *Independent Chronicle*, Jan. 5, 1792.

51. *Ibid.*; Letter Extract from Le Cap François, Dec. 28, 1791, in *Maryland Journal and Baltimore Advertiser*, Feb. 14, 1792.

52. Letter Extract from Le Cap François, Nov. 16, 1791, in Baltimore *Daily Repository*, Dec. 27, 1791.

53. Letter Extract from Le Cap François, Dec. 28, 1791, in *Maryland Journal and Baltimore Advertiser*, Feb. 14, 1792.

54. The mulattoes most faithful to the whites in North Province were those at Port-de-Paix and Le Cap François, the two places where white power was strongest. In areas where the whites were weak in North

Province, the mulattoes were often in rebellion. Boston *Independent Chronicle*, Oct. 18, 1792, and March 28, 1793; Newport *Mercury*, March 26, 1792.

55. Letter Extract from Le Cap François, Dec. 28, 1791, in *Maryland Journal and Baltimore Advertiser*, Feb. 14, 1792.

56. Letter from Le Cap François to a Correspondent in Philadelphia, April 13, 1792, in *ibid.*, May 18, 1792; Letter Extract from Le Cap François, Jan. 2, 1792, in Baltimore *Daily Repository*, March 5, 1792; Boston *Independent Chronicle*, March 15 and May 3, 1792.

57. Letter Extract from Le Cap François, Dec. 28, 1791, in *Maryland Journal and Baltimore Advertiser*, Feb. 14, 1792; Edwards, *San Domingo*, 102–103.

58. Gros, *Récit historique*, 28–31, 36, 39–40; Alexis, *Black Liberator*, 40.

59. Letter Extract from Le Cap François, Dec. 28, 1791, in *Maryland Journal and Baltimore Advertiser*, Feb. 14, 1792.

60. *Ibid.*

61. *Ibid.*; Gros, *Récit historique*, 41–42.

62. Letter from Le Cap François, Jan. 3, 1792, in Baltimore *Daily Repository*, March 10, 1792; Lacroix, *Mémoires*, I, 156–57.

63. Letter Extract from Le Cap François, Dec. 28, 1791, in *Maryland Journal and Baltimore Advertiser*, Feb. 14, 1792; *Le Moniteur*, April 10, 1792; Gros, *Récit historique,* 46–47.

64. Gros, *Récit historique*, 47.

65. Alexis, *Black Liberator*, 11–17, 34–35.

66. *Ibid.*, 35–38, 41–42; Gerard M. Laurent, ed., *Toussaint Louverture à travers sa correspondance, 1794–1798* (Madrid: Gerard Laurent, 1953), 104; H. P. Davis, *Black Democracy* (New York: Dial Press, 1928), 48.

67. Delaire to Pickering, Aug. 10, 1798, Consular Dispatches, Cap-Haitien, vol. 1; Baltimore *Daily Repository*, May 9, 1792; Perkins, *Reminiscences*, 30; Letter from Le Cap François, April 13, 1792, in *Maryland Journal and Baltimore Advertiser*, May 18, 1792.

68. Letter from Le Cap François, April 13, 1792, in *Maryland Journal and Baltimore Advertiser*, May 18, 1792.

69. Newport *Mercury*, June 18, 1792.

70. Boston *Independent Chronicle*, April 5, 1792; Letter Extract from Les Cayes, n.d., in Providence *Gazette and Country Journal*, March 31, 1792.

71. Providence *Gazette and Country Journal*, April 19, 1792. One group of 200 blacks, calling themselves the Zuzards, gave the mulattoes especially close and loyal support. The *gens de couleur*, in return, promised them their freedom. But when their usefulness ended, the Zuzards were betrayed and deported by the mulattoes. Like "The Swiss," the Zuzards found out too late that the mulattoes were not to be trusted. This is another example of the failure of the *gens de couleur* to unite with the blacks, perhaps their greatest failure. Letter Extract from Le Cap François, Jan. 22, 1792, in Baltimore *Daily Repository*, March 31, 1792.

72. Letter Extract from Port-au-Prince, March 16, 1792, in Newport *Mercury*, April 16, 1792.

73. *Ibid.*, March 26, 1792; Letter Extract from Le Cap François, Jan. 24, 1792, in Baltimore *Daily Repository*, March 2, 1792.

74. Boston *Independent Chronicle*, Sept. 6, 1792.

75. Perkins, *Reminiscences*, 30.

CHAPTER FOUR

The White Collapse, 1792-1793

With so much bad news reaching France from Saint-Domingue, the Legislative Assembly began to despair. On March 24, Gaudet took the floor and asked, "What will stop the revolt of the slaves in Saint-Domingue?"[1] What, indeed! Answering his own question, Gaudet maintained that peace could be achieved only with the "reunion of the men of color and the colonial whites."[2] The Assembly agreed and voted in favor of full citizenship for all mulattoes. Furthermore, a new governor, Desparbes, was appointed to replace Blanchelande, and a new three-member executive commission and seven thousand soldiers were to accompany him. The commissioners— Léger Félicité Sonthonax, Etienne Polverel, and Jean-Antoine Ailhaud—possessed the real power, for they could dissolve the Colonial Assembly in order to make it more representative of the *gens de couleur*. Louis XVI signed these measures into law on April 4, 1792.[3]

One of the most forceful and radical figures of the Haitian Revolution was Sonthonax, leader of the new commission. Born into a well-to-do family in Oyannax, France, Sonthonax became a Jacobin and was closely associated with the *Amis des Noirs*.[4] Even though he had no intention of freeing the slaves, he did intend to exceed his instructions by eradicating royalism from Saint-Domingue. Royalism and the white man, according to Sonthonax, were equated; therefore, he was antiwhite.[5] Moreover, Sonthonax personified the increasingly radical swing of the French Revolution: France declared war against Austria on April 20, the *sans-culottes* destroyed the last vestiges of crown authority on August 10, and the National Convention held its first meeting on September 20. Despite the continuing bourgeois nature of the Convention, the stage was being set for the dominance of a powerful Jacobin–*sans-culotte* alliance.[6] By the time Desparbes and the second commission reached Saint-Domingue in late September 1792, much of this leftward drift had already taken place.[7]

When Desparbes and the commissioners arrived in Le Cap François, an immediate power struggle began. Because he was the new governor, Desparbes was received with "all the civil and military honors which he merited elsewhere."[8] The commissioners, especially Sonthonax, were jealous, but their feelings went deeper than envy. Sonthonax saw that Desparbes had the support of many whites, and so he grouped them as royalists and turned to the mulattoes for support.[9] By now the commissioners had decided that only a dictatorship—with themselves at the helm, of course—could save the sagging Haitian Revolution.[10]

They worked with amazing speed. To lull the colonial whites into inaction, Sonthonax decreed in late October that slavery should be protected in Saint-Domingue and that the institution would be safe after the expulsion of "agitators." He then began to deport "agitators" who were both hated by the whites and feared by the commissioners. Blanchelande and Joseph-Paul Cambefort, commander of the Le Cap François regiment, were among Sonthonax's first victims of deportation to France. Cambefort later stood trial but was acquitted; Blanchelande, not so fortunate, would have a rendezvous with "Madame Guillotine." The commissioners had only begun the purge of their opponents, real or potential.[11]

In weaving his web of dictatorship, Sonthonax was careful to stay within his legally constituted powers. In late October, therefore, the Colonial Assembly held its last meeting, as the commissioners replaced it with the Intermediate Commission. The whites, unaware of what was happening, were joyous at the prospect of peace and unity.[12] One observer wrote that "the Intermediate Commission . . . values much the confidence of the public, which it will endeavor to deserve."[13] But the commissioners held the power of appointment, making the colonial legislature nothing more than their tool. Sonthonax had constructed his dictatorship.[14]

Once he had achieved supreme power, Sonthonax worked to secure his position. Desparbes, too old to take vigorous action, largely submitted to Sonthonax's authority, especially since most of his seven thousand soldiers had died. Furthermore, Sonthonax established Jacobin clubs within Saint-Domingue and deported many white soldiers. Those of any importance who remained were often bribed to support the dictatorship. Within the commission itself, Sonthonax pushed Ailhaud into obscurity, while Polverel was content with a prominent but secondary position.[15]

The major pillar of Sonthonax's strength was the mulatto. Enticing the latter's support, he recognized only "two distinct and separate classes: free men without distinction of color and slaves."[16] At this point Sonthonax was careful not to include the slave with the mulatto, for even he did not want to go that far; besides, it would have destroyed his alliance with the *gens de couleur*. The mulattoes responded to the overtures, and large crowds gathered whenever the commissioners passed through their vicinity. According to one disgusted white, Sonthonax and Polverel, "with smiles on their lips and fury in their hearts, caressed them and promised them help and protection in the name of the French Republic and of Heaven."[17] Within a year, however, Sonthonax would desert the mulatto for the slave.

The great tragedy of Sonthonax's policy was not dictatorship, which was perhaps the only means to social order, but destruction of the whites.[18] Sonthonax was too busy rooting out royalism to realize that the whites, despite their sins, were an integral part of the colony; Toussaint would not make the same mistake. One eighteenth-century critic who sensed Sonthonax's main weakness concluded that no one blamed the Jacobin leader for loving mulattoes and blacks, "but no one would think it wrong if . . . [he] loved the white man, too."[19]

At first the situation under Sonthonax did not appear hopeless. His field commander, General Etienne Laveaux, was able and energetic.[20] In one campaign around Le Cap François, the Insurgents were so badly beaten by Laveaux's forces that they were driven from much of the Plaine du Nord and into the mountains. Some planters believed that they might even return to their estates by early 1793.[21]

Soon optimism turned to despair, for in 1793 France declared war on England and Holland on February 1 and on Spain on

March 7. Moreover, Jean François, Biassou, and Toussaint formally joined the Spanish. To make the situation worse, the Insurgents once again reoccupied most of the Plaine du Nord and pressed Le Cap François. By May 1793 Sonthonax must have known that his alliance with the mulattoes had not brought needed stabilization to the colony. Perhaps he was already looking at the Insurgents and contemplating a new type of alliance.[22]

In the meantime the white caste was literally disintegrating in its own recriminations. As one witness put it, "The common . . . enemy to the white people, the rebel Negroes, are nearly forgotten —and the colonists are totally absorbed in animosity against each other."[23] Suspicion among the whites became so deep that Captain Decker of the *Sally* reported that Le Cap François was in a state of virtual civil war. On November 19, 1792, observed Decker, 2,800 whites were mustered at the Place d'Armes "for the purpose of sending those they knew were clandestinely supplying the rebel Negroes with arms and ammunition as prisoners to Europe."[24] Forty-three high-ranking officials were purged, but the National Guard of Le Cap François, commanded by Gagnon, came to their rescue. Gagnon, however, was confronted by another force led by Desparbes. A fight ensued in which Desparbes' force was completely victorious. Gagnon himself was hacked apart, and the crowd dipped torn pieces of his clothing "in his blood, tied them to their shoe strings and then exultingly paraded the streets with their bloody trophies."[25]

This was not all. The whites were so disorganized and rebellious that one frustrated commander committed suicide when his detachment mutinied. Furthermore, the mulattoes of Le Cap François, traditionally allied with the whites, showed signs of growing restlessness. Sonthonax continued his relentless pressure on the whites, frequently using royalism as an excuse to carry out continued purges. Typical was his decree of April 19, 1793, forbidding the military to wear the Cross of St. Louis. Behind this decree was Sonthonax's rather obvious motive of destroying any remaining vestiges of white military power.[26] With Sonthonax aligned against them and with no prospect of security within the French Empire, many white colonials looked to England as their salvation. "The white people," said one eyewitness, "begin too late to see their folly, and every individual, democrat or aristocrat, looks forward to the protection of England as their only refuge."[27] The whites' only refuge, however, would arrive too late.

The decisive contest between Sonthonax and the whites began on May 7, 1793, when General Galbaud, the new governor, arrived at Le Cap François. In the beginning it appeared that Galbaud might even be successful, for Sonthonax and Polverel were too occupied with revolts at Port-au-Prince and Jacmel to react immediately and Galbaud had time to solidify his position. His object, of course, was to win the support of the whites, since Sonthonax had that of the mulattoes.[28] As one observer noted, the whites "were pleased to see that the people of colour were kept at a great distance from him [Galbaud], and that no one amongst them were admitted at his table."[29]

Despite his efforts, Galbaud had built the foundation of his authority on quicksand. For instance, he could never unite the whites in a common front against Sonthonax—partly because of his conflict with the merchants of Le Cap François over the disposal of their produce. Galbaud compounded the antagonism by calling the merchants an "aristocracy of the opulent men."[30] Furthermore, Galbaud did not anticipate the shrewdness of Sonthonax and Polverel, who arrived at Le Cap François on June 10. Galbaud told them that his instructions were issued by the "executive," probably referring to the Committee of Public Safety, and that the commissioners had no other choice but to recognize his superior authority. Sonthonax, however, maintained that his authority was superior since it had come directly from the National Convention. Besides, Sonthonax pointed out, Galbaud owned a local plantation; therefore he was violating a French law that prohibited a proprietor from governing the colony in which his property was located. Sonthonax then ordered Galbaud to embark and leave with a French fleet then in port. Galbaud, realizing that his authority was destroyed, obliged, and the commissioners appointed Adrien-Nicola de la Salle, a puppet, as Galbaud's replacement. But the deposed governor had not lost the struggle, for the French fleet, at anchor in the harbor, would soon give him new hope.[31]

Two events played into Galbaud's hands. First, the merchants of Le Cap François turned against Sonthonax when he levied a heavy fine against them. Moreover, many whites, despite their reservations about Galbaud as a leader, saw him as the lesser of two evils. For the first time since the beginning of the slave rebellion, the colonial whites seemed firmly united. The second event involved a growing antagonism between sailors of the fleet and the mulattoes of Le Cap François. Sonthonax, to avoid trouble, imposed a curfew on the sailors but did nothing when mulattoes badly slashed three seamen.[32] According to Captain Jones, skipper of an American vessel, "complaints were made to the commissioners in vain, for they were totally devoted to the mulattoes' interest, and would scarcely hear a word from a white person."[33]

With the support of the fleet and of the whites of Le Cap François, Galbaud made his play for power. On the afternoon of June 20 he landed with a force of well over two thousand men.[34] The struggle had begun. At first neither side seemed to be winning, but slowly Sonthonax was forced to take refuge in the governor's mansion, amid much destruction and loss of life. That night the fighting was even more violent, and it became impossible to distinguish friend from foe.[35] As one witness reported, "Whites destroyed whites and blacks destroyed blacks throughout the night, and one constant and incessant firing of musketry, with incessant roaring of cannon, was heard in every direction and even at our own door till daylight."[36]

As a new day began to break, Galbaud's chances of success waned. The sailors, though good fighters, were hard drinkers. During the night many had raided various wine cellars, and by dawn a large number of seamen had taken themselves out of the combat. Furthermore, white unity once more proved to be an illusion. Many *petits blancs*, perhaps considering the *grands blancs* "aristocrats" and themselves "revolutionaries" or perhaps simply wishing to join the winning side, switched their allegiance to Sonthonax.[37] Noting the break in white unity, one *grand blanc* recorded that "I saw dragoons proudly leading us and haranguing us into excitement, who, when they had accompanied us as far as the batteries of the enemy, turned upon us a murderous fire and retired amidst the ranks of our adversaries, laughing at our credulity."[38]

The decisive factor in the struggle, however, was not in Le Cap François but in the murky dusk of the Plaine du Nord—the Insurgent! During the night Sonthonax promised freedom to all black warriors joining the Republican cause. Macaya took his offer and in the dark hours of early morning attacked the war-torn city.[39] Suddenly a horrified white, hearing terrible shrieks, saw that "a great brightness lit the black skies. From the summit of the mountains down the road to the plain, came immense hoards of Africans. They arrived with torches and knives and plunged into the city. From all sides flames were lifted as in a whirlwind and spread everywhere."[40]

Le Cap François was in total confusion. Whites and sailors ran toward the harbor and jumped into the sea, hoping that they would be rescued by the fleet. Amid "the whistling of bullets, the explosions of powder, [and] the crumbling of houses," the white caste collapsed in Saint-Domingue.[41] Captain Eggar, a Yankee skipper, noted that "one fourth of the town remained standing, but entirely deserted by the white inhabitants, who had fled in every direction to avoid the melancholy scene."[42] In all, more than ten thousand people were killed, a large portion of them whites. A few days later the fleet, with thousands of whites on board, sailed for Baltimore.[43]

What was the reasoning of Sonthonax in granting freedom to the Insurgent? Obviously, despite his attachment to the *Amis des Noirs*, he only planned to use the black to support his dictatorship. Like Ogé, he had the naïve belief that he could control the unleashed power of the slaves. Sonthonax thought that he could rescue his weakening position by granting freedom to a few thousand Insurgent allies without uprooting slavery itself.[44] He made this clear in a proclamation on June 21: "We declare that the will of the French Republic, and that of its delegates, is to give liberty to all the Negro warriors who will fight for the Republic under the orders of the Civil Commissioners."[45] Yet in the same proclamation Sonthonax emphasized that most slaves could only expect improved conditions, with some hope of gradual freedom. Furthermore, he intended his June 21 proclamation to be applicable solely to North Province.[46]

The interests of his mulatto allies also made Sonthonax careful not to abolish slavery. In fact, after the destruction of Le Cap François, he continued to play for mulatto support. In South Province, for example, he supported André Rigaud, making him commander in chief of the South and allowing him to slaughter whites indiscriminately. Moreover, white executions such as those committed by Polverel at Port-au-Prince were largely intended to tighten the mulatto alliance through vengeance.[47]

Nevertheless, Sonthonax had lost his grip on the Haitian Revolution. The Insurgents believed that his decree of June 21 was intended to abolish slavery completely. With the Spanish and their black allies closing in, Sonthonax had no other choice but to agree with this interpretation. How else could he defend his position? On August 29 Sonthonax decreed the general abolition of slavery. Even so, he attempted to keep the economic structure of Saint-Domingue from collapsing, just as Toussaint would later do. According to Sonthonax, blacks had to remain on the plantations to which they were attached and receive wages for their work.[48] He warned them, moreover, that liberty also means duty; after all, "in France everyone is free, but all work for their living—at St. Domingo, subject to the same laws, you shall follow the same example; return to your work or to your former owners."[49] In spite of Sonthonax's desire to keep the plantation intact, he failed because of the lack of machinery to enforce his system. Toussaint would not make the same mistake.[50]

The abolition of slavery by no means solved Sonthonax's problems. Few blacks actually joined the commissioners, perhaps doubting their sincerity, and a Spanish army was literally at the gates of Le Cap François. Furthermore, England invaded the colony in September and at first seemed invincible. If Sonthonax was to maintain his control of Saint-Domingue, he needed the answers to two vital questions: would the National Convention support his abolition of slavery, and if so, would this act convince large numbers of Insurgents to join the side of France? All Sonthonax could do was wait and endure.[51]

NOTES FOR CHAPTER FOUR

1. *Le Moniteur*, March 25, 1792.

2. *Ibid.*

3. *Ibid.*, March 26, 1792; Edwards, *San Domingo*, 106–108; Letter Extract from Le Cap François, Sept. 18, 1792, in *Maryland Journal and Baltimore Advertiser*, Oct. 16, 1792; Parham, *My Odyssey*, 80.

4. Claude Perroud, ed., *J. P. Brissot, Correspondance et Papiers*, 2 vols. (Paris: Alphonse Picard et Fils, 1912), II, 331–34; Alexis, *Black Liberator*, 46.

5. Captain Monteynaez to Laveaux, n.d., Laveaux Papers; Sonthonax to M. Allouis, July 5, 1796, Léger Félicité Sonthonax Correspondence (Library of Congress and Bibliothèque Nationale); *Le Courrier de L'Amérique* (Philadelphia), Dec. 25, 1792.

6. Even the Jacobins were predominantly *bons bourgeois*; however, in comparison with the "Girondins," the Jacobins were "closer to the people, more flexible in their attitudes, and more able and willing to yield gracefully to popular pressure." Rudé, *Revolutionary Europe*, 134.

7. *Ibid.*, 130–32; Lefebvre, *French Revolution*, I, 221.

8. Parham, *My Odyssey*, 80.

9. *Ibid.*; Edwards, *San Domingo*, 110–11; Newport *Mercury*, Nov. 26, 1792.

10. Sonthonax and the other members of the commission seemed to identify the Haitian Revolution mostly with that of the French.

11. *Le Courrier de L'Amérique*, Dec. 25, 1792; *Le Moniteur*, Oct. 27, 1792; Letter Extract from London, April 21, 1793, in *State Gazette of South Carolina*, July 15, 1793.

12. Letter Extract from Le Cap François, Oct. 28, 1792, in *State Gazette of South Carolina*, Nov. 17, 1792.

13. *Ibid.*

14. Edwards, *San Domingo*, 111; *Le Courrier de L'Amérique*, Jan. 1, 1793.

15. *Le Courrier de L'Amérique*, Jan. 1, 1793; Parham, *My Odyssey*, 81–83; *The Times* (London), Dec. 25, 1792; Delaire to Pickering, Aug. 10, 1798, Consular Dispatches, Cap Haitien, vol. I; Lacroix, *Mémoires*, II, 221–22.

16. Lacroix, *Mémoires*, II, 218.

17. Parham, *My Odyssey*, 85.

18. There is some evidence that the whites, at long last, were willing to accept the mulattoes as equals. But instead of working for mulatto-white consolidation, the commissioners deliberately used the *gens de couleur* to subdue the whites. Baltimore *Daily Repository*, Aug. 16, 1792; *The Times* (London), Dec. 25, 1792.

19. *Courrier de la France et des Colonies* (Philadelphia), Oct. 15, 1795.

20. General Etienne Laveaux had served under Charles Dumouriez in

the fight against the royalists at Valmy and Jemmapes. His tenacity as a commander saved Sonthonax on a number of occasions. Later he would be one of Toussaint's closest friends and supporters. Alexis, *Black Liberator*, 46.

21. Letter Extract from Le Cap François, Feb. 18, 1793, in Boston *Independent Chronicle*, March 28, 1793; Newport *Mercury*, April 1, 1793.

22. Providence *Gazette and Country Journal*, June 1, 1793; García y Moreno to Jean François, July 10, 1793, Laveaux Papers; *The Times* (London), Sept. 11, 1794; Sydenham, *French Revolution*, 141–42; Perroud, *Brissot*, II, 334.

23. Newport *Mercury*, Nov. 26, 1792.

24. *Ibid.*, Dec. 3, 1792.

25. *Ibid.*

26. Providence *Gazette and Country Journal*, June 1, 1793; *State Gazette of South Carolina*, June 14, 1793; Letter Extract from Le Cap François, Feb. 18, 1793, in Boston *Independent Chronicle*, March 28, 1793.

27. Gilbert Franchlyn to General Adam Williamson, April 14, 1793, C. O. 137/50.

28. Henry Shirley to Edward Shirley, July 22, 1793, *ibid.*

29. *Ibid.*

30. *Ibid.*; Perkins, *Reminiscences*, 32–33; *The Times* (London), Oct. 3, 1793.

31. Baltimore *Daily Repository*, July 16, 1793; Newport *Mercury*, July 23, 1793; H. Shirley to E. Shirley, July 22, 1793, C. O. 137/50; Providence *Gazette and Country Journal*, July 13, 1793.

32. Providence *Gazette and Country Journal*, July 20, 1793; Perkins, *Reminiscences*, 34; Parham, *My Odyssey*, 87–88; *State Gazette of South Carolina*, July 29, 1793.

33. *State Gazette of South Carolina*, July 29, 1793.

34. *Ibid.*

35. Perkins, *Reminiscences*, 36.

36. *Ibid.*, 37.

37. H. Shirley to E. Shirley, July 22, 1793, C. O. 137/50; Edwards, *San Domingo*, 115.

38. Parham, *My Odyssey*, 89–90.

39. Edwards, *San Domingo*, 116. After making the agreement with Macaya, Sonthonax left Le Cap François and made his headquarters at the Charrier plantation not far from the city. Probably Sonthonax did not want to get caught up in the general massacre of Le Cap François, which he knew was soon to come. H. Shirley to E. Shirley, July 22, 1793, C. O. 137/50.

40. Parham, *My Odyssey*, 90.

41. *Ibid.*

42. Newport *Mercury*, July 30, 1793.

43. Providence *Gazette and Country Journal*, July 13 and Aug. 3, 1793; *The Times* (London), Oct. 3, 1793.

44. Citizen Want to Citizen Genêt, Sept. 24, 1793, in Boston *Independent*

Chronicle, Nov. 21, 1793; Sonthonax to Jean Pierre, June 6, 1796, Sonthonax Correspondence.

45. Proclamation of the Civil Commissioners, Le Cap François, June 21, 1793, in Providence *Gazette and Country Journal*, Aug. 10, 1793.

46. *Ibid.*

47. *Ibid.*, July 27, 1793; Perkins, *Reminiscences*, 54; Newport *Mercury*, Oct. 8, 1793.

48. Proclamation of Sonthonax, Civil Commissioner, Aug. 29, 1793, in Newport *Mercury*, Oct. 29, 1793.

49. *Ibid.*

50. Laveaux to Sonthonax, Aug. 28, 1793, Laveaux Papers.

51. Boston *Independent Chronicle*, Aug. 1, 1793; Newport *Mercury*, July 30, 1793; Edwards, *San Domingo*, 146; Great Britain, War Office, *Bulletins of the Campaign, 1793–1815*, 20 vols. (London: A. Strahan, 1794–1816), I, 224–26.

CHAPTER FIVE

Toussaint and the British Invasion, 1793-1798

From 1791 to 1793 Great Britain's Prime Minister William Pitt the Younger and Secretary of War Henry Dundas closely followed events both in the West Indies and in Europe. Pitt's decision to invade Saint-Domingue, defying simple explanation, was based upon the occurrences of two continents.

Pitt was sensitive to the fact that the Saint-Domingue slave rebellion posed a threat to the rejuvenated British Caribbean, especially to Jamaica with its nearly 300,000 slaves.[1] Sensitivity turned to fear when white Jamaicans rushed military aid to Saint-Domingue and even attempted to prevent French planters and their "infected" slaves from migrating to English territory.[2] By 1793 the feeling of the British ministry was best expressed by Dundas: "Had not St. Domingo been attacked, Jamaica would not have been worth one year's purchase."[3] Understandably, the Earl of Spencer, First Lord of the Admiralty, emphasized the security of Jamaica as the foremost reason for invading Saint-Domingue.[4]

Other West Indian influences were also at work. White colonial agents who traveled constantly between the Franco-Caribbean and the British ministry emphasized the desire of French planters to join England. Not only Saint-Domingue, but all the French West Indies were represented. Moreover, Pitt was aware that Spain might conquer Saint-Domingue and that British occupation of the French Caribbean would be diplomatically valuable in any negotiated peace with France. Also, Great Britain traditionally followed the policy of seeking to capture the colonial empires of its European opponents while leaving the struggle on the Continent to a strong ally, such as Prussia. Therefore Pitt formulated a plan to seize the French West Indies and to minimize England's involvement in Europe. Part of the plan included dividing Saint-Domingue with Spain. Le Cap François and much of the interior of North and West provinces would be Spanish, while England would get most of the important ports and South Province.[5]

In Europe war had erupted on April 20, 1792, when France and Austria began their hostilities. By early March 1793 the First Coalition—Austria, Prussia, Spain, Holland, and England—confronted France. Of even greater interest to Pitt's cabinet was the disintegration taking place within France itself. The peasants of the Vendée and the Chouans rose in rebellion against the Paris-dominated revolution; at about the same time, the important ports of Bordeaux, Toulon, and Marseilles began their fight against the French capital. Civil conflict threatened France more than did the First Coalition.[6]

While Pitt and Dundas planned to conquer the French Caribbean, Secretary-at-War William Windham wanted to exploit conditions in strife-torn France. He was much opposed to West Indian involvement and sought to concentrate British aid on the Vendeans and Chouans. In his opinion, the sprawling Caribbean plans of Pitt and Dundas invited military disaster.[7] A Yankee ship captain, unknown to the British ministry, upheld the apprehensions of Windham, predicting that "it would cost a kingdom to pay the expenses of getting a tolerable footing on St. Domingo with an army."[8] With the exception of Toulon and the fiasco in 1795 on the Quiberon Peninsula, Windham's policy was largely ignored.[9]

Preparing the way for conquests in the Caribbean, the British ministry signed a series of treaties with the French West Indies, represented by planter-agents. Duluc and Clairfontaine consummated the first agreements by surrendering Martinique and Guadeloupe to England in February 1793. Other French colonies followed, including Saint-Domingue on August 18.[10] With the illusion of unanimous planter support and easy conquest, Pitt and Dundas began their West Indian campaign by capturing Tobago in April 1793. Great Britain, despite the warnings of Windham, was headed toward a severe military defeat.[11]

The invasion of Saint-Domingue, under the direction of General

Adam Williamson, began on September 20. At first all went according to plans. Lieutenant-Colonel John Whitelocke's British forces and Baron de Montalambert's army of white planters seized Jérémie without a struggle. Three days later Commodore John Ford captured Môle Saint Nicolas, "the Gibraltar of the Antilles," with the collusion of the city's white inhabitants. When Sonthonax attempted to counterattack, the British blockaded his expedition at Port-au-Prince. On October 4 Williamson experienced the first of many frustrations when his forces failed to take Tiburon. But by the end of the year Great Britain held the parishes of Jean Rabel, Saint Marc, Arcahaye, and Léogane, while putting great pressure on the French at Port-au-Prince. The Laveaux-led army of Sonthonax, contained no more than twenty-five hundred men, was hard pressed; its annihilation seemed only a matter of time.[12]

Early 1794 did not bring a change in the military fortunes of Sonthonax. The British, having well over five thousand regulars and colonial militia, continued their rapid offensive. On February 2 Whitelocke attacked Tiburon, captured it, and forced its defenders to fall back toward Les Cayes. At Port-au-Prince, however, Sonthonax stubbornly held out against British assaults and postponed the city's capture. Only for a moment did the British stall, and L'Acul, an important French fort near Léogane, fell to the attacking forces of Whitelocke on March 2. In late April, English troops led by Captain Matthews cornered Polverel and eight hundred of his soldiers at Les Cayes. Ingloriously Polverel surrendered; perhaps he had even connived with the British.[13] Late in May, General John Whyte, Whitelocke's replacement, led two thousand English and colonial troops against Port-au-Prince. On June 1 the city fell; Sonthonax, Polverel, and Montbrun barely escaped to Croix-des-Bouquets. Furthermore, Martinique, Guadeloupe, Tobago, and St. Lucia were all under England's control by April, largely due to the efforts of Admiral Sir John Jarvis and General Sir Charles Grey.[14] The British appeared on the verge of total victory in the French West Indies.[15]

In the meantime the Spanish were pressing Sonthonax from the east. From the beginning Spanish Santo Domingo had encouraged disruptions in Saint-Domingue, but war between France and Spain served as the occasion for actual invasion. A Spanish army of fourteen thousand men under the direction of Captain-General Joaquín García y Moreno launched a two-pronged offensive toward Le Cap François and Port-au-Prince. The latter assault was slowed, but in North Province, Spanish conquest was especially rapid after June 1793. Soon Spain controlled most of the north, except for British-held Môle Saint Nicolas and French-held Le Cap François and Port-de-Paix.[16]

The Spaniards depended heavily upon their black allies. Jean François and Biassou had been closely attached to Spain since the start of the slave rebellion, partly because both men desired power. With these two blacks, thousands of Insurgents joined the Spanish. Among them was Toussaint Louverture.[17]

The date Toussaint enlisted in the Spanish effort is not clear, but by May 1793 he was actively fighting on the side of Spain. Nor can one be sure about the depth of Toussaint's attachment to emancipation at that time because he proudly became a knight in the Order of Isabella and generally told the Spanish what they wanted to hear.[18] Historians, nonetheless, have sometimes looked only at the black leaders rather than at the masses of former slaves who began to equate the Haitian Revolution with emancipation. Perhaps as early as mid-1793 the blacks would not tolerate any victory—whether French, Spanish, or English—which failed to abolish slavery.[19]

Despite uncertainty about Toussaint's early view on emancipation, there can be no doubt about his skillful fighting ability. Within a short period his forces had conquered Dondon, La Marmelade, Plaisance, and Gonaives. The latter position gave him an outlet on the Gulf of Gonave and severed the French forces, Laveaux and Sonthonax commanding those in the north and Rigaud those in the south. The real reasons for Toussaint's rapid victories, however, were his wise choice and control of able subordinates. One was the vicious Jean Jacques Dessalines, who had been mistreated as a slave and who hated both whites and mulattoes. Another was Moyse, whom Toussaint affectionately called his "nephew"; like Dessalines, he despised the white man. Both Moyse and Dessalines represent the radical limits of the Haitian Revolution; that Toussaint harnessed their energies is a tribute to his skill.[20]

Even while resisting British and Spanish invasions, Sonthonax weakened the French further by indulging himself in an internal power struggle with General Montbrun, mulatto commander of Port-au-Prince. In March 1794 Sonthonax officially visited the city to check its defenses against the English; unofficially he had come to displace Montbrun. To his disappointment, however, Sonthonax found the mulattoes solidly in favor of their leader. Using whites and freed criminals, the commissioner formed the Battalion d'Artois to oppose Montbrun's Corps of Equality. In a fierce struggle Sonthonax was badly beaten and many of his white supporters were slaughtered. Moreover, the conflict damaged the defenses of Port-au-Prince, making the city easier prey for the British. Fortunately for the French, the National Convention recalled Sonthonax and Polverel to face charges of misconduct. The two commissioners left for France on June 15. Laveaux was left to face the invaders alone, but he had potent hidden allies: dissension, yellow fever, and cruelty.[21]

Dissension in many forms plagued the British and Spanish from the outset. One was tension between the planters and the British. Often the planters refused to join the struggling English, and those who did sometimes claimed to be in the company of pompous glory-seekers.[22] One indignant *grand blanc* claimed that the French colonials did all the fighting but that the British got all the credit. Nevertheless, the English would not be such bad fellows, he believed, provided one did not trample their egos:

> It would be easy to live amicably with our Britannic comrades. All that is needed is to drink strictly hard liquor with them each day, and not to contradict when they repeat to satiety that the English nation is the greatest in all the world in war, commerce, agriculture, manufacture, customs, sciences, arts, manly strength, womanly charm, social accomplishments, et cetera—and there are countless et ceteras. But, unfortunately for the tranquility of the country, there are among us a few who do not admit all of these claims.[23]

The British, of course, often saw the planters as no better. Lieutenant Howard, believing the planters to be too concerned with personal vices to concentrate their efforts on the enemy, contemptuously noted that they "have so much to do in decorating their pretty persons and debauching the wives and daughters of the honest citizens that it would be horrid to take up one moment of their precious time."[24]

Yellow fever and malaria were as potent as dissension in playing havoc among Spanish and British forces. Bathing one's feet in warm water, drinking vinegar diluted with water, bleeding, and regular usage of James's Powder were all recommended remedies for the dreaded tropical diseases.[25] Still British and Spanish soldiers "dropped like the leaves of autumn."[26] So many Englishmen died that often the British could only maintain defensive positions; furthermore, they were forced to supplement their ranks with blacks, including slaves requisitioned from the planters. To attract Negroes, the British offered them freedom, and many blacks responded. In several cases more Negroes than whites composed British forces. Thus disease and the English themselves contributed to the spreading of abolition as a goal of the revolution.[27]

Cruelty also damaged the waning chances of a British or Spanish victory. Both Englishmen and Spaniards often refused to recognize the valor of their opponents and treated many whom they captured as something less than human. Rigaud complained that the British were deporting his troops from South Province to Jamaica, where they were being sold as slaves. At Port-au-Prince, on June 8, 1794, General Whyte even threatened to execute those Insurgents who refused to surrender. When the blacks did surrender, however, they sometimes faced execution anyway. At La Charbonier this happened when a group of Insurgents offered to surrender if they were pardoned. The British accepted their offer, took them into custody, and promptly massacred them. The Spanish were no better, for they deported hundreds of Negroes and mulattoes and condemned others to forced labor. At Fort Dauphin, however, the Spaniards would prove to have no peers in cruelty.[28]

When the Spanish began their invasion of Saint-Domingue, they sent proclamations to many cities in the United States asking refugee planters to "come and rally under the flag of His Catholic Majesty."[29] Many Spanish-held areas had received large numbers of them by early 1794, especially Fort Dauphin, thirty-nine miles from Le Cap François. Commandant Don Casalola, however, conspired with Jean François to enter the town and slaughter the French planters. The reason for this act of treachery is not clear, but there is some evidence that the Spanish may have used it to tighten their alliance with François. After all, many blacks in Spanish ranks must have felt uneasy about the return of their former masters.[30]

Early in July 1794 Jean François rode into Fort Dauphin, leading a detachment of six hundred men.[31] "The splendor of jewels and the high polish of silver rendered his black, wrinkled skin and gross features more hideous."[32] Drawing his troops up in formation at the town square, François harangued the blacks to start killing the French and not to listen to any pleas for mercy. With the full compliance of the Spaniards, the blacks fell on the planters, turning the town into a slaughterhouse.[33] Eight hundred whites died before the Negroes would complain "that they could not find more . . . on whom to vent their rage."[34] Obviously such actions weakened further an already feeble Spanish and British alliance with the planters.

Disease, dissension, cruelty, and the French forces might not have been enough to defeat England and Spain had Toussaint not defected in mid-May 1794. History is more than the biography of great men, but certainly Toussaint deserves much credit for leading Saint-Domingue to independence and the slave to freedom.

One of the most important preparations for Toussaint's defection to the French was the National Convention's abolition of slavery. Sonthonax had sent Dufay, Jean Baptiste Mills, and Mars Belley to the Convention to uphold his emancipation decrees in Saint-Domingue. Fortunately for Sonthonax, the Girondins were purged and Maximilien Robespierre, closely associated with the *Amis des Noirs,* dominated the Committee of Public Safety.[35] Under such favorable conditions, the Convention enthusiastically received the three agents, and on February 4, 1794, Arnaud Levasseur made the motion that "slavery be abolished in all the territory of the Republic, including Saint-Domingue."[36] Such feelings of emotion gripped the Convention that Levasseur's recommendation was unanimously approved by acclamation. Even Abbé Grégoire, leader of the *Amis des Noirs* after Brissot's execution, was

BATTLE OF RAVIN-À-COULEUVRE. *The Bettmann Archive.*

CAPTURE OF TOUSSAINT LOUVERTURE BY THE GENERAL OF THE FRENCH
EXPEDITION. *The Bettmann Archive*.

surprised that the abolition of slavery came so quickly. Perhaps it would not have without the prodding of Sonthonax.[37]

The Convention's abolition of slavery, according to Lacroix, "persuaded Toussaint to join Laveaux, for now France had taken the lead in the Negroes' interest."[38] To stop here, as some historians have done, is a mistake because Toussaint was more complex than that. Often historians have looked only at Toussaint the humanitarian, advocate of black liberty, but Toussaint the Machiavellian was just as important.[39]

As long as Toussaint remained with the Spanish, his advancement was blocked by Biassou and Jean François. In the last few months preceding his defection to the French, Toussaint began a power struggle with Biassou; Pierre, the former's brother, was killed in the conflict. Toussaint must have noticed the better opportunity for his promotion with the French, since Laveaux was their only able leader. In fact, Toussaint was in contact with Laveaux before the Convention took action on slavery. In one letter, dated January 3, he already seemed close to defection. At about the same time he was sending out agents to win over the followers of François and Biassou. Toussaint was both a power-seeker and a sincere abolitionist; by joining the French, he served both purposes.[40]

Suddenly, after several months of heavily guarded secrecy, Toussaint struck with the fierceness of a tornado. At Saint-Raphael on May 6, 1794, he surprised the Spanish as they came from Mass and slaughtered many before fleeing toward Gonaives. Then he turned and drove the Spanish eastward and the British toward the sea; soon Toussaint possessed much of the Artibonite Valley. Meanwhile Laveaux and Villatte made junction in North Province, raising Spanish sieges at Port-de-Paix and Le Cap François. To the south Rigaud renewed his efforts against the British with new inspiration.[41] Already many agreed with Captain Wickham, a Yankee sea captain, that "Toussaint is a brilliant officer; indefatigable in action; cautious in his proceedings; and is not careless and negligent."[42]

On May 18 Toussaint made his change of allegiance official in a letter to Laveaux. In this document, marked for public consumption, Toussaint claimed that he had fought on the side of the Spaniards for Negro freedom. The Spanish, he maintained, refused to liberate the blacks and "have caused us to fight each other in order to diminish our numbers and to overwhelm the remainder with chains."[43] Toussaint also made it clear that he had sympathy and respect for the suffering whites. Within a few years this remarkable black man gained their support.[44]

In an emotional meeting at Dondon on July 27, Toussaint and Laveaux personally greeted each other for the first time. A long friendship had begun between two men who learned the meaning of mutual love and respect. Yet Toussaint never allowed his feelings for Laveaux to block his drive for black freedom and personal power. Not surprising, therefore, was his early request to increase his military strength by four regiments.[45] Laveaux agreed and became a useful instrument in Toussaint's rise to power.[46]

From the outset of his alliance with the French, Toussaint demonstrated an unusual grasp of political and military tactics. Never fight, he believed, without first propagandizing your opponent to surrender peacefully. Typical was a warning he gave on February 16, 1795, to planters still in British service: "Frenchmen, the alarm bell sounds, awake from the fatal errors into which you have been plunged. This is the last time that you can leave England and regain your dignity as a French citizen."[47] When words failed, shooting began, but Toussaint was careful to alter his military tactics to fit his situation. Lieutenant Colonel Thomas Brisbane, one of the most able English commanders, was about to discover how versatile Toussaint could be.[48]

In September 1794 Brisbane, joined by Spaniards to the east, launched an offensive to recapture the Artibonite Valley. Toussaint, seeing little chance of openly withstanding an enemy assault of several thousand soldiers, resorted to guerrilla tactics.[49] One British officer noted that Insurgent tactics consisted "chiefly in ambuscades for which the face of the country is particularly calculated."[50] During this offensive and others, Toussaint used guerrilla tactics so well that Brisbane's attack "was like a vessel traversing the ocean—the waves yielded indeed for the moment but united again as the vessel passed."[51]

As Brisbane's offensive waned, Toussaint shifted to frontal attacks to obtain his objectives. At Saint-Raphael and Saint-Michel, near Marmelade, Toussaint faced seven thousand Spanish soldiers. Striking through hails of grapeshot, Toussaint led his forces in an assault on enemy entrenchments. By October 21 both towns were in his possession, and Jean François failed to regain them in a counterattack. By early 1796 Toussaint controlled much of North and West provinces; despite repeated attempts, he could not be dislodged and every day seemed to grow more powerful.[52]

To the south Rigaud was putting tremendous pressure on the British. From Léogane mulattoes informed Rigaud that their city awaited liberation from the British. Reaching Léogane with over a thousand soldiers, he found the English defenders alerted by two of the mulatto conspirators. Undeterred by his situation, Rigaud resolved to attack anyway; courage in the face of adversity was one of his finest qualities. On October 6, 1794, his army stormed the city and received only light casualties. The British had to make a hasty retreat to Port-au-Prince, but not before they had slaughtered over one hundred captives and dumped them into the sea.[53]

Encouraged by the fall of Léogane, Rigaud aimed an offensive at Port-au-Prince, key to the British position in West Province. On December 5, 1794, he assaulted the port with a force of two thousand men, suffered many losses, and was forced to withdraw. Undismayed by defeat, Rigaud redirected his offensive toward Tiburon, a key port in South Province.[54]

Preparatory to attack, Rigaud blockaded Tiburon with a small fleet of eight ships. On December 26 he attacked the city, garrisoned by one thousand English soldiers. When the British commandant, Bradford, saw that he was outnumbered four to one and that there was no chance for a withdrawal by sea, he ordered his forces to break through the mulatto encirclement. As they came out, the mulattoes fell on them, wiping out almost the entire garrison. By June 1795 English forces held only Saint Marc and Port-au-Prince in West Province, Jérémie in South Province, and Môle Saint Nicolas in North Province. British counterattacks had no more success with Rigaud than with Toussaint.[55]

At the pinnacle of his power Rigaud began to demonstrate the qualities of command that marked him as inferior to Toussaint. Rigaud personified the mulatto drive for vengeance and saw little use for blacks or whites. When mulatto forces lost a battle, he would often blame defeat on the whites in his ranks; sometimes he even resorted to mass executions of the "traitors." Nor did the blacks fare much better. One Insurgent leader, General Dudonait, was so angry at Rigaud and the mulattoes that he offered to join the British to destroy the *gens de couleur*. Even though mulattoes captured and executed Dudonait, Rigaud never achieved the unity of Toussaint's zones of occupation. For Toussaint, all colors were part of Saint-Domingue.[56]

While Rigaud and Toussaint rose in power, Great Britain's plans of West Indian conquests neared total collapse. In June 1794, Victor Hugues recaptured Guadeloupe for France and freed the island's slaves. Soon he began to threaten other areas under British control. To make matters worse for England, a serious maroon rebellion broke out in Jamaica in 1795, which tied up much needed reinforcements for Saint-Domingue. Moreover, on July 22, 1795, Spain officially withdrew from the First Coalition and ceded Santo Domingo to France. When news of these agreements in the Treaty of Basle reached the Spanish planters and Jean François, they refused to stop their fight against the French; nevertheless, Spain's official participation in the Saint-Domingue campaign was at an end. Even British naval supremacy, at least around Saint-Domingue, was in jeopardy. In June 1796 the commander of the Jamaica station complained that he did not have enough ships to prevent French supplies and reinforcements from landing regularly. Two months later the British suffered a naval defeat off the coast of Saint Marc. By 1796 the English ministry began to revaluate the invasion of Saint-Domingue; millions of pounds and perhaps as many as twenty thousand British lives had already been lost. England vainly continued to struggle, however, before finally withdrawing two years later.[57]

With the decline of European power in Saint-Domingue, an ever widening power vacuum began to appear. Toussaint aspired to fill the void, but whether he could was not certain. One by one he eliminated his strong rivals for power with amazing finesse. The first to go was Villatte, mulatto commander of Le Cap François.

Villatte viewed Toussaint with alarm. Toussaint had the support of Laveaux, had great military power, and began to demonstrate his skill as a competent reconstructionist. He even sent his own aide-de-camp, Meharon, to communicate with the National Convention. This act of superiority must not have escaped Villatte and the other mulattoes. During June 1795 Villatte intrigued with Joseph Flaville to overthrow Toussaint. But at Marmelade, Flaville and his followers met the army of Toussaint and were defeated. Perhaps Villatte would have given up in despair had Rigaud not offered him participation in a more daring conspiracy.[58]

Rigaud saw Laveaux as the basis of Toussaint's rising power and believed that overthrow of the Frenchman would guarantee mulatto supremacy. Communicating with Villatte through an agent, he proposed that Laveaux be removed and himself made governor; for his cooperation Villatte would become Rigaud's successor. Two clear implications in the plot were that the mulattoes planned to inherit the former position of the whites and that slavery itself might be restored. Villatte agreed to the plot, and a struggle began which ended in mulatto defeat.[59]

On the morning of March 20, 1796, a hundred mulattoes, armed with pistols and swords, entered the government palace at Le Cap François and broke into the bedroom of Laveaux. Grabbing the governor-general and Henri Perroud, an adviser, the *gens de couleur* beat their victims and humiliated them by dragging both men through the streets. With Laveaux in prison the conspiracy neared success, but suddenly Toussaint, informed of the plot, struck one of his characteristic lightning blows. What appeared to be a mulatto victory actually became nothing more than a stepping stone in his quest for power.[60]

Toussaint was at his headquarters at Gonaives when news of Laveaux's imprisonment arrived. Immediately he ordered Pierre Michel, Moyse, Dessalines, and Bélair to converge on Le Cap François with ten thousand men. Toussaint himself soon followed and demanded that Laveaux be released within a half-hour or else he would storm the city. On March 22 the mulattoes responded by releasing Laveaux, and Villatte fled with six hundred of his followers into the oblivion of an outcast.[61]

More resulted from the mulatto conspiracy than just the restoration of Laveaux to the governorship. Toussaint had eliminated

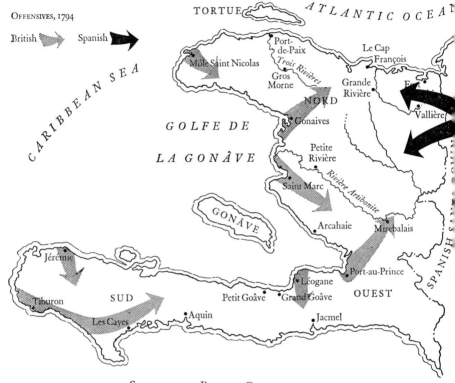

British   Spanish

ATLANTIC OCEAN

CARIBBEAN SEA

TORTUE

Port-de-Paix

Le Cap François

Môle Saint Nicolas

Trois Rivières

Gros Morne

Grande Rivière

NORD

Vallière

GOLFE DE

Gonaives

LA GONÂVE

Petite Rivière

Saint Marc

Rivière Artibonite

Mirebalais

GONÂVE

Arcahaie

Jérémie

Port-au-Prince

Tiburon

SUD

Léogane

Petit Goâve   Grand Goâve

OUEST

SPANISH

Les Cayes

Aquin

Jacmel

SPANISH AND BRITISH OFFENSIVES, 1793–94

Villatte and thwarted Rigaud; of greater importance, the governor depended on his support. As a result Laveaux ceremoniously conferred the office of lieutenant governor upon Toussaint on April 1.[62] From that moment Laveaux became Toussaint's puppet. Moreover, the new lieutenant governor could expand his military strength at his own discretion. On April 2 Toussaint increased his army with five new regiments and a personal bodyguard of one hundred men; soon he would have a well-trained army of more than twenty thousand men.[63]

One conflict was hardly over before another followed. On May 11, 1796, Sonthonax returned as the head of a five-member commission.[64] Thousands of blacks demonstrated their affection for their white emancipator by crowding Sonthonax's carriage as it wheeled through the streets of Le Cap François. As they shouted, *"Vive la République! Vive la liberté générale! Vive notre ami Sonthonax!"* Toussaint must have realized that here was perhaps his greatest threat: a man who could command the black masses.[65] Getting rid of Sonthonax would be a delicate operation, but the hand of Toussaint proved steady and dexterous.

At first Toussaint tried to ease Sonthonax out gently. The French Constitution of the Year III allowed Saint-Domingue representation in the Council of Five Hundred. Toussaint nominated Sonthonax and Laveaux. The latter, although nothing but a puppet governor, was potentially dangerous because of his position. Using political methods common in Saint-Domingue, Toussaint threatened to destroy Le Cap François if the electors did not accept his choices. They did, and in mid-August the delegates were notified of their "elections." Laveaux, bearing no ill will toward Toussaint, took the opportunity to leave on October 13, but Sonthonax remained.[66]

Faced with the dilemma of letting Sonthonax stay or openly flouting French authority with his removal, Toussaint waited for conditions to change. Sonthonax himself was a large contributor to the success of this strategy because he was his own worst enemy. He failed to exercise adequate control over economic matters, especially in trade relations with the United States. Early in 1797 Toussaint went to Sonthonax and demanded that all privateering against American vessels be stopped; otherwise a major trade artery might be cut off. Even the black cultivators protested against the lack of protection for American shipping, and some resorted to economic boycotts and rebellion. Sonthonax also held a series of conferences with Toussaint in which he advocated independence for Saint-Domingue and white extermination. The latter point gave Toussaint reinforcement for his decision that Sonthonax must go; the future of Saint-Domingue, he believed, depended upon both black and white. The former point gave Toussaint material for propaganda.[67] By making Sonthonax appear to be leading Saint-Domingue to independence, Toussaint could pose as the defender of French interests.[68] He later rationalized that "the interest of France and the health of the colony rendered his [Sonthonax's] departure necessary."[69]

Sonthonax committed his biggest blunder, however, in his relationship with Rigaud. Instead of encouraging the mulatto leader
to join him to counterbalance Toussaint's power, Sonthonax acted
despotically toward Rigaud. In July 1796 he sent a small army and
a group of agents to Les Cayes to reform its municipal government
and cast Rigaud aside. Furious at his shabby treatment, Rigaud
staged a successful uprising on August 28 and regained his authority. This indicated to Toussaint that Rigaud would support
rather than oppose a *coup d'état* against Sonthonax.[70]

Events in France also had a heavy bearing on the struggle for
power. After the overthrow of Robespierre, reactionaries gained
strength. Among them were many planters, one being Barbé-
Marbois, former intendant of Saint-Domingue, now president of
the Council of Elders. With growing reaction came the desire to
return the colonies, especially Saint-Domingue, to their former
status during the *ancien régime*. By early 1797 colonial delegates
to the French legislature found it increasingly difficult to be seated,
and there was a growing disposition in favor of the restoration of
slavery. There were frequent emotional attacks upon Sonthonax,
centering on emancipation and loss of colonial prosperity.[71] On
January 5 Vaublanc stood before the Council of Elders and condemned Sonthonax's laws as "so barbaric that Robespierre himself
would have disavowed them."[72] On June 12 the French legislature
recalled Sonthonax, Roume, and Raimond.[73]

Toussaint viewed the reaction in France with mixed emotions.
Obviously he was appalled by the apparent drift toward the restoration of slavery. In a letter dated May 21 he reminded the
French legislature that he and France had only endeavored "to
restore men to the liberty which He [God] gave them, and which
other men would have deprived them."[74] He even sent his two
sons, Isaac and Placide, to France for an education, probably believing that it might improve his image among French reactionaries. Toussaint the humanitarian must have felt great relief
when on September 4, known in French history as 18 Fructidor,
many on the extreme right were purged. For the moment Saint-
Domingue was safe from slavery.[75]

Toussaint the power seeker viewed French reaction from a dif-

ferent perspective than Toussaint the humanitarian. Contrary to
C. L. R. James's belief, Toussaint did not "sacrifice" Sonthonax
to France only to stall approaching slavery; reaction actually served
to cushion the fall of the white emancipator. By removing Sonthonax, Toussaint would simply be upholding the decision of the
French legislature. Furthermore, Toussaint would gain the favor
of French government, making the restoration of slavery more re-
mote and the achievement of his dictatorial power closer at hand.
Toussaint may have reasoned that he could even use feelings
against Sonthonax to destroy both the man and his position. On
October 21 he went so far as to send Colonel Vincent to the French
legislature to ask that no more agents be appointed for Saint-
Domingue. France, however, refused to make that concession.[76]

Hoping to stave off the collapse of his power, Sonthonax installed Toussaint as the new governor-general in place of Laveaux
on May 2, 1797, but Toussaint's determination to remove Sonthonax did not abate.[77] On August 16 Toussaint marched a large army
to the outskirts of Le Cap François and demanded that Sonthonax
return to France as a delegate from Saint-Domingue. Sonthonax
hesitated and then prepared to resist. Toussaint waited, believing
that he could avoid bloodshed. On August 27 the hard-pressed
commissioner, realizing the futility of resistance, made his way
through crowds of sorrowful blacks to the vessel *L'Idien*, about to
weigh anchor for France. Amid thundering salutes, the ship
slowly made its way to open sea. Toussaint had eliminated a
major opponent.[78]

While Toussaint struggled with Villatte and Sonthonax, the
British renewed their attempts to conquer Saint-Domingue.
Pleased with their new commander, General Gordon Forbes, Pitt
and Dundas had reason to believe that the year 1796 might bring
a favorable change in British military fortunes. Once again they
miscalculated. Forbes might win occasional battles, but the elusive
Toussaint continued to apply unrelenting pressure against English forces.[79]

Forbes launched his first major offensive toward Rigaud in
South Province and quickly learned that blacks and mulattoes
were tough fighters. From Port-au-Prince a British armada of

twenty ships arrived off the coast of Léogane, gateway to South Province. For nine hours on March 21 the fleet laid down a heavy bombardment. Then Colonel James Grant and Major General Bowyer landed and began a two-pronged drive toward the battered city. Renaud, one of Rigaud's best subordinate officers, stood his ground and forced the British to retreat. During the next day Bowyer and Grant attempted a frontal assault against Léogane but lost hundreds of men and had to withdraw. Deciding to embark his troops, Forbes left Baron de Montalambert with a force of white colonials as a rear guard. Renaud, however, routed Montalambert's detachment and slashed into the retreating British army. In great confusion, Englishmen ran toward the shore, seeking the safety of their ships.[80]

Soon Forbes encountered two other formidable opponents, yellow fever and malaria. Planning to push Toussaint back in West Province, Forbes ordered a concentration of troops at Saint Marc. The offensive was a failure before it began. Hundreds of soldiers died as the stinging mosquitoes took their toll, some units losing 80 percent of their personnel.[81] So depressed did the British soldiers become that "some ... gave themselves up for lost and instead of attempting to stop the progress of the disease did everything in their power to promote it in order to be the sooner out of their misery."[82] Seeing that his opponent was weak, Toussaint counterattacked and bottled up the British in Port-au-Prince and Saint Marc.[83]

The English forces did have some success. On June 10 they captured Fort Bombardé, pushing Toussaint's army back from Môle Saint Nicolas. In August, Forbes undertook a major offensive in West Province which pushed Toussaint into the interior and almost trapped his Fourth Regiment. In South Province, Rigaud's October offensive against Jérémie failed. Yet Toussaint and Rigaud seemed no closer to defeat, and England's expenses and losses were mounting. Disenchanted with Forbes, the British ministry replaced him with Lieutenant General John Simcoe, who arrived in Saint-Domingue on February 28, 1797.[84]

Simcoe, an able commander, had well over thirty thousand men, but the armies of Rigaud and Toussaint had the initiative.[85] In April 1797 Toussaint seized Mirebalais and swept toward Port-au-

Prince. With hard fighting, the British prevented the blacks from scaling the mountains overlooking the important port. In the south Rigaud struck at Jérémie but had to retreat with a loss of about twelve hundred men.[86]

Encouraged by his successful defensive stands, Simcoe believed Toussaint was vulnerable to a swift counterattack. The thrust of the offensive, he decided, would be aimed at Mirebalais in an attempt to push Toussaint deep into the interior of West Province. Simcoe began his drive on May 30 and soon learned that Toussaint and the terrain were worthy opponents.[87] The British suffered from lack of water and from sunstroke, and "at every instant the obstructions were becoming more formidable without mentioning those the enemy might throw in the way."[88] On May 31 Mirebalais fell to English forces without a shot being fired, but the blacks left the city a charred ruins. Suddenly Toussaint whirled his army around and launched a counteroffensive toward Saint Marc; Simcoe was forced either to abandon his plans or to lose the valuable city. Choosing to forsake his plans, he rushed back to Saint Marc in a grueling forced march and parried Toussaint's assault.[89] Simcoe now decided to maintain only defensive positions along the coast from Môle Saint Nicolas to Jérémie. Toussaint could have the interior.[90]

In England, meanwhile, feeling began to mount against the British invasion of Saint-Domingue. On May 18, 1797, St. John took the floor of the House of Commons to point out the need for reinforcements at home and the great expense of the Saint-Domingue campaign. Even though Commons voted overwhelmingly against withdrawal, the British ministry decided to curtail England's West Indian involvement.[91] The campaign had cost over ten million pounds and perhaps as many as 100,000 casualties.[92] England retained the important deep-water port Môle Saint Nicolas but sacrificed the remainder of its conquests in Saint-Domingue. In March 1798 General Thomas Maitland arrived in Saint-Domingue to carry out the new policy. Obviously the British were through; now only Rigaud stood in Toussaint's way.[93]

NOTES FOR CHAPTER FIVE

1. Fear of the Saint-Domingue slave rebellion and of the French Revolution contributed to the decline of British support for the abolition of the slave trade. By 1794 the Committee for the Abolition of the Slave Trade met only occasionally; from 1797 to 1804 it did not meet at all. Not until 1808 did England end her commerce in slaves. Coupland, *British Anti-Slavery*, 101.

2. Newport *Mercury*, April 16, 1792; Julian Corbett, ed., *Private Papers of George, Second Earl of Spencer: First Lord of the Admiralty* (London: Navy Records Society, 1913), 139; Letter Extract from Kingston, Jamaica, Nov. 10, 1794, in Philadelphia *Aurora*, Jan. 3, 1795.

3. *The Times* (London), May 19, 1797.

4. Corbett, *Spencer Papers*, 139.

5. *Ibid.*; Bayard to Lady in Annapolis, April 8, 1795, Gibson-Maynadier Papers (Maryland Historical Society); Hubert Cole, *Christophe, King of Haiti* (New York: Viking, 1967), 42; Providence *Gazette and Country Journal*, Aug. 3, 1793.

6. Rudé, *Revolutionary Europe*, 139; Sydenham, *French Revolution*, 141–42, 145, 166, 175.

7. Corbett, *Spencer Papers*, xviii–xix.

8. *State Gazette of South Carolina*, July 29, 1793.

9. Georges Lefebvre, *The Thermidorians and the Directory* (New York: Random, 1964), 164–66.

10. Great Britain, *Bulletins*, I, 226; *State Gazette of South Carolina*, May 13, 1793.

11. Many French planters rationalized their support of the British invasion as the only way to achieve order. "To carry arms against the revolting slaves of Saint-Domingue," one planter maintained, "is not to be traitorous to one's country; it is to serve it." Parham, *My Odyssey*, 143.

12. Great Britain, *Bulletins*, I, 224–26, 237–39; II, 91; Edwards, *San Domingo*, 149; Alexis, *Black Liberator*, 54.

13. One cannot be certain that Polverel was traitorous on this occasion. Yet there did seem to be an uncertain amount of tension between Sonthonax and Polverel over the abolition of slavery, the latter being a bit more hesitant. Alexis, *Black Liberator*, 55; Baltimore *Intelligencer*, Oct. 29, 1793.

14. As the Caribbean conquests of Great Britain neared completion, Pitt assigned to Lord Charles Hawkesbury, president of the Board of Trade, the task of providing a plan for their government. Influenced by his earlier efforts to centralize the colonial administration of India through a governor-general and by the fair treatment of Catholics in Canada, Hawkesbury designed a political system for the French West Indies which was both just and strong. Each of the former French colonies was to have a governor-

general in whom all civil and military executive powers were vested. Of only nominal importance was an advisory council, for the governor-general had the power to appoint and remove its members and could veto its measures. The remainder of the Hawkesbury program, moreover, generally conformed with French tradition: the Roman Catholic faith was to be maintained, the British Treasury would impose no new revenues, and the local laws of 1789 were to be observed. In two important respects, however, the program departed from French tradition: the former French colonies became part of the British Navigation System and the *gens de couleur* were promised the same civil rights as the mulattoes of the Anglo-Caribbean.

Even though British government in the French West Indies was never fully established, it still set important constitutional precedents for other areas which Great Britain conquered, such as Cape Colony, Ceylon, and Maritius. Thus one of the lasting effects of Pitt's West Indian policy was upon the administrative institutions of the British Empire. Vincent Harlow, *The Founding of the Second British Empire, 1763–1793*, 2 vols. (London: Longmans, 1964), II, 774–79; Vincent Harlow and Frederick Madden, eds., *British Colonial Developments, 1774–1834: Select Documents* (Oxford: Clarendon, 1953), 83–87.

15. Great Britain, *A Collection of State Papers Relative to the War Against France Now Carrying on by Great Britain*, 10 vols., ed. John Debrett (London: n.n., 1794–1801), II, 136–38; William Burn, *The British West Indies* (London: Hutchinson House, 1951), 104; *State Gazette of South Carolina*, Feb. 18 and May 19, 1794; Newport *Mercury*, May 20, 1794; Boston *Independent Chronicle*, May 19, 1794.

16. Boston *Independent Chronicle*, April 10, 1794; Alexis, *Black Liberator*, 58; *L'Étoile Américaine* (Philadelphia), April 1, 1794; *The Times* (London), Oct. 3, 1793.

17. *The Times* (London), Sept. 11, 1794; Captain-General Joaquín García y Moreno to Admiral Jean François, July 10, 1793, Laveaux Papers; H. Shirley to E. Shirley, July 22, 1793, C. O. 137/50; Parham, *My Odyssey*, 128.

18. Alexis, *Black Liberator*, 48, 58–59; Cole, *Christophe*, 43.

19. *The Times* (London), Oct. 14 and Sept. 11, 1794; Deputy Laplace to Captain-General Joaquín García y Moreno, April 4, 1794, Laveaux Papers.

20. Cole, *Christophe*, 70–71; Great Britain, *Bulletins*, II, 91.

21. *State Gazette of South Carolina*, Oct. 5, 1793; Baltimore *Intelligencer*, May 17, 1794; Newport *Mercury*, May 20, 1794. Sonthonax even threatened trade connections with the U.S. Alexander Hamilton recommended that aid to the colony be reduced and that "care should be taken . . . to avoid the explicit recognition of any regular authority in any person." Harold Syrett, ed., *The Papers of Alexander Hamilton*, 13 vols. (New York: Columbia Univ. Press, 1961–67), XIII, 171.

22. According to C. L. R. James, "All propertied San Domingo rushed to welcome the British, the defenders of slavery." James is incorrect, for the

planters were mixed in their response to the British. Besides, the planters were seriously weakened after Galbaud's departure in June 1793. James, *Black Jacobins*, 135; Edwards, *San Domingo*, 144.

23. Parham, *My Odyssey*, 145–46.

24. "Journal of Occupation," II, 71–72.

25. *Ibid.*, I, 41; *The Times* (London), Aug. 15, 1794.

26. Edwards, *San Domingo*, 162.

27. *The Times* (London), Oct. 14, 1794 and Sept. 5, 1795; Letter Extract from Saint Marc, Feb. 1, 1795, in Boston *Independent Chronicle*, March 26, 1795.

28. Great Britain, *State Papers*, II, 110–11; Letter Extract from Môle Saint Nicolas, July 11, 1794, in Baltimore *Intelligencer*, Aug. 7, 1794; *L'Étoile Américaine* (Philadelphia), April 1, 1794; Philadelphia *Aurora*, Jan. 7, 1795.

29. Parham, *My Odyssey*, 121

30. *The Times* (London), Oct. 14, 1794.

31. *Ibid.*

32. Parham, *My Odyssey*, 127.

33. *Ibid.*, 128, 130.

34. *Ibid.*, 132.

35. McCloy, *French West Indies*, 79–80;; Rudé, *Revolutionary Europe*, 138; Sydenham, *French Revolution*, 170.

36. *Le Moniteur*, Feb. 5, 1794.

37. *Ibid.*; Abbé Henri-Baptiste Grégoire, *Mémoires de Grégoire, ancien évêque de Blois, député à Assemblée Constituante*, 2 vols. (Paris: A. Dupont, 1837), I, 390–91.

38. Lacroix, *Mémoires*, I, 299.

39. Ralph Korngold and C. L. R. James both committed this error. After receiving news in May of the Convention's ratification of emancipation, Toussaint "did not," according to James, "hesitate a moment but at once told Laveaux that he was willing to join him." Such statements as this have done much to hide Toussaint's character behind a cloud of altruism. James, *Black Jacobins*, 143; Korngold, *Citizen Toussaint*, 105–106.

40. Laplace to García y Moreno, April 4, 1794, and Toussaint to Laveaux, Jan. 3, 1794, Laveaux Papers.

41. Cole, *Christophe*, 43; Alexis, *Black Liberator*, 67–69.

42. Charleston *City Gazette*, Feb. 20, 1802.

43. Toussaint to Laveaux, May 18, 1794, Laveaux Papers.

44. *Ibid.*

45. Henry Christophe joined Toussaint at this time and soon showed expert leadership in wielding raw recruits into a well-disciplined fighting machine. Christophe was born on Oct. 6, 1767, in British-held Grenada. Well treated as a slave and a cook by occupation, Christophe did not join the Insurgents until Toussaint defected to the French. Cole, *Christophe*, 30–33, 43–44.

46. *Ibid.*, 43–44; Alexis, *Black Liberator*, 70. Even at this early date,

Laveaux realized that French power in Saint-Domingue depended upon the blacks. When putting down a local rebellion or when cornering enemy forces, he would exclude the blacks from any threats of extermination. Laveaux's delicate position played a large role in Toussaint's eventual dictatorship. Laveaux to Inhabitants of Saint Marc, Sept. 13, 1794, Laveaux Papers.

47. Toussaint to the French encamped on Mosere Plantation, Feb. 16, 1795, Laveaux Papers.

48. Howard, "Journal of Occupation," II, 39; Philadelphia *Aurora*, Jan. 27, 1795.

49. Edwards, *San Domingo*, 165–66.

50. Howard, "Journal of Occupation," II, 39.

51. Bryan Edwards, *History, Civil and Commercial of the British Colonies in the West Indies,* 4 vols. (Philadelphia: James Humphreys, 1806), IV, 227.

52. *Ibid.*, 226–27; Philadelphia *Aurora*, Jan. 27, 1795; *Le Moniteur*, June 2, 1795.

53. Baltimore *Intelligencer*, Feb. 23, 1795.

54. Edwards, *San Domingo*, 167.

55. Philadelphia *Aurora*, Feb. 11, 1795; Newport *Mercury*, Feb. 24, 1795; *Le Moniteur*, June 2, 1795; Great Britain, *Bulletins*, IV, 77–78.

56. Great Britain, *Bulletins*, IV, 319–20; Edwards, *British West Indies*, IV, 227.

57. *The Times* (London), Feb. 2, 1797; Ragatz, *British Caribbean*, 225–26; Parry and Sherlock, *West Indies*, 165–66; Corbett, *Spencer Papers*, 283–84; Boston *Price-Current*, Aug. 29, 1796.

58. Philadelphia *Aurora*, Feb. 7, 1795; Toussaint to Laveaux, n.d., and Toussaint to Laveaux, June 18, 1795, Laveaux Papers.

59. Korngold, *Citizen Toussaint*, 119–20; Great Britain, *State Papers*, V, 1.

60. Great Britain, *State Papers*, V, 1; Letter Extract from Môle Saint Nicolas, May 2, 1796, in *The Times* (London), June 8, 1796.

61. Alexis, *Black Liberator*, 80–82; Laveaux to Perroud, March 1796, in Boston *Independent Chronicle*, May 23, 1796; Letter Extract from Port-de-Paix, March 24, 1796, in Baltimore *Federal Gazette*, April 19, 1796.

62. Laveaux in an emotional speech maintained that he had dreamed that Toussaint was the very man predicted by Abbé Raynal as the avenger of the wrongs sustained by the blacks. This statement, according to James Delaire, an observer, contributed to Toussaint's image as protector of the blacks. Delaire to Pickering, April 27, 1799, Consular Dispatches, Cap-Haitien, vol. 1.

63. Alexis, *Black Liberator*, 83; Letter Extract from Le Cap François, April 10, 1797, in Boston *Independent Chronicle*, May 18, 1797.

64. Sonthonax was one of those unusual politicians who could maintain his power under almost any circumstances. He and Polverel arrived in France on Aug. 2, 1794, to stand trial before the National Convention. In

danger of following Robespierre to the guillotine, Sonthonax was able to convince the Convention of the justice of his actions. On Aug. 6 he and Polverel were acquitted and given seats in the Convention. Despite periodic attacks afterward, Sonthonax was selected to head a new commission to Saint-Domingue, probably because he stood a good chance of controlling Toussaint and the blacks. Other members of the commission were Raimond, Roume, Leblanc, and Giraud. *Courrier Français*, May 17, 1796; *The Times* (London), Aug. 22 and Sept. 11, 1794; *Le Moniteur*, Sept. 24, 1795.

65. Sonthonax to Minister of Marine, May 18, 1796, in *Le Moniteur*, July 29, 1796.

66. Alexis, *Black Liberator*, 95–96; Korngold, *Citizen Toussaint*, 126–27.

67. Even though Toussaint would later lead Saint-Domingue close to independence, there is no evidence that he seriously considered it at this time.

68. Boston *Price-Current*, March 30, 1797; Boston *Independent Chronicle*, June 15, 1797; Philadelphia *Courrier Français*, Oct. 12, 1797.

69. Toussaint to Citizens of North Province, Sept. 8, 1797, in Philadelphia *Courrier Français*, Oct. 10, 1797.

70. Address of Citizens of Les Cayes and Neighboring Plantations to Commissioners of French Government, n.d., in Baltimore *Federal Gazette*, Oct. 20, 1796; Alexis, *Black Liberator*, 92; Philadelphia *Aurora*, Oct. 20, 1796.

71. Lefebvre, *Thermidorians and the Directory*, 304; *Le Moniteur*, Sept. 8, 1797.

72. *Le Moniteur*, Jan. 6, 1797.

73. James, *Black Jacobins*, 193.

74. Toussaint to French National Legislature, May 21, 1797, in Charleston *City Gazette*, July 8, 1797.

75. Sonthonax to Toussaint, July 3, 1796, Sonthonax Correspondence; Rudé, *Revolutionary Europe*, 174.

76. James, *Black Jacobins*, 193; Toussaint to Citizen Vincent, Oct. 21, 1797, in *Le Moniteur*, Jan. 18, 1798.

77. One indication that Toussaint's appointment to the governorship did not influence his plan to remove Sonthonax was the deportation of General Desfourneaux. Rigaud and the mulattoes hated Desfourneaux, and one observer believed his removal served to cement a pact of friendship between the *gens de couleur* and Toussaint. Philadelphia *Courrier Français*, June 17, 1797.

78. *Ibid.*; Letter Extract from Môle Saint Nicolas, Dec. 24, 1797, in *Bahama Gazette* (Nassau), Feb. 10, 1798; Korngold, *Citizen Toussaint*, 133–37.

79. Forbes to Henry Dundas, Oct. 9, 1796, in *The Times* (London), Dec. 21, 1796; Edwards, *British West Indies*, IV, 229.

80. Boston *Independent Chronicle*, May 23, 1796; Philadelphia *Aurora*, May 10, 1796.

81. Howard, "Journal of Occupation," I, 51, 64.

82. *Ibid.*, 62.

83. *Ibid.*, 68, 76.

84. *Ibid.*, II, 28; Boston *Independent Chronicle*, July 18, 1796; Toussaint to Laveaux, Aug. 13, 1796, Laveaux Papers; Great Britain, *Bulletins*, IV, 320–21.

85. Toussaint had about 20,000 troops and Rigaud 12,000. Moreover, the cooperation between Rigaud and Toussaint was good. Edwards, *British West Indies*, IV, 231–32.

86. *The Times* (London), July 15, 17, 1797; Great Britain, *State Papers*, VI, 76–77; *Minerva and Mercantile Evening Advertiser* (New York), March 20, 1797.

87. Howard, "Journal of Occupation," II, 46.

88. *Ibid.*, 49.

89. *Ibid.*, 60–61.

90. Edwards, *British West Indies*, IV, 230.

91. *The Times* (London), May 19, 1797.

92. One cannot be positive about the total number of British casualties. The estimates range from 54,000 to 100,000 men. The latter estimate, which Fortescue made, seems more accurate since the British lost 6,000 men in Martinique during one summer alone. Moreover, as the Saint-Domingue campaign became deadlocked, the British lost increasing numbers of men. Based on Howard's reports, some unit hospitals were losing 50 men a day, and one regiment lost 500 men in five months. Silas Talbot to Timothy Pickering, Oct. 12, 1796, U.S., Dept. of State, Consular Dispatches, Kingston, Jamaica, vol. 1 (National Archives); John W. Fortescue, *A History of the British Army*, 13 vols. (London: Macmillan, 1899–1930), IV, pt. 1, 565; Howard, "Journal of Occupation," I, 62, 64; II, 1.

93. Cole, *Christophe*, 53; Edwards, *British West Indies*, IV, 231.

CHAPTER SIX

The Consolidation of Power, 1798-1801

Holding the coast from Jérémie to Môle Saint Nicolas, the British military desperately clung to its defenses. No longer did the English have any doubts about the fighting ability of Toussaint's black army.[1] As Lieutenant Howard succinctly put it, the "Negroes are called Brigands and are infinitely the most formidable enemy the British arms have to encounter."[2]

Toussaint, too competent to relax until the British were completely defeated, continued to press his military advantage. With the close support of the mulattoes of South Province, the black commander-in-chief decided to launch major offensives at the British salient extending from Port-au-Prince to Mirebalais and at Jérémie.[3] If successful, Toussaint would collapse the British center and right flank.[4]

Early in February 1798 two large black armies began to march, one toward Mirebalais and the other toward Jérémie. The former, under the direction of Toussaint himself, met stiff resistance from a perimeter of forts near Mirebalais. Fort Borough, the "Interior Gibraltar," and Fort Escahobe were the keys to this seemingly impregnable British defense. Toussaint demonstrated tireless determination in sending Moyse and Dessalines against the two forts in attack after attack. For twenty days and thirty-five assaults, Fort Escahobe withstood black onslaughts before it collapsed on March 7. On March 9 the Insurgents stormed Fort Borough and killed over half of its garrison. The salient melted away and the road to Port-au-Prince was open. Meanwhile the other black army assaulted Jérémie on February 19, failed to take the city, and suffered heavy casualties. The repulsed Negro force still managed to cut land communications between Jérémie and Port-au-Prince. Bottled up inside those two cities, two large groups of the British army faced possible annihilation. This was the situation when General Thomas Maitland, outspoken veteran of the West Indies, arrived in Saint-Domingue on March 21, 1798.[5]

Maitland attempted to boost sagging British morale, stating that "the rumors that we are going to pull out are falsehoods and everyone should remain faithful to the King to show that they deserve his paternal care."[6] Still a mood of defeatism gripped the British soldiers and their planter allies. Many began to flee: "Everyone packs up. Some carry away something; others nothing."[7] Maitland clearly saw that he must withdraw from West Province as rapidly as possible or face unconditional surrender.[8]

On April 22 negotiations began on board H.M.S. *Abergavenny* off the coast of Port-au-Prince; the representatives were Huin for Toussaint and Nightengale for Maitland. The British agreed to evacuate Port-au-Prince, Saint Marc, Arcahaye, and Croix-des-Bouquets, leaving all military installations intact. In return Toussaint promised to protect the lives and property of all those who did not withdraw with the English. Both sides agreed to a maximum truce of five weeks while the arrangements were carried out. On April 30 the agreement was signed, and within a week the last British troops left Port-au-Prince. Now England held only Jérémie in the south and Môle Saint Nicolas in the north. Just after the British left, Toussaint entered Port-au-Prince in triumph; West Province was his.[9]

Maitland, however, was not completely passive. He reasoned that total British defeat in Saint-Domingue would pose a threat to Jamaica. Toussaint might attempt to break the shackles of slavery throughout the West Indies. Maitland saw that South Province, closest point to Jamaica, was the logical area from which such an invasion might be launched. Therefore, leaving Môle Saint Nicolas on the defensive, he undertook a major offensive to secure the western tip on the peninsula-shaped province.[10]

Early in June, Major Churchill broke through the mulatto encirclement of Jérémie and pushed a large *gens de couleur* force

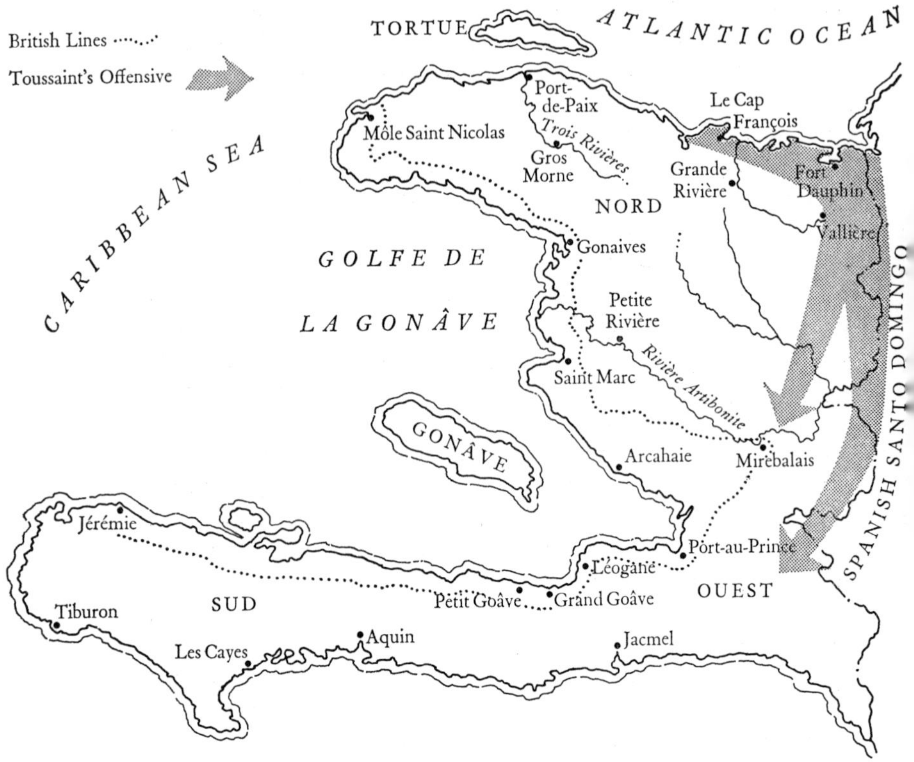
British Lines
Toussaint's Offensive
TORTUE
ATLANTIC OCEAN
CARIBBEAN SEA
Port-de-Paix
Môle Saint Nicolas
Trois Rivières
Gros Morne
Le Cap François
Grande Rivière
Fort Dauphin
Vallière
NORD
Gonaives
GOLFE DE LA GONÂVE
Petite Rivière
Rivière Artibonite
Saint Marc
GONÂVE
Arcahaie
Mirebalais
SPANISH SANTO DOMINGO
Jérémie
Port-au-Prince
Léogâne
SUD
Petit Goâve
Grand Goâve
OUEST
Tiburon
Les Cayes
Aquin
Jacmel

Toussaint's Spring Offensive, 1798

into Tiburon. From the land side Churchill's command applied heavy pressure on the defenses of the city, while an English fleet laid down a devastating bombardment and prevented relief or escape. On June 12 the second phase of the offensive began when Colonel Dessources landed his British force at Cape Irois, on the western end of South Province, and drove toward a rendezvous with other English troops at Bay des Anglois. Toussaint rushed aid to Rigaud, and the staggered mulatto leader quickly launched his own counteroffensive; Toussaint also drew British forces away from the south with attacks on Môle Saint Nicolas. For the moment Toussaint and Rigaud stood together, and the British offensive collapsed as quickly as it had begun. Maitland was now convinced that England must leave Saint-Domingue, all the more so because of the program of the French special agent Théodore Hédouville.[11]

On March 29, 1798, Hédouville arrived at the capital of Spanish Santo Domingo to confer with Roume about the complicated task of holding Toussaint in check until the Directory could re-establish its control over Saint-Domingue.[12] Hédouville, famous as the pacifier of the Vendée, probably disclosed the Directory's strategy of using Rigaud to counterbalance Toussaint and of luring the black commander-in-chief to invade Jamaica or even the southern United States. Attacking the U.S. and Jamaica would serve a double purpose: Toussaint and his black army would be swallowed up, and it would be a punishing blow to either the United States or England, both engaged in hostilities with France.[13] But Hédouville jeopardized his mission by arrogantly announcing to Julien Raimond, Toussaint's puppet, that "the government should remain intact until his [Hédouville's] arrival."[14] The implication was clear. Toussaint must have realized that for him to recognize such authority might undo his rising position. Hédouville's unguarded statement allowed the astute Toussaint a glimpse of the Frenchman's mission.

Sometime after Hédouville arrived at Le Cap François in mid-April, Maitland learned of the French plans to invade Jamaica. Maitland believed that England's continued presence in Saint-Domingue would only antagonize Toussaint and drive him toward Hédouville's project. On the other hand, Maitland saw distinct advantages in a British withdrawal: England could pose as Toussaint's ally and perhaps even force a wedge between the black commander-in-chief and Hédouville. Once again British diplomats were to prove more dangerous than British soldiers.[15]

Late in July, Maitland commenced his new strategy by sending Lord Harcourt to Port-au-Prince to open negotiations with Huin, Toussaint's representative. By August 10 Maitland had agreed to withdraw completely from Saint-Domingue during a truce of forty-two days; moreover, Môle Saint Nicolas would be surrendered to Toussaint, while Rigaud would be given the honor of occupying Jérémie. In the meantime Maitland conducted negotiations with Hédouville which duplicated many of the agreements with Huin. Toussaint complained, and Maitland withdrew from his arrangements with Hédouville. But Maitland had accomplished his purpose: he had intensified the growing tension between the French special agent and Toussaint.[16]

Seeing his plans take shape, Maitland attempted to deliver a diplomatic *coup de grâce* in discussions with Toussaint. On August 31 the two men met in a series of secret conferences at Pointe Bourgeoise, a few miles from Môle Saint Nicolas. During the parley Toussaint agreed upon a preliminary secret treaty: England would trade with Saint-Domingue and promised not to invade the colony again; American commerce with the blacks would have British support; and Toussaint pledged never to attack Jamaica. Maitland also offered Toussaint the protection of the British navy if he would declare the independence of Saint-Domingue. Should the black leader accept his proposal, Maitland reasoned, it would destroy forever the Directory's plans to invade Jamaica. Toussaint, however, declined the offer.[17] The idea of independence probably had already occurred to him, but he was unable to act because Hédouville, Rigaud, and Spanish Santo Domingo blocked his way.

On September 2 Maitland feted Toussaint at Môle Saint Nicolas with a reception befitting a sovereign. When the black commander approached the gates of the city, many inhabitants went out in holy procession to offer Toussaint their escort. Toussaint, quite religious by nature, "gravely accepted a place by the side of the pontiff [bishop], and in entering the Môle he carried the precious burden [a cross], which the seduced multitude adored with as much piety as fanaticism."[19] Troops passed in review, banquets were held, salutes thundered. Toussaint was impressed and expressed his pleasure: the Republic, he claimed, had never shown him as much honor as did the king of England. Perhaps Toussaint also intended his statement as a gentle warning for Hédouville to leave the status quo in Saint-Domingue alone, for seldom did he speak publicly without calculation.[20]

By early October the last British troops had left Saint-Domingue. Militarily, England had suffered an embarrassing and costly defeat. Yet British diplomacy had turned defeat to advantage: English trade with Toussaint would be maintained, the grip of France on the colony was weakened, and Jamaica was safe. The British military itself could not have hoped for much more. As one Englishman explained it:

> This new order of things, by keeping away from St. Domingo the Republican troops of France, suppresses every apprehension with respect to the invasion of Jamaica, while it secures almost exclusively to Great Britain the trade of the vast and rich colony of St. Domingo, without any expense, or the necessity of employing any additional force; the arrangement made by the Government relative to that island must be considered of the most judicious and beneficial nature.[21]

While Toussaint reached a new rapport with the British, his relationship with Hédouville deteriorated. When the special agent arrived at Le Cap François in mid-April 1798, he tried to win the confidence of Toussaint with compliments: "The Republican virtues of the general-in-chief are no less useful to Saint-Domingue than his military talents, for I see the confidence placed in him and the restoration of tranquility."[22] Toussaint was unmoved by such public utterances and seemed fully aware that General Hédouville had come to block his quest for power. In a series of parries and probes, each man searched for the weakness in the other's defense.[23]

Hédouville at first tried to control Toussaint through constant harassment. He attempted to discredit Toussaint by claiming that the black leader had improperly conducted the evacuation of Port-au-Prince; the British, Hédouville claimed, had removed too many cannons. Then during the British negotiations with Toussaint for the surrender of Môle Saint Nicolas, Hédouville willingly conducted discussions with Maitland on the surrender. Hédouville hoped that such duplicity would corrode Toussaint's authority, but Toussaint complained to Maitland, who in turn dropped negotiations with Hédouville. After the surrender of Môle Saint Nicolas, Hédouville thought that the *émigré* problem might at last be the chink in Toussaint's political armor.[24]

Many of the whites of Saint-Domingue were classified as *émigrés* according to French law, which meant their property could be confiscated and they could be exiled. Despite such legal technicalities, Toussaint needed the skills and experience of the white men to reconstruct ravaged Saint-Domingue. He was determined to let the "past bury itself" and would accept anyone willing to work for a unified and peaceful colony.[25]

When the British surrendered Môle Saint Nicolas, therefore, Toussaint not only pardoned those *émigrés* within English ranks but made many of them officers in his own army. Hédouville took quick counteraction against Toussaint's policy, hoping that the weight of French law might crush the black leader's authority. He declared that all *émigrés* must leave the colony, giving up their property; in anger Toussaint feigned resignation and had mobs of blacks attack the warehouses of merchants faithful to France. Hédouville quickly abandoned this course of action, for Toussaint had made his point: if the French meant to unseat him, it would cost them their colony.[26] It was now clear, as General Maitland observed, that "Hédouville though possessed with great nominal powers was in truth possessed of no real authority."[27] Nevertheless the special agent continued his intrigues.

In a series of meetings with Toussaint, Hédouville attempted to interest the black leader in leading an invasion of Jamaica. Toussaint realized that such a project might destroy him and that "the old system might then be restored in St. Domingo and slavery re-established."[28] Besides, Toussaint knew that he would be acting in violation of the agreements he had made with England. Seeing that Toussaint was inflexible on the subject, Hédouville decided to approach Rigaud. This was Hédouville's last chance to counterbalance Toussaint's authority.[29]

At first Rigaud seemed to be anything but receptive to the schemes of Hédouville. Remembering his clashes with Sonthonax, Rigaud viewed Hédouville as a potential enemy; the special agent nonetheless slowly began to win the support of the mulatto chief in a series of private conferences. Hédouville convinced Rigaud that Toussaint must be defeated and Jamaica invaded. Rigaud, flattered by the special agent's attention, disregarded the extreme dangers of an alliance with the Directory. Not only would England and the United States, in opposition to the Directory, side with Toussaint, but a mulatto victory was no guarantee against the actions of France.[30] Maitland believed that had Hédouville overthrown Toussaint, "it was perfectly apparent that his next attempt would have been to have gotten rid of Rigaud."[31]

Toussaint, well informed of the alliance between Rigaud and Hédouville, braced himself for a conflict which he welcomed. That Toussaint viewed the coming collision as an opportunity to expand his authority to include the mulattoes was revealed in a conversation with Lacroix.[32] On September 20, 1798, Rigaud approached Toussaint's headquarters and could easily have been arrested. Toussaint realized that such an action would be useless because the *gens de couleur* would still be unsubdued; also, the mulattoes "might find a better man."[33]

The league between Rigaud and Hédouville constituted an imposing threat to the black commander-in-chief's quest for power, "but neither the nominal powers of Hédouville nor the cunning and talents of Rigaud . . . were sufficient to enable them to cope with Toussaint."[34] Using the axiom of divide and conquer, Toussaint planned to expel Hédouville from Saint-Domingue before turning his attention to the titanic struggle with Rigaud. At Fort Liberté, near Le Cap François, a group of angry blacks and their commander provided Toussaint with the opportunity to remove the special agent.[35]

The Negro Fifth Regiment, commanded by Moyse, endured the pangs of starvation at the French stronghold. This and the belief that Hédouville had ordered the assassination of Moyse combined to bring a confrontation between the Fifth and a regiment of white and mulatto "compatriots," the Eighty-fourth.[36] In mid-October fighting broke out in which the white commander of the Eighty-fourth was killed, but the Fifth was routed. Hédouville declared Moyse an outlaw and ordered Toussaint to converge on Fort Liberté with his troops. Instead, Toussaint seized upon the situation to force Hédouville from the colony. After spreading the rumor that the special agent wished to restore slavery, Toussaint led his army and thousands of Negro cultivators to Le Cap François.[37]

With a horde of angry blacks threatening to storm the city, Hédouville had no choice but to flee from Saint-Domingue. On

October 22, 1798, the Frenchman and one thousand of his followers embarked upon three ships for France. Before his departure, however, Hédouville absolved Roume and Rigaud from any allegiance to Toussaint; moreover, he addressed a proclamation to the citizens of Saint-Domingue, warning them of a developing plot for independence. England and the United States, he believed, were ready to back Toussaint in such a move.[38]

Hédouville was close to the truth. Maitland had promised British support for the independence of Saint-Domingue late in August 1798. Even the United States, deeply involved in the Quasi-War, began to uphold the British position. Secretary of State Timothy Pickering, along with other Federalists, saw that the support of Toussaint might be a guarantee against a black invasion of the South,[39] an encouragement to American trade with Saint-Domingue, and an injury to French colonialism.[40]

On June 13, 1798, the United States Congress had passed a trade embargo against France and its empire; about a month later the embargo was amended to allow the President to use his discretion in reopening commercial relations with areas under French control. Yet the United States would not officially restore trade with Saint-Domingue until Hédouville, symbol of French authority, had fled to France.[41] Quickly Pickering took advantage of the special agent's removal to appoint Edward Stevens as consul general to Saint-Domingue. Part of Stevens' instructions was to encourage Toussaint to declare his independence from France.[42] Pickering also told Jacob Mayer, American consul in Le Cap François, that he hoped that "good policy doubtless suggests to the chiefs, and especially to the amiable and respectable Toussaint . . . a system of peace towards Great Britain and her dependencies as well as to the United States."[43] The independence of Saint-Domingue would draw Toussaint closer to both England and the United States and make Pickering's "good policy" a reality.[44]

Toussaint greatly valued American friendship and saw the United States as playing an important economic role in the reconstruction of Saint-Domingue. The United States was a young nation and was more sympathetic and less dangerous than Great Britain. For these reasons, Toussaint sent Joseph Bunel as his representative to Philadelphia and openly received Edward Stevens; clearly the black commander-in-chief had acted as a sovereign. Such lapses were only occasional, for Toussaint had to maintain his charade of allegiance to France. He could do little else until Rigaud was out of his way. Perhaps, as a Spanish observer maintained, a declared war between the United States and France would have forced Toussaint to choose the former and to declare his independence from the latter. Such a dilemma, however, never faced the black leader.[45]

Immediately upon Hédouville's departure, Toussaint tried to convince the Directory of his loyalty to France. To dispel the fear that he might be moving toward independence, Toussaint proclaimed that all inhabitants of Saint-Domingue must remain faithful to the laws and constitution of France.[46] Then on November 5, 1798, he began a propaganda campaign to make the special agent's departure appear in the best interest of France: "Hédouville has caused trouble and civil war by his impolitic measures and arbitrary acts, which he exercised in the name of laws."[47] Of greater importance, Toussaint wanted to maintain a veil of legality and asked Philippe Roume, French agent to Santo Domingo, to replace Hédouville. Roume complied because the Directory had secretly appointed him as Hédouville's successor; after all, until France could muster an invasion force, Toussaint must not be encouraged to dispense with the last symbol of French authority. Early in 1799 Roume arrived in Le Cap François to assume his new duties.[48]

Roume soon proved to be nothing more than a front for Toussaint's authority. In a speech on January 24, 1799, he even promised not to act without Toussaint's consent.[49] Edward Stevens reported that Roume "dare not do otherwise. He is, at present, no better than a dignified person at the Cape."[50] The French agent would be useful in seconding Toussaint's edicts, Stevens added, but once Rigaud was defeated, "Roume will be sent off and from that moment the power of the Directory will cease in this colony."[51]

While Roume took up the duties of his powerless post, Toussaint worked to prepare the stage for his showdown with Rigaud. Of particular concern to Toussaint was his relationship with England and the United States. From April to mid-June he sought a series of alliances which would guarantee him economic and military assistance while isolating Rigaud. Early in May 1799 Toussaint made a major diplomatic concession by allowing armed American vessels to use the ports of Saint-Domingue; the French navy, on the other hand, was banned from the "colony." The black commander-in-chief was coming perilously close to dropping his pretense of loyalty to France, but he had to take the chance, for the actual independence of Saint-Domingue would have to be built on the bedrock of friendship with England and the United States.[52]

On May 22 Toussaint signed a tripartite treaty with Britain and the United States. The pact excluded Rigaud's South Province from Anglo-American trade, protected Jamaica and the southern United States from attack by the blacks, and guaranteed that the British navy would neither interrupt commerce nor molest Toussaint's small navy.[53] On June 13 the pact was amended to include the Heads of Regulations, an Anglo-American statement opposing the indoctrination of the slaves of both nations with "dangerous principles."[54] On the eve of civil war with Rigaud, Toussaint had the assurance of foreign support.[55]

The actions of Toussaint shocked Roume, despite his knowledge of developing Negro independence. Roume claimed that the treaty should not have been made because England and France were at war, that Stevens had exceeded his powers as consul general, and that Toussaint was endangering his good image in France. But Toussaint fixed his gaze on Rigaud in South Province and ignored the protests of the powerless magistrate.[56]

Because Roume realized that France stood to lose if either Rigaud or Toussaint seized complete control of Saint-Domingue, he had attempted an earlier conference between the two warriors.[57] Late in January 1799 the two leaders and their followers met at Port-au-Prince. The major issue was whether Toussaint or Rigaud had title to two border towns, Grand and Petit Goâve. Roume proposed that both places be recognized as within Toussaint's territory. Furious at Roume's recommendation, Rigaud bolted the conference.[58] Afterward Toussaint demonstrated his growing distaste for the *gens de couleur* by summoning "all the people to meet him in the church. He ascended the pulpit and harangued them for two hours. He was bitter against the mulattoes."[59] With the breakdown of the parley, Rigaud and Toussaint awaited the occasion of their final rupture.

From February to mid-June 1799 Toussaint and Rigaud laid the grounds for civil war in a torrent of charges and counter-charges. Each claimed the other to be a rebel: Toussaint accused Rigaud of insubordination; Rigaud indicted Toussaint for disloyalty to France. The charges of the mulatto leader were well founded, for if "French territory is still crowded with its enemies it is not in the Department of the South; neither their agents nor their ships are seen there."[60] Rigaud stretched the truth into a falsehood, however, by having his agents in Môle Saint Nicolas publish a bogus treaty between the British and Toussaint. One paragraph, Stevens claimed, contained the statement that "St. Domingo was to be sold to the British Government, and once more brought under the yoke of slavery."[61]

Tired of verbal combats, Rigaud broke off all communications with Toussaint early in June; in retaliation Toussaint forced Roume to declare Rigaud in rebellion. Saint-Domingue fell into an uneasy silence—a silence about to be broken by the tocsins of war.[62] The personal conflict was secondary to the main question: would all three castes finally find grounds of common interest and understanding under Toussaint, or would the mulattoes rule alone under Rigaud? That the two leaders personified a crossroads for Saint-Domingue did not escape the notice of Stevens:

> Both wish to reign, but by different means, and with different views. Rigaud would deluge the country with blood to accomplish this favorite point, and slaughter indiscriminately whites, blacks, and even the leading chiefs of his own colour. The acquisition of power with him is only because it would enable him to indulge, without restraint, his cruel and sanguinary passions. Toussaint, on the contrary, is desirous of being confirmed in his authority by the united efforts of all the inhabitants, whose friend and protector he wishes to be considered and, I am convinced, were his power uncontrolled he would exercise it in protecting commerce, encouraging agriculture, and establishing useful regulations for the internal government of the colony.[63]

Rigaud struck first. After slaughtering many whites in South Province to secure his rear, he hurled a brutal offensive at Petit and Grand Goâve on June 16. Laplume, Toussaint's commander at the two outposts, narrowly escaped capture as his army collapsed in a flurry of confusion and desertions. Taking no prisoners, the mulattoes put blacks and whites to the sword. The blood bath and race war known as the War of Knives had begun.[64]

Toussaint reacted immediately to Rigaud's offensive and marched an army of twenty thousand men to Léogane. Before he could spring a counteroffensive, the mulattoes of North and West provinces rose in rebellion on signal from Rigaud. Frustrated and furious, Toussaint had to break off his southern offensive to pacify the north. Leaving Dessalines and Henry Christophe to face Rigaud's advancing army, Toussaint personally led his troops in suppressing the mulatto uprisings which threatened his rear. For once Toussaint permitted the passions of revenge to overcome his usual humanitarian temper.[65] "Toussaint gave the word," claimed Captain Riggs, "that not one mulatto should be suffered to reside within his territory. . . . Everyone of that description that could be found was either shot or drowned."[66]

Beginning his purge at Port-au-Prince, Toussaint summarily executed many conspirators.[67] Some faced death by cannon while hundreds of others were herded on board vessels, "carried some distance from the shore, stabbed with the bayonet, and were thrown into the sea. The shores were lined with their bodies."[68] The mulattoes tried to seize Le Cap François but failed; in retaliation Toussaint executed fifty of their number on August 4, including Pierre Michel, Pierre Paul, Louis Nicolas Moline, and Barthélemy Leveille—all of them important civil and military officials. On October 29 Toussaint reconquered Môle Saint Nicolas; five hundred *gens de couleur* were executed, including two hundred who had surrendered to Toussaint in an attempt to remain neutral. With the capture of Môle Saint Nicolas, he could now concentrate his efforts on the south.[69]

By late October preparations were "being made by Toussaint to attack Rigaud in every part of the South."[70] Massed for an attack was a black army of fifty-five thousand men. Early in November, Christophe led one wing of the army against Jacmel, and

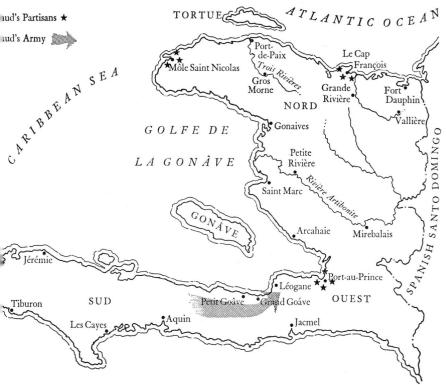

ATLANTIC OCEAN

TORTUE

Port-de-Paix

Le Cap François

★ Môle Saint Nicolas

Trois Rivières

Gros Morne

Grande Rivière

Fort Dauphin

NORD

Vallière

CARIBBEAN SEA

GOLFE DE

Gonaives

LA GONÂVE

Petite Rivière

SPANISH SANTO DOMINGO

Saint Marc

Rivière Artibonite

GONÂVE

Arcahaie

Mirebalais

Jérémie

Port-au-Prince

Léogane ★ ★

Tiburon

SUD

Petit Goâve

Grand Goâve

OUEST

Les Cayes

Aquin

Jacmel

THE "WAR OF KNIVES": RIGAUD'S INVASION OF TOUSSAINT'S TERRITORY, 1799

Dessalines led another one to recapture Grand and Petit Goâve. No small part in the black offensive was played by an American fleet, which destroyed Rigaud's marauding barges, transported blacks to the southern front, and bombarded mulatto positions. To the United States, Rigaud's ties to France represented a threat to American commerce and a chance that Hédouville's program might be carried out.[71]

By mid-November, Toussaint's southern offensive was stalled at Jacmel, symbol of mulatto resistance. In one of the most heroic episodes of the Haitian Revolution, the tenacious mulattoes of Jacmel and their able commander, Alexandre Pétion, refused to succumb to fierce attacks by the blacks. Early 1800 found the city almost without food but still repulsing the slashing assaults of

Dessalines' army; one time the blacks even broke inside the beleaguered city, only to be cut off and slaughtered by the mulatto defenders.[72]

Toussaint now decided to close in on Jacmel in a coordinated land and sea operation. For months he had been building a small naval squadron around *La Diligente*, a captured French frigate rechristened *Bâtiment d'État*. Yet when the small fleet made its way from Léogane toward Jacmel, it was intercepted by British ships under the command of Admiral Sir Hyde Parker.[73] Hugh Cathcart, British agent in Port-au-Prince, was surprised at Parker's actions, maintaining that "in no case whatever, can I allow Rigaud to gain the ascendancy over Toussaint."[74] Parker maintained that Toussaint had violated his agreements with Maitland by launching an attack by sea. The main reason for the British action, however, was the discovery of secret agents in Jamaica; Roume had sent them there to stir rebellion and prepare the way for an invasion from Saint-Domingue. Actually Toussaint did not intend to permit an attack on Jamaica but stopped the agents only after the sharp British reaction. One must conclude that in the light of available evidence the British seizure of Toussaint's fleet was justified.[75]

The capture of the black armada left a gap that was filled by the navy of the United States. The American frigates *Boston, Connecticut, Constitution,* and *General Greene* gave Toussaint's army close support and destroyed the privateering barges of Rigaud. Toussaint especially cited the aid rendered him by Captain Raymond Perry of the *General Greene*. On the night of March 11, 1800, Pétion hacked his way out of Jacmel, but the blacks fell on his retreating army and killed or captured hundreds of mulatto soldiers. The resistance of the *gens de couleur* was all but crushed.[76]

Just as Toussaint was preparing the final offensive against the mulattoes, France attempted to rescue Rigaud from almost certain destruction. This was the very thing that Toussaint had hoped to prevent until he could force Rigaud's unconditional surrender. He had maintained some semblance of loyalty by allowing Roume to prepare an expedition against Jamaica but had resolved not to receive any more commissioners from the Directory. Napoleon

Bonaparte, however, not the Directory, now controlled France. News of the political change reached Toussaint in late January 1800; from the beginning he had a healthy respect for the First Consul. Thus when Toussaint was confronted by a new commission, he received it and a letter from Pierre Forfait, the minister of marine, but expressed his displeasure to Stevens.[77]

In the letter the minister of marine informed Toussaint that Bonaparte had confirmed his position as commander-in-chief of the army of Saint-Domingue, "but in doing so the First Consul expects that these forces will never be employed against any other than the English."[78] Bonaparte "expects by the first dispatches . . . from Saint-Domingue," Forfait added, "to be informed that he [Toussaint] has made peace with Rigaud, and restored tranquility to the colony."[79] Despite the First Consul's apparent concern over the civil war and his guarantee of Negro freedom, Toussaint was not deceived. After all, the Constitution of the Year VIII (December 26, 1799) seemed to indicate the return of the *ancien régime* for Saint-Domingue.[80] Until he was ready to declare the independence of the colony, however, Toussaint had to obey Bonaparte's direct orders.[81]

On June 20, 1800, Toussaint offered clemency to South Province, which "will remain entire, and the inhabitants will, after a tempest so dreadful, enjoy a state of perfect tranquility."[82] Toussaint followed up his proclamation by sending Vincent, Arrault, and Philippe César to Petit Goâve to confer with three agents sent there by Rigaud. Through his peace commissioners Toussaint offered pardons to those who had joined the mulatto army, exile and brief imprisonment for some of the *gens de couleur* leaders, safety for Rigaud's family, and even permission for Rigaud himself to remain in Saint-Domingue.[83] One reason for Toussaint's leniency toward the mulatto commander was that "Rigaud at Cayes would undoubtedly be less of a menace than Rigaud in France."[84]

Rigaud, in a state of despondency during much of Toussaint's counteroffensive, marshaled new courage and refused to surrender. Seeing that Rigaud must be crushed, Toussaint ordered Dessalines to attack Les Cayes, and the mulatto defenses began to crumble.

On July 29 Rigaud fled to France. With mulatto resistance completely shattered, Toussaint entered Les Cayes in triumph on
August 1.[85]

After the defeat of Rigaud, Toussaint the humanitarian probably
would have stood by his declarations of clemency; but Toussaint
the Machiavellian needed to purge the mulattoes to secure his
position. When the two dispositions conflicted, the latter usually
prevailed. To break mulatto power, therefore, Toussaint appointed the brutal Dessalines to govern South Province. Thus the
black commander-in-chief could avoid direct involvement in the
purge and any loss of his popularity while having the assurance
that his program would be thoroughly completed. Although estimates of the number of people killed by Dessalines range from
two hundred to ten thousand, the result was the same: Toussaint
had placed an indelible crimson stain on his record in order to
gain power.[86]

Toussaint's drive for dictatorial power was incomplete, however,
as long as Santo Domingo remained under de facto Spanish control, despite the Treaty of Basle. For many years the relationship
between French Saint-Domingue and Santo Domingo had been
strained. The eastern colony had served as a base for operations
against Saint-Domingue; captive blacks from the French colony
were sold into slavery by the Spaniards; and as early as June 1796
Sonthonax had seriously considered an invasion of the Spanish
territory. All these irritants served to camouflage Toussaint's very
real fear of the French using Spanish Santo Domingo as a base
from which to launch an invasion of Saint-Domingue. In April
1800 Toussaint was horrified by the information that a French
expedition of fifteen thousand men was sailing to Santo Domingo. Although the news proved false, the black leader decided
to strike.[87]

Even while crushing Rigaud, Toussaint was preparing for the
conquest of Santo Domingo. The affront to French authority,
which such preparation necessitated, was disguised by Roume's
cooperation.[88] Early in March 1800 Roume appeared to lend Toussaint willing support by replacing the First Consul's representative in Santo Domingo, General Kerversau, with General Antoine
Chanlatte. Kerversau had staunchly opposed Toussaint's plans to

conquer Santo Domingo. But once Roume understood the black leader's designs for the Spanish colony, he resisted. Still needing a façade of legality, Toussaint was more determined than ever to have the support of the French agent—at the point of a sword if necessary.[89]

Early in April 1800 Toussaint "invited" Roume to lend his support to the war effort against South Province by residing in Port-au-Prince. Roume realized that open support of one part of Toussaint's program might imply blanket approval for all of it. Wisely the French agent declined the invitation. Taking quick counteraction lest Roume's new-found courage might become a habit, Toussaint instigated a mob uprising against the French agent at Le Cap François. Roume was humiliated and imprisoned at Haut-du-Cap, not far from Le Cap François.[90] Finally, after his authority appeared on the verge of total destruction, the French agent, according to the American consul, "promised to cooperate with Toussaint in all his plans for promoting the good of the colony."[91]

On April 27 Roume, for the "good of the colony," approved Toussaint's plan to seize Santo Domingo: Adjutant General Agé and a body of three hundred white soldiers would assume authority over the area, leaving Spanish society intact.[92] Toussaint the humanitarian seemed to hope for a peaceful conquest of Santo Domingo, for perhaps he was sick of carnage.

In late May, Agé left with his small detachment of troops for the capital of Santo Domingo. Captain-General Don Joaquín García y Moreno, however, had no intention of turning over his domain to Negro rule; with the wholehearted support of the Spanish planters, he summoned eight hundred soldiers to block the intrusion. Once the Spaniards had accomplished their mission, they permitted Agé to proceed unaccompanied to a meeting with García.[93]

At the conference the captain-general said that he would gladly deliver the colony to Toussaint but that he would need a period of six months to make arrangements for evacuation and to receive exact orders from Madrid. Obviously García was stalling, hoping that France might intercede.[94] After three days of futile discussion and with Spanish mobs growing more threatening, Agé returned to Saint-Domingue. He and Toussaint were now convinced that only a swift invasion would subdue the Spaniards.[95]

Heartened by the stubborn Spanish stand, Roume rescinded his approval of Toussaint's planned occupation of Santo Domingo. Toussaint, in no mood to tolerate resistance, had Moyse imprison the special agent at Dondon. By late November, Moyse had "convinced" Roume to issue a second decree in favor of an invasion of Santo Domingo. From November 1800 to September 1801 Toussaint continued to hold Roume captive and would not even allow him the appearance of authority.[96] Trying to justify his actions to the First Consul, Toussaint claimed that Roume had plotted to maintain Santo Domingo as a Spanish colony; he promised Bonaparte that the special agent would be returned to France "whenever you shall claim him."[97] The major reason for Roume's rough treatment is clear: Toussaint wanted him powerless during the conquest of Santo Domingo and the consolidation of black rule.

Massing his invasion forces, Toussaint directed Moyse to attack in the north of St. Jago, and Paul Louverture, Toussaint's brother, to assault Spanish positions farther to the south. Early in January 1801 the two black forces, totaling eight thousand soldiers, crossed into the Spanish colony. Captain-General García seemed to suffer from indecision and only half-heartedly opposed the Negro invasion. Perhaps, as Gerbier maintained, García was indecisive because he tried to serve two masters, France and Spain.[98] With the Spanish forces completely scattered after several skirmishes, Toussaint entered the capital of Santo Domingo on January 26; many observers were shocked by his easy triumph because it was generally believed, as Stevens put it, that the "Spaniards are too numerous and too much opposed to the domination of the blacks."[99] Almost the only consolation for the Spaniards was the great humanity Toussaint showed them: of the social institutions only slavery was abolished, and the conquest had been practically bloodless.[100]

With the entire island now in his grasp, Toussaint turned to the problem of constitution making. On February 5 he appointed a Central Assembly of ten members to draft the document. Bernard Borgella, white mayor of Port-au-Prince, was the chairman, and the Central Assembly contained seven whites and three mulattoes;

such favorable representation for the whites and the mulattoes was part of Toussaint's scheme to win their support. The blacks, of course, were more than favorably represented, since Toussaint guided the hand of the Central Assembly as it wrote a constitution for Saint-Domingue.[101]

Completing its work by early July, the Toussaint-controlled Central Assembly unveiled a form of government which concentrated authority in the executive. The Constitution of 1801 made Toussaint governor-general for life, with the power to name his successor. It abolished slavery, ordered all males from fourteen to fifty-five years of age to enroll in the militia, recognized Catholicism as the state religion, attempted to rescue the plantation from economic collapse, and permitted the importation of blacks to augment the decimated population. Of interest was the probable influence of Alexander Hamilton upon the constitution; in suggestions forwarded to Toussaint, Hamilton had recommended a lifelong executive and the enrollment of all males in the militia.[102]

The one obvious omission from the constitution was a statement of independence from France. Toussaint's island was to remain nominally a French colony, in a sort of dominion status.[103]

Why did Toussaint fail to declare the independence of Saint-Domingue? The answer lies in his system of alliances. In late 1798 the black commander-in-chief had the firm support of England and the United States and would have separated Saint-Domingue from France then if the internal situation of the colony had been stabilized. As quickly as Toussaint consolidated the island under his rule, foreign support for independence deteriorated. After mid-June 1799 Great Britain stopped encouraging him to separate Saint-Domingue from France; black independence would be a bad example for the British colonies.[104] The new English policy, therefore, was to keep Toussaint in "a state of real independence, but without declaring it."[105] The new British diplomacy, furthermore, was reinforced when England and France began peace negotiations in the spring of 1801.[106]

Like Great Britain, the United States found that a shifting relationship with France dictated a change in its position on the issue of independence for Saint-Domingue. On September 30, 1800, the Treaty of Mortefontaine ended the Quasi-War; also the rise of Jeffersonian Democracy brought a friendlier relationship with France and a decline of the old Federalist commercial emphasis. The new feeling was best expressed by James Madison, Jefferson's secretary of state: "The United States would withdraw from Saint-Domingue rather than hurt relations with France."[107]

Author C. L. R. James contends that Toussaint committed a major error in not informing the black masses of his plans for independence: "They did not understand what he was doing or where he was going."[108] What else could Toussaint have done? With the erosion of his diplomatic foundations for independence, he had to settle for dominion status within the French Empire.

Toussaint promulgated the constitution on July 16, 1801, without the prior approval of Bonaparte. The black leader was now at the peak of his power: he had eliminated his rivals for leadership, conquered the entire island, and had his authority legalized with a constitution. It was an uneasy victory, however, with an angry First Consul in France and restless black generals at home.[109]

NOTES FOR CHAPTER SIX

1. Not all historians have had a high opinion of the black army. T. Lothrop Stoddard relied on an account by General Becker, a Frenchman, to prove that the black forces were inferior to those of the whites. Becker, like many French militarists of that time, was probably incapable of judging Toussaint's army with objectivity. Many other accounts contradict Becker, especially those written by Toussaint's English enemies. Stoddard, *San Domingo*, 288; Edwards, *British West Indies*, IV, 231–32; Howard, "Journal of Occupation," II, 38.

2. "Journal of Occupation," II, 38.

3. Despite C. L. R. James's contention that Toussaint and Rigaud were in "complete solidarity," one must remember that a common enemy was the cement of that bond. Once the British were eliminated, the two leaders would collide attempting to gain control of Saint-Domingue—only one could emerge as the victor. James, *Black Jacobins*, 203; Edwards, *British West Indies*, IV, 232.

4. *Le Moniteur*, June 28, 1798; Alexis, *Black Liberator*, 108–109.

5. General Moyse to Citizen Commissioners of Le Cap François, March 1798, in *Bulletin Officiel de Saint-Domingue* (Le Cap François), March 9, 1798; Charleston *City Gazette*, March 21, 1798; Toussaint to Brigadier General Agé, Feb. 14, 1798, and Toussaint to Raimond, March 9, 1798, in Boston *Independent Chronicle*, April 23, 1798.

6. Great Britain, *State Papers*, X, 295.

7. Letter Extract from Môle Saint Nicolas, July 3, 1798, in Baltimore *Federal Gazette*, July 25, 1798.

8. Great Britain, *Bulletins*, V, 113–17.

9. General Thomas Maitland to Henry Dundas, May 10, 1798, in *The Times* (London), June 27, 1798; Letter Extract from Jérémie, May 12, 1798, in St. George's *Chronicle and Grenada Gazette*, Sept. 14, 1798.

10. Maitland to Dundas, Dec. 26, 1798, Public Record Office, Colonial Office 245/1, San Domingo Correspondence (hereafter cited as C. O. 245/1).

11. *Ibid.*; Alexis, *Black Liberator*, 113–14; Consul General Edward Stevens to Maitland, May 23, 1799, Consular Dispatches, Cap-Haitien, vol. 1; Boston *Independent Chronicle*, July 30, 1798; Edwards, *British West Indies*, IV, 235.

12. Roume was the French commissioner to Spanish Santo Domingo. His role was largely that of an adviser in the nominally French colony.

13. Maitland to Dundas, Dec. 26, 1798, C. O. 245/1; Stevens to Pickering, Sept. 30, 1799, Consular Dispatches, Cap-Haitien, vol. 1; Robert Harper to an unknown recipient, March 20, 1799, Miscellaneous Papers (Maryland Historical Society); General Theodore Hédouville to Citizen Julien Raimond, March 30, 1798, in *Bulletin Officiel de Saint-Domingue*, April 8, 1798.

14. Hédouville to Raimond, March 30, 1798, in *Bulletin Officiel de Saint-Domingue*, April 8, 1798.

15. Maitland to Dundas, Dec. 26, 1798, C. O. 245/1.

16. *The Times* (London), Jan. 15, 1799; Alexis, *Black Liberator*, 119.

17. Lacroix, *Mémoires*, I, 346; Secret Convention between Toussaint and General Maitland, n.d., Consular Dispatches, Cap-Haitien, vol. 1; Korngold, *Citizen Toussaint*, 151.

18. According to Ralph Korngold (p. 125), by mid-1796 Toussaint had "seen the vision of an independent Negro state." Korngold, however, did not base his statement on evidence. One simply cannot be sure of when Toussaint decided to strive for independence or of the exact ideas which he had in mind.

19. Charleston *City Gazette*, April 11, 1799.

20. *Ibid.*; *Le Moniteur*, Dec. 23, 1798; *The Times* (London), Jan. 15, 1799.

21. St. George's *Chronicle and Grenada Gazette*, April 26, 1799.

22. Hédouville to Citizen Julien Raimond, n.d., *Bulletin Officiel de Saint-Domingue*, April 23, 1798.

23. Korngold, *Citizen Toussaint*, 157–58; Stevens to Pickering, Sept. 30, 1799, Consular Dispatches, Cap-Haitien, vol. 1; Charleston *City Gazette*, March 23, 1798.

24. *The Times* (London), Jan. 15, 1799; *Le Moniteur*, Dec. 24, 1798.

25. Charleston *City Gazette*, April 11, 1799.

26. *Ibid.*; Alexis, *Black Liberator*, 127–28.

27. Maitland to Dundas, Dec. 26, 1798, C. O. 245/1.

28. Stevens to Pickering, Sept. 30, 1799, Consular Dispatches, Cap-Haitien, vol. 1.

29. Stevens to Maitland, May 23, 1799, *ibid.*; Roume to Minister of Marine and Colonies, July 4, 1799, Roume Papers.

30. *Le Moniteur*, Aug. 19, 1798; Stevens to Maitland, May 23, 1799, Consular Dispatches, Cap-Haitien, vol. 1; Maitland to Dundas, Dec. 26, 1798, C. O. 245/1.

31. Maitland to Dundas, Dec. 26, 1798, C. O. 245/1.

32. Lacroix, *Mémoires*, I, 353.

33. *Ibid.*

34. Maitland to Dundas, Dec. 26, 1798, C. O. 245/1.

35. Bouvier, The State of St. Domingo, April 27, 1799, Consular Dispatches, Cap-Haitien, vol. 1.

36. The rumor of assassination was perhaps accurate because Hédouville was determined to replace Moyse and disband the black army. James, *Black Jacobins*, 218–20; Charleston *City Gazette*, April 11, 1799.

37. Charleston *City Gazette*, April 11, 1799; *Le Moniteur*, Dec. 24, 1798; *The Times* (London), Jan. 15, 1799; Korngold, *Citizen Toussaint*, 165; Alexis, *Black Liberator*, 129–30.

38. Great Britain, *State Papers*, VIII, 131–32; Baltimore *Federal Gazette*, Dec. 3, 1798; J. B. Oyarzabal to Stevens, Jan. 7, 1799, Consular Dispatches, Cap-Haitien, vol. 1; Roume to Citizen Bruin, Minister of Marine, Nov. 22, 1798, Roume Papers.

39. The American fear of an invasion of the South from Saint-Domingue was quite strong. According to Congressman Henry Lee, "the proximity of St. Domingo to our Southern States, weak from their peculiar condition, had its effect in producing the law forming twelve regiments." Speech of Henry Lee, Sixth Congress, Jan. 7, 1800, *Annals of Congress, 1789–1824*, 42 vols. (Washington, D.C.: Gales and Seaton, 1834–56), X, 276–77.

40. Alexander DeConde, *The Quasi-War: The Politics and Diplomacy of the Undeclared War with France, 1797–1801* (New York: Scribners, 1966), 133; Harper to an unknown recipient, March 20, 1799, Miscellaneous Papers; Pickering to Jacob Mayer, June 27, 1798, Consular Dispatches, Cap-Haitien, vol. 1.

41. Pickering to Mayer, Nov. 30, 1798, Consular Dispatches, Cap-Haitien, vol. 1; Pickering to Stevens, March 7, 1799, Rufus King Papers (Henry E. Huntington Library).

42. Pickering to Stevens, March 4, 1799, Rufus King Papers; Henry C. Lodge, ed., *The Works of Alexander Hamilton*, 12 vols. (New York: Putnam's, 1904), X, 345; DeConde, *Quasi-War*, 136; Stevens to James Yard, Aug. 22, 1799, Consular Dispatches, Cap-Haitien, vol. 1.

43. Pickering to Mayer, Nov. 30, 1798, Consular Dispatches, Cap-Haitien, vol. 1.

44. The threat of Saint-Domingue to the British West Indies and to the

southern U.S. drew English and American foreign policies closer together. Early in April 1799 both nations agreed that Great Britain and the U.S. had "a common interest in preventing the dissemination of dangerous principles among the slaves of their respective countries." "Heads of Regulations and Points understood between the British and American Governments as settled in Philadelphia," April 20, 1799, *ibid.*

45. Charleston *City Gazette*, June 3, 1799; Don Carlos Martínez de Irujo to Sr. Mariano Luis de Urquizo, Aug. 1, 1800, Spain, Sección de Estado, Legajo 3897 (Archivo Histórico Nacional and Library of Congress); Roume to Minister of Marine, May 7, 1799, Roume Papers; Baltimore *Federal Gazette*, Dec. 3, 1798.

46. Baltimore *Federal Gazette*, Dec. 3, 1798.

47. Great Britain, *State Papers*, VIII, 153–54.

48. Roume to Inhabitants of Saint-Domingue, Jan. 24, 1799, in Charleston *City Gazette*, April 27, 1799.

49. *Ibid.*

50. Stevens to Pickering, June 24, 1799, Consular Dispatches, Cap-Haitien, vol. 1.

51. *Ibid.*

52. Stevens to Pickering, May 3, 1799, *ibid.*; DeConde, *Quasi-War*, 207–208.

53. British naval superiority was a major reason for close cooperation between Britain and the U.S. in dealing with Toussaint. Without the support of English frigates, Secretary of State Pickering knew that trade with Saint-Domingue would be extremely hazardous. For that reason, he concluded, "we are bound . . . to act in perfect concert with Great Britain in all this business respecting St. Domingo." Pickering to Stevens, April 20, 1799, Consular Dispatches, Cap-Haitien, vol. 1.

54. Secret Agreements with Toussaint, May 22, 1799, *ibid.*; Charleston *City Gazette*, Aug. 31, 1799; DeConde, *Quasi-War*, 207–208.

55. The Federalist policy of support for Toussaint had much opposition. Even Attorney General Charles Lee had "no more confidence in the black Frenchmen than in white." James Delaire, representing many Southerners, maintained that "however advantageous the independence of these revolters might appear to the mercantile faction, I am very far from coinciding with such erroneous opinion." Lee to Pickering, Feb. 20, 1799, and Delaire to Harper, Jan. 11, 1799, Consular Dispatches, Cap-Haitien, vol. 1.

56. Roume to Pickering, June 3, 1799, *ibid.*; Roume to Toussaint, May 28, 1799, and Roume to Minister of Marine, May 7, 1799, Roume Papers.

57. Both England and the U.S. attempted to counteract Roume's efforts for a peaceful settlement. War would prevent Rigaud from giving his attention to such external matters as Hédouville's invasion plans. Maitland, therefore, directed Lieutenant Colonel James Grant, England's representative in Saint-Domingue, to "prevent any amicable arrangement from taking

place between Rigaud and Toussaint, of which I see no possible chance."
Maitland to Grant, June 17, 1799, Consular Dispatches, Cap-Haitien, vol. 1.

58. Bouvier, State of St. Domingo, April 27, 1799, *ibid.*; Charleston *City Gazette*, April 20, 1799.

59. Bouvier, State of St. Domingo, April 27, 1799, Consular Dispatches, Cap-Haitien, vol. 1.

60. Address of Rigaud to his fellow Citizens, June 3, 1799, in Charleston *City Gazette*, Aug. 13, 1799.

61. Stevens to Pickering, June 24, 1799, Consular Dispatches, Cap-Haitien, vol. 1.

62. *Ibid.*; *The Times* (London), Dec. 13, 1799; Roume to Minister of Marine, July 4, 1799, Roume Papers; Rigaud to his fellow Citizens, June 3, 1799, in Charleston *City Gazette*, Aug. 13, 1799.

63. Stevens to Pickering, June 24, 1799, Consular Dispatches, Cap-Haitien, vol. 1.

64. *Ibid.*; Charleston *City Gazette*, Aug. 13, 1799.

65. Charleston *City Gazette*, Aug. 26, 1799; Toussaint to John Adams, Aug. 14, 1799, Consular Dispatches, Cap-Haitien, vol. 1.

66. Charleston *City Gazette*, Nov. 14, 1799.

67. *Ibid.*, Aug. 26, 1799.

68. Letter Extract from Port-au-Prince, n.d., in Providence *Gazette and Country Journal*, Oct. 26, 1799.

69. Charleston *City Gazette*, Sept. 21, 1799, and Nov. 14, 1799; *The Times* (London), Dec. 5, 1799.

70. Stevens to Pickering, Oct. 26, 1799, Consular Dispatches, Cap-Haitien, vol. 1.

71. *Ibid.*; Stevens to Pickering, Dec. 3, 1799, Consular Dispatches, Cap-Haitien, vol. 2; Don Carlos Martínez de Irujo to Don Mariano Luis de Urquizo, Dec. 26, 1800, Spain, Legajo 3897; U.S., Dept. of Navy, *Naval Documents related to the Quasi-War between the United States and France*, 7 vols. (Washington, D.C.: Government Printing Office, 1935–38), VI, 139–40.

72. Alexis, *Black Liberator*, 143; *Mirror of the Times and General Advertiser* (Wilmington, Del.), March 8, 1800.

73. Stevens to Captain Little of the *Boston*, Dec. 4, 1799, Consular Dispatches, Cap-Haitien, vol. 2; Toussaint to Lord Balcarres, Dec. 21, 1799, C. O. 137/50.

74. Cathcart to Parker, Dec. 21, 1799, C. O. 137/50.

75. Parker to Cathcart, Dec. 20, 1799, *ibid.*; Stevens to Pickering, Jan. 16 and Jan. 29, 1800, Consular Dispatches, Cap-Haitien, vol. 2.

76. Toussaint to Commodore Silas Talbot, March 17, 1800, Silas Talbot Papers (Marine Historical Association); Providence *Gazette and Country Journal*, May 24, 1800; Charleston *City Gazette*, May 24, 1800; *Mirror of the Times and General Advertiser*, April 23, 1800.

77. *Mirror of the Times and General Advertiser*, March 1, 1800; Stevens

to Little, Dec. 4, 1799, and Forfait to Toussaint, n.d., in Stevens to Pickering, May 24, 1800, Consular Dispatches, Cap-Haitien, vol. 2.

78. Stevens to Pickering, May 24, 1800, Consular Dispatches, Cap-Haitien, vol. 2.

79. *Ibid.*

80. The Constitution of the Year VIII, unlike the Constitution of the Year III, did not recognize the colonies as part of the French nation. Gershoy, *French Revolution*, 350–53.

81. J. Christopher Herold, ed., *The Mind of Napoleon: A Selection from His Written and Spoken Words* (New York: Columbia Univ. Press, 1955), 186; Great Britain, State Papers, X, 146–47.

82. Toussaint to Inhabitants of South Province, June 20, 1800, in *The Times* (London), Oct. 22, 1800.

83. Great Britain, *State Papers*, X, 161–64.

84. Alexis, *Black Liberator*, 151.

85. Great Britain, *State Papers*, X, 163–64; Toussaint to Stevens, Aug. 5, 1800, and Stevens to John Marshall, Aug. 2, 1800, Consular Dispatches, Cap-Haitien, vol. 2; *Mirror of the Times and General Advertiser*, Aug. 30, 1800.

86. Lacroix, *Mémoires*, I, 393–94; James, *Black Jacobins*, 236–37; Korngold, *Citizen Toussaint*, 184–85.

87. Toussaint to Laveaux, Jan. 30, 1796, Laveaux Papers; Sonthonax to Rigaud, June 30, 1796, Sonthonax Correspondence; Stevens to Pickering, April 27, 1800, Consular Dispatches, Cap-Haitien, vol. 2.

88. Not only did the Directory oppose a black invasion of Santo Domingo, but so did Napoleon. France, Ministère de la Guerre, *Correspondance de Napoléon ler*, 32 vols. (Paris: Henri Plom, 1858–70), VI, 497.

89. Roume to Stevens, March 5, 1800, and Stevens to Pickering, April 24, 1800, Consular Dispatches, Cap-Haitien, vol. 2.

90. Stevens to Pickering, April 19 and 27, 1800, *ibid.*

91. Stevens to Pickering, April 24, 1800, *ibid.*

92. Stevens to Pickering, April 27, 1800, *ibid.*

93. Charleston *City Gazette*, Aug. 14, 1800; Irujo to Urquizo, Aug. 1, 1800, Spain, Legajo 3897.

94. García actually had only a few military resources after the departure of Biassou and Jean François in 1796. The former fled to Florida and the latter to Spain. Alexis, *Black Liberator*, 76.

95. Korngold, *Citizen Toussaint*, 189–90; Stevens to Pickering, May 28, 1800, Consular Dispatches, Cap-Haitien, vol. 2.

96. Tobias Lear to James Madison, Sept. 9, 1801, Consular Dispatches, Cap-Haitien, vol. 3; Toussaint to Citizens of Saint-Domingue, Nov. 26, 1800, in Charleston *City Gazette*, Jan. 12, 1801; Toussaint to Bonaparte, Feb. 12, 1801, in *The Times* (London), Oct. 21, 1801.

97. *The Times* (London), Oct. 21, 1801.

98. Toussaint to Citizens of Saint-Domingue, Feb. 3, 1801, in Charleston *City Gazette*, March 31, 1801; Gerbier to General Charles Victor Emmanuel

Leclerc, Aug. 3, 1801, Donatien Rochambeau Papers (Univ. of Florida Research Library); N. S. Fletcher to Stevens, Jan. 5, 1801, Consular Dispatches, Cap-Haitien, vol. 3.

99. Stevens to Pickering, May 28, 1800, Consular Dispatches, Cap-Haitien, vol. 2.

100. Gerbier to Leclerc, Aug. 3, 1801, Rochambeau Papers; Alexis, *Black Liberator*, 160–66.

101. Korngold, *Citizen Toussaint*, 220; Toussaint to Bonaparte, July 16, 1801, in *The Times* (London), Oct. 21, 1801.

102. Lear to Madison, July 7, 1801, Consular Dispatches, Cap-Haitien, vol. 3; Charleston *City Gazette*, Nov. 27, 1801; *Mirror of the Times and General Advertiser*, Nov. 21, 1801; Hamilton to Pickering, Feb. 21, 1799, in Lodge, *Works of Hamilton*, X, 344. Why Hamilton was selected to devise a plan of government for Saint-Domingue is not certain, but Hamilton was the leader of the Federalist Party, a West Indian by birth, and an advocate of strong central government.

103. Charleston *City Gazette*, Aug. 20, 1801, and Jan. 18, 1802; Korngold, *Citizen Toussaint*, 220.

104. Maitland to Grant, June 17, 1799, Consular Dispatches, Cap-Haitien, vol. 1.

105. *Ibid*.

106. Gershoy, *French Revolution*, 364.

107. Madison to Lear, Feb. 28, 1802, Consular Dispatches, Cap-Haitien, vol. 4.

108. *Black Jacobins*, 240.

109. Charleston *City Gazette*, Jan. 18, 1802; Lear to Madison, July 7, 1801, Consular Dispatches, Cap-Haitien, vol. 3; Toussaint to Bonaparte, Feb. 12, 1801, in *The Times* (London), Oct. 21, 1801.

CHAPTER SEVEN

Toussaint's New Order, 1797-1801

After ten years of constant conflict, Saint-Domingue, once the "Pearl of the Antilles," was "only a picture of endless desolation."[1] Thousands of people, nearly a third of the population, had been killed.[2] Many of the survivors lived like outcasts in the rubble-littered towns and cities. Mary Hassal, an American observer, noted that the homeless inhabitants of Le Cap François made "a kind of shelter by laying a few boards across the half-consumed beams."[3] This was the Saint-Domingue which many wished to return to commercial glory. Several attempted the feat, but only one temporarily succeeded—the remarkable Toussaint Louverture.

A man of many talents, Toussaint soon demonstrated the qualities that made him a leader; one was his enormous capacity for work. Sometimes sleeping no more than three hours a night, Toussaint usually arose at dawn. After a period of prayerful meditation he would turn his attention to administrative duties, especially to correspondence. Often his dictations were quite extensive, and his letters, despite his semiliteracy, were models of subtle but powerful expression. After he finished his correspondence, Toussaint frequently mounted his favorite horse, Bel-Argent, and rode off to inspect the countryside. No one knew where the mysterious black leader might suddenly appear, but this was Toussaint's device to avoid assassination and to strike the fear of uncertainty in supporters and opponents alike. His prodigious activity is even more amazing because at the height of power he was in his late fifties, an age of rapid decline for many men in the tropics.[4]

Tireless and steady labor constituted only one facet of Toussaint's personality. A deeply religious nature, bordering on mysticism, was another. Peter Chazotte, an American eyewitness, sought an interview with Toussaint and soon discovered that "the best place . . . to meet him would be in the church, as he went there every morning to hear Mass."[5] So devoutly Catholic was Toussaint that he attempted to suppress voodoo, abolished the calendar of the French Revolution in order to restore the observance of the Sabbath as a holy day, encouraged Christian marriage vows, and extolled the virtues of labor.[6] He also opposed the common practice of concubinage, especially among officials of government. Such puritanical abnegation was intended only for others, however, for he kept three white mistresses: Madame Valabrègue, Madame Lartigne, and the latter's daughter.[7]

Closely related to Toussaint's religious nature was his generally humanitarian disposition. Often he offered amnesty to his most vehement enemies, and if it was accepted, his conduct usually was "uniformly so accurate and so perfectly conformable to the terms he agreed to."[8] Of course, Toussaint sometimes let the wrath of revenge overcome his humanitarianism. This was particularly true in regard to the mulattoes, a group he distrusted because of their reluctance to fuse with the rising blacks. In one case he executed a mulatto for wounding a black before he learned that the Negro was a criminal attempting to elude capture. Yet Toussaint wanted the mulattoes to be part of the emerging black state and harbored no plans for their extermination.[9] An occasional outburst of brutality, furthermore, prevented the mulattoes from interpreting kindness as weakness, for Toussaint "believed that to rule men they must be lashed and caressed in turns."[10] That such strategy was effective is undeniable. Tobias Lear, an American consul, observed Toussaint's adoration "by all the inhabitants of all colours; whether this proceeds from fear or love I cannot yet tell; but all speak of him as a just man."[11]

Toussaint also had an aristocratic temperament. Perhaps this characteristic stemmed from his autocratic control of Saint-Domingue, his admiration for white society, the political necessity of elevating the black generals above the masses, and a desire to imitate Bonaparte. Whether at Le Cap François or at some other important city, Toussaint frequently conducted two types of fairly exclusive social gatherings—the "small circle" and the "great circle." Only those with special invitations could attend gatherings of the small circle; for the great circle no invitation was necessary, but Toussaint would hold audience only with those of his choice, after "inviting" them to his study.[12] Like Bonaparte, Toussaint sometimes wore an undress uniform to give a plebeian appearance in contrast to his ornately clad guests.[13] Such gatherings were generally stilted affairs, as an observer of a great circle noted:

> Everybody seemed to have a mask, or at least so cramped were his features as to appear a different person from that which he would have been taken to be in the common circles of society, because his sable monarch was expected to enter the hall in state attire: therefore, a respectful silence was kept during his long anticipated entrance. . . . This state of suspense continued until eight o'clock, when his coloured female waiter, who was also his head wife and chief cook, came in and announced that her master would receive the present company in his large business room. Whilst this large assemblage were making ceremonies and low bows about who should have precedence, I hurried into his presence.[14]

Autocrat, aristocrat, tireless worker, mystic, and humanitarian all partly describe the amazingly complex personality that was Toussaint Louverture. He more than any other man reconstructed and remolded society in Saint-Domingue. Hubert Cole, biographer of Henry Christophe, called Toussaint "no revolutionary."[15] Yet Cole failed to distinguish between two revolutions. By the standards of the French Revolution, Toussaint did appear to be either conservative or reactionary at times, especially in his acceptance of white *émigrés*, but in relation to Saint-Domingue such an appearance was necessary for Toussaint to establish his new order. Toussaint was most certainly a revolutionary, but of the Haitian, not the French, Revolution.[16]

From 1793 to 1797 Léger Félicité Sonthonax, the white radical commissioner from France, attempted to rebuild and to reshape Saint-Domingue. He undertook the development of a fully integrated school system and reminded the blacks that "labour . . . is absolutely necessary to him who wishes to preserve his rights and enjoy his liberty."[17] But Sonthonax was baffled by the attitude of the blacks that "being freemen, they would only work where and as long as they pleased."[18]

Part of Sonthonax's frustration was due to inherent weaknesses in his social and economic programs. Despite his proclamation that "all three classes were now French citizens,"[19] Sonthonax failed to make effective use of either whites or mulattoes. In his opinion most whites were enemies of the French Revolution, and instead of using their skills and experience he harassed and exiled them.[20] Sonthonax also realized that the economic future of Saint-Domingue was in the plantation; yet he allowed "the cultivator to shift from one plantation to another and to divide the produce with the proprietor at whose plantation he might momentarily inhabit."[21] Such permissiveness threatened the colony's economy, but Sonthonax viewed any coercion of the blacks as an infringement on their liberty.[22]

Sonthonax's programs, however, were not complete failures. The need to educate the masses inspired him to make literacy a prerequisite for citizenship. This idea, which met with some success, made an impression on Toussaint and on his plans for Saint-Domingue. Perhaps no man in the colony valued education more or understood the limitations of illiteracy better than did Toussaint. But the successful elements of Sonthonax's economic program interested him even more.[23]

Fermage, a system of seizing abandoned plantations and renting them, was adopted by Sonthonax.[24] Half of the profits of a rented plantation went to the state, while the remainder was equally divided between worker and proprietor. Other features of the system included regulation of working hours, government permission for a worker to quit a plantation, and Sonthonax's advice that the planter should labor among his "children." Even though Sonthonax never made the system operative, Toussaint understood that the flaw was in the operator, not in the design. Several instances showed Toussaint that Sonthonax failed because he did not coerce the blacks. For example, Laveaux made *fermage* succeed by forcing the blacks back to work on the Plaine du Nord during Sonthonax's return to France after mid-1794; similarly Christophe and Vincent used rigid control of the worker in a section of North Province and proved that *fermage* could be quite effective if properly enforced.[25]

After Sonthonax left Saint-Domingue on August 27, 1797, Toussaint was in a position to formulate clear plans for the colony. One key to both his social and his economic goals was the return of the *émigré* planter. Contrary to T. Lothrop Stoddard's biased assertion that Toussaint needed the whites' "superior intelligence," the black leader actually wanted the planters for their administrative experience and as teachers. Time and education, Toussaint believed, would lift the black from the ignorance of slavery to equality with the whites.[26]

As early as 1794 Toussaint began to encourage the return of absentee planters. By providing that the returning plantation owners could regain the net profits from their lands, he attracted hundreds of whites to Saint-Domingue. Even Bayon de Libertad, former manager of Bréda plantation, returned. Moreover, Toussaint protected the whites regardless of whether their antagonists were Sonthonax or Hédouville or wrathful blacks such as Moyse or Dessalines.[27]

Toussaint made it clear, however, that the old position of the planters had been radically altered. In several decrees and in the Constitution of 1801 he clarified the new duties of the planters. The proprietor would share the produce of his estate with the laborers; he had to tend to their needs; he could not use the whip; and he was not to consider the workers as slaves, even though they were under rigid three-year contracts and needed the planter's permission to leave.[28] He further decreed that the proprietors "must on all occasions conduct themselves as good family men. They are to encourage the cultivators to form legitimate marriages by making them feel that it is the best means of assuring themselves the enjoyment of all the advantages of society."[29] Legitimate families, Toussaint felt, would encourage social stability.[30]

Another white group included in the plans of Toussaint was the Americans. That the black leader intended to use the United States as the bedrock of Saint-Domingue's independence was discussed in an earlier chapter; of equal importance were commercial relations. With France unable to supply the colony's needs and with England wavering in its fear for Jamaica, Toussaint desperately needed American trade, particularly because Saint-Domingue had mostly an export economy. So valuable did trade with the United States become that it was not uncommon to hear the blacks refer to Americans as "good whites."[31]

Although American shipping had been continuously active in Saint-Domingue since the beginning of the Haitian Revolution, Toussaint wanted to give it formal standing. This was partly the reason for sending Joseph Bunel as his representative to Philadelphia in mid-1798.[32] Many important Federalists were quite receptive to Bunel's offer of an alliance with Saint-Domingue because the United States would guarantee the blacks "their independence, furnish them with necessaries, and stipulate for the exclusive carriage of their produce."[33] On May 22, 1799, as discussed earlier, Toussaint signed a tripartite treaty with Great Britain and the United States, establishing formal trade relations with the United States. From 1799 to 1801 American trade became so active that it played no small role in promoting "the happiness and prosperity of St. Domingo."[34] On a single day early in July 1801 no less than thirty-two American vessels were counted at Le Cap François alone.[35]

After the end of the Quasi-War and the rise of Jefferson to the presidency, however, Toussaint found both his economic and political relations with America in sharp decline. The United States would no longer support the independence of Saint-Domingue, and Toussaint sarcastically asked if the change in administrations had destroyed all the American ships.[36] For all practical purposes it had, for Jefferson could see the coming of Bonaparte to the colony as well as could Toussaint.[37]

Without the regimentation of the blacks, even the temporary success of Toussaint's commercial alliance would have been impossible. In several decrees culminating in the Constitution of 1801, Toussaint protected the plantation from dismemberment, sentenced vagabonds and criminals to forced labor, greatly curtailed worker migrations, and subjected the cultivators to military discipline. In return for his regimentation, the black was guaranteed a quarter share of the plantation's produce, given regulated and reasonable working hours, and protected from abuse by the proprietors.[38] Undeniably, the system was effective because idle blacks all through the colony were forcibly returned to the plantations; soon Toussaint had "re-established the agricultural and economic pursuits of the colony."[39] Even the ruined plantation of the Marquis de Beauharnais was restored and its profits forwarded to its new owner, Josephine Bonaparte.[40]

Despite Saint-Domingue's return to economic prosperity, Toussaint's labor program contained great evils.[41] One problem that it bred was corruption among the black military. Instead of encouraging a wide distribution of plantation proprietorships and acting only as policemen of the system, the black commanders centralized land ownership in their own hands. The desire for affluence caused many black generals to be blinded by the gilded glare of self-interest: Henry Christophe amassed a fortune of $250,-000; Dessalines controlled over thirty plantations; and there is evidence that even Toussaint himself indulged in the race for personal wealth. Eventually more than two-thirds of the land in Saint-Domingue was state controlled.[42]

The corruption of the military was exceeded only by its brutality to the worker. One observer noted that "great attention is paid by the military and civil officers to keep the cultivators employed and steady to their work, and in some cases not a little severity is used."[43] Dessalines became inspector general, a type of collective plantation overseer. Accompanied by mounted guards, he ranged vast areas to keep the blacks steady at their labors. For minor offenses, since the whip was outlawed, Dessalines administered lashes "with a strong knotted limb of the lemon tree upon the bare backs."[44] Sometimes he even buried victims alive and committed mass murder to force the blacks to remain on the plantations.[45] Such a heavy hand led Roume to the conclusion that "the cultivators were oppressed more under Toussaint than under their old masters."[46]

T. Lothrop Stoddard claimed that the blacks were now "slaves of the state."[47] Was he correct? Saint-Domingue was no different than most countries whose citizens are subject to martial law in times of great peril. Toussaint had no other choice because France was closing in from the outside and anarchy was threatening collapse from the inside. It was a question of priority, and order outweighed both corruption and brutality. Perhaps Toussaint grimaced at the furious efficiency of Dessalines and looked forward to the end of conditions which he considered temporary. The black masses must have sensed that this was Toussaint's policy, or they probably would have been more restive.[48] After all, Toussaint was trying to ensure that the blacks would never "again submit to the yoke of slavery."[49]

Any permanent social and economic achievements, however, depended upon political stabilization. Unless Toussaint could veil his dictatorial authority with a constitution, he would be faced with the growing independence and power of his generals. Bonaparte, moreover, might better accept Saint-Domingue's autonomy; at least he would clearly be faced with that decision. Thus on July 16, 1801, as mentioned previously, Toussaint uncovered his political order for everyone to see.[50]

All important powers belonged to Toussaint. He controlled major appointments, both civil and ecclesiastical, and each of the six departmental governors, as well as other chief administrators, communicated directly and only with him.[51] In this way he could isolate the members of his administration, lessening the chance of conspiracy. Even the Central Assembly was only a façade for Toussaint's power: it could not initiate legislation, and although it had the power to reject legislation, no delegate dared to try.[52]

The system was not without weaknesses. By not including a French agent in his plans, Toussaint was making his challenge to Bonaparte obvious. It would have been less offensive to France had he made provision for one with nominal powers. The greatest weakness of the system, however, was the overcentralization of power in the hands of one man,[53] for as governor-general for life, Toussaint refused to delegate much authority: "Everything at this time," U. S. consul Tobias Lear explained, "is done by his special authority."[54] Perhaps Toussaint felt that he could trust only himself, but such a burden was overwhelming.

Yet the Saint-Domingue that emerged after ten years of conflict was largely a tribute to the abilities of Toussaint. He had brought the colony to the threshold of independence and had placed it on the road to recovery. The problem of race, furthermore, seemed solvable because all three castes—black, mulatto, and white—showed signs of fusing. It was because of these achievements that an American observer enthusiastically proposed that Toussaint should be "considered as a phenomenon which every century does not produce."[55] But the "phenomenon," at the pinnacle of his political career, was about to fall from power.

NOTES FOR CHAPTER SEVEN

1. Parham, *My Odyssey*, 169.
2. Stoddard, *San Domingo*, 289.
3. *Secret History*, 2.
4. Korngold, *Citizen Toussaint*, 166, 217; Alexis, *Black Liberator*, 164; James, *Black Jacobins*, 249; Lacroix, *Mémoires*, I, 406.
5. *Sketches of the Revolution*, 19.
6. Philadelphia *Courrier Français*, Oct. 10, 1797; *The Times* (London), Dec. 15, 1801; Cole, *Christophe*, 66; Korngold, *Citizen Toussaint*, 209.
7. Korngold, *Citizen Toussaint*, 209.
8. Maitland to Grant, June 17, 1799, Consular Dispatches, Cap-Haitien, vol. 1.
9. Chazotte, *Sketches of the Revolution*, 19; Baltimore *Federal Gazette*, June 11, 1798.
10. Alexis, *Black Liberator*, 145.
11. Lear to Madison, July 20, 1801, Consular Dispatches, Cap-Haitien, vol. 3.
12. Bouvier, State of St. Domingo, April 27, 1799, *ibid.*; James, *Black Jacobins*, 246; Korngold, *Citizen Toussaint*, 216–17.
13. It was not uncommon for 19th-century Latin American dictators to imitate Napoleon. Such martial emulation encouraged Francisco Solano López of Paraguay to plunge his nation into a reckless war against Argentina, Brazil, and Uruguay. Santa Anna, the devious Mexican leader, even went so far as to call himself the Napoleon of the West. Like Toussaint, Santa Anna sought to imitate the First Consul's simplicity of dress, and so he had his staff donned in glittering uniforms and six colonels stood behind his chair when he dined in state. Henry Parkes, *A History of Mexico* (Boston: Houghton, 1966), 198, 208.
14. Chazotte, *Sketches of the Revolution*, 18.
15. *Christophe*, 55.
16. Letter Extract from St. Domingo, Dec. 6, 1798, in Providence *Gazette and Country Journal*, Feb. 16, 1799; *The Times* (London), March 10, 1802.
17. Proclamation of Sonthonax, Julien Raimond, Marce Antoine Alexis

Giraud, Pierre-Georges Leblanc, and Philippe Roume, May 15, 1796, in Boston *Independent Chronicle*, June 13, 1796.

18. *The Times* (London), Sept. 12, 1796.

19. Proclamation of Sonthonax and others, May 15, 1796, in Boston *Independent Chronicle*, June 13, 1796.

20. Sonthonax to Minister Plenipotentiary near the U.S., n.d., *ibid.*, June 20, 1796; Sonthonax to Allouis, July 5, 1796, Sonthonax Correspondence; Charleston *City Gazette*, July 31, 1797; Baltimore *Federal Intelligencer*, March 20, 1795.

21. Observations of General-in-Chief Leclerc, June 13, 1802, Charles Victor Emmanuel Leclerc Papers (Univ. of Florida Research Library).

22. Sonthonax to the Commander of the National Guard at Dondon, July 30, 1796, Sonthonax Correspondence.

23. Proclamation of Sonthonax and Pascal, n.d., in Philadelphia *Aurora*, June 4, 1796; James, *Black Jacobins*, 175, 246.

24. The origin of *fermage* is not clear. A Negro named Brossard, according to James, had the confidence of both blacks and whites on a plantation in the Plaine du Nord and got them to employ the system. Another viewpoint, that of Hubert Cole, finds *fermage* beginning with Christophe and Vincent. There is some evidence, however, that General Laveaux may have started the practice early in 1795. James, *Black Jacobins*, 186; Cole, *Christophe*, 51; Philadelphia *Aurora*, Feb. 7, 1795.

25. Philadelphia *Aurora*, Feb. 7, 1795; Proclamation of Sonthonax and others, May 15, 1796, in Boston *Independent Chronicle*, June 13, 1796; *The Times* (London), Nov. 7, 1794; Cole, *Christophe*, 51; Letter Extract from Le Cap François, April 10, 1797, in Philadelphia *Aurora*, May 6, 1797.

26. Law Concerning Plantation Police Regulations and Reciprocal Obligations of Proprietors or Farmers and Cultivators, July 24, 1798, Rochambeau Documents; Stoddard, *San Domingo*, 292; Providence *Gazette and Country Journal*, June 28, 1800.

27. Providence *Gazette and Country Journal*, June 28, 1800; Toussaint to Municipality and Military Commandant of Gros Morne, Dec. 13, 1794, Laveaux Papers; *The Times* (London), March 11, 1802; Great Britain, *State Papers*, X, 146–47; Korngold, *Citizen Toussaint*, 214–15.

28. Korngold, *Citizen Toussaint*, 207; Alexis, *Black Liberator*, 167; Law of July 24, 1798, Rochambeau Documents.

29. Law of July 24, 1798, Rochambeau Documents.

30. *Ibid.*

31. Richard Yates to Pickering, April 30, 1797, vol. 1; Toussaint to Lear, July 14, 1801, Consular Dispatches, Cap-Haitien, vol. 3; Pickering to Stevens, March 7, 1799, King Papers; *Gazette Officielle de Saint-Domingue* (Le Cap François), Aug. 21, 1802.

32. Charleston *City Gazette*, June 3, 1799; DeConde, *Quasi-War*, 135; Cole, *Christophe*, 57.

33. Adams to William Vans Murray, July 14, 1798, in Worthington C.

Ford, ed., *The Writings of John Quincy Adams*, 7 vols. (New York: Macmillan, 1913–17), II, 336.

34. Stevens to Marshall, Sept. 10, 1800, Consular Dispatches, Cap-Haitien, vol. 2.

35. Lear to Madison, July 7, 1801, *ibid.*

36. Jefferson's policy is more fully discussed in the next chapter.

37. Lear to Madison, Aug. 4 and Nov. 9, 1801, vol. 3; Madison to Lear, Feb. 28, 1802, Consular Dispatches, Cap-Haitien, vol. 4.

38. Lear to Madison, Oct. 22, 1801, vol. 3; Lear to Madison, Jan. 17, 1802, Consular Dispatches, Cap-Haitien, vol. 4; Chazotte, *Sketches of the Revolution*, 16; Alexis, *Black Liberator*, 167; Law of July 24, 1798, Rochambeau Documents; Henry Addington, *The Crisis of the Sugar Colonies, or an Inquiry into the Probable Effects of the French Expedition on the West Indies* (London: J. Hatchard, 1802), 16; Korngold, *Citizen Toussaint*, 206.

39. *Le Moniteur*, April 11, 1799.

40. Korngold, *Citizen Toussaint*, 234–35.

41. There are several statistics that indicate that prosperity returned. From 1796 to 1797 the value of Saint-Domingue's exports rose from $700,000 to $3,000,000, and from 1800 to 1801 Saint-Domingue's exports almost doubled. *The Times* (London), Oct. 10, 1797, and June 15, 1801.

42. Cole, *Christophe*, 67; Korngold, *Citizen Toussaint*, 205, 217; Alexis, *Black Liberator*, 169; Benjamin Dandridge to Madison, July 23, 1801, Consular Dispatches, Cap-Haitien, vol. 3.

43. Lear to Madison, July 20, 1801, Consular Dispatches, Cap-Haitien, vol. 3.

44. Chazotte, *Sketches of the Revolution*, 21.

45. Cole, *Christophe*, 67; W. L. Whitfield to Edward Corbett, June 13, 1801, C. O. 137/50.

46. Roume to Minister of Marine Forfait, Sept. 25, 1801, Roume Papers.

47. *San Domingo*, 292.

48. Letter Extract from Le Cap François, Jan. 1, 1799, in Baltimore *Federal Gazette*, March 15, 1799; Charleston *City Gazette*, Aug. 20, 1801; Letter Extract from Jamaica, Dec. 6, 1801, in *The Times* (London), Jan. 26, 1802; New York *Evening Post*, March 22, 1802; Stevens to Marshall, Sept. 10, 1800, Consular Dispatches, Cap-Haitien, vol. 2.

49. Lear to Madison, Jan. 17, 1802, *ibid.*, vol. 4.

50. Stevens to Pickering, Dec. 2, 1799, *ibid.*; *The Times* (London), Oct. 21, 1801; Means Proposed to the French Government for the Reorganization of that Colony by its Agent to St. Domingue, June 12, 1800, Roume Papers; Charleston *City Gazette*, Jan. 18, 1802.

51. Charleston *City Gazette*, Nov. 27, 1801; Alexis, *Black Liberator*, 166; *Mirror of the Times and General Advertiser*, Nov. 21, 1801; James, *Black Jacobins*, 264.

52. James, *Black Jacobins*, 264; Chazotte, *Sketches of the Revolution*, 17–18.

53. Charleston *City Gazette*, Jan. 18, 1802; Lear to Madison, July 25, 1802, Consular Dispatches, Cap-Haitien, vol. 4.

54. Lear to Madison, July 25, 1802, Consular Dispatches, Cap-Haitien, vol. 4.

55. An American at Le Cap François to Gentleman in Providence, R.I., April 14, 1800, *ibid.*

CHAPTER EIGHT

The French Invasion,
1801-1802

On January 29, 1802, an armada of French frigates and transports carrying twelve thousand soldiers anchored in Samaná Bay, on the east coast of Hispaniola. From the heights surrounding the harbor, a stunned Toussaint saw that his black state was being crushed by a force of destruction. It would be incorrect to assume that France struck Saint-Domingue like a bolt of lightning; instead the French expedition was more like the jaws of a vise which had been slowly closing over a period of six years.[1]

The Directory, long before the colonial projects of Bonaparte, planned to restore French authority in Saint-Domingue. In 1795 France had obtained Spanish Santo Domingo and commenced negotiations for Louisiana, both indications that the Directory was becoming increasingly interested in the Antilles. Even as a French invasion force prepared in 1797 to seize Egypt, which historian J. M. Thompson considered as compensation for French losses in the West Indies, the Directory itself never forgot Saint-Domingue. Early in 1798 the Directory sent Hédouville to the colony in an attempt to destroy Rigaud and Toussaint by playing one against the other; then French authority could be re-established by default. If Hédouville failed, the Directory was prepared to use the force of arms against Saint-Domingue. That the Directory never sent a military expedition to the troubled colony was perhaps more attributable to the French memory of Admiral Nelson and the Battle of the Nile rather than to any possible growing disinterest in the Caribbean.[2]

When Bonaparte overthrew the Directory on November 9, 1799, he inherited its West Indian policy—a policy which stressed the

recovery of Saint-Domingue. Whether the First Consul would continue such a course, however, was by no means certain. Had he
been able to stand by his enthusiastic observation in 1797 that
"Egypt was to supply the place of Saint-Domingue,"[3] he no doubt
would have de-emphasized the Directory's Caribbean policy. Yet
1799 was not 1797, and Bonaparte's dreams of an Eastern empire
were melting away in the blowing sands and scorching heat of
the Egyptian desert. Being a realist as well as a dreamer, Bonaparte was forced to continue the Directory's policy of interest in
Saint-Domingue.[4]

Initially the First Consul took a conciliatory attitude toward
Saint-Domingue, since he could do little else while France remained at war with England.[5] Early in January 1800 he sent a
proclamation to the citizens of the colony, promising never to return the blacks to slavery and warning "that the French people
alone recognize your liberty and the equality of your rights."[6]
Even Toussaint, whose abilities Bonaparte respected, was allowed
to retain some political power, and in late April of the same year
the First Consul made Toussaint second-in-command to General
Mathieu, who was supposed to occupy Saint-Domingue with an
expedition of 4,600 men. When the venture failed to materialize,
Bonaparte recognized the black leader as the commander-in-chief
of the Army of Saint-Domingue. By March 4, 1801, he went so far
as to acknowledge Toussaint's *de facto* military and political control of the colony by appointing him captain-general, an office
second only to the minister of marine and to Bonaparte himself.
Bonaparte may have been influenced by the efficiency with which
Toussaint was restoring economic prosperity to Saint-Domingue,
but he never sent a letter of confirmation because his policy soon
shifted from one of conciliation to one of force. The reason for the
change lay in a coalescence of influences upon the First Consul.[7]

One influence was that of the planters. From the moment that
Bonaparte overthrew the Directory, West Indian proprietors del-
uged him with arguments in favor of the restoration of slavery
and the destruction of Toussaint's authority. Only slavery, they
insisted, could restore the former wealth of the French West
Indies because the cost of rebuilding the plantation system would

preclude the hiring of black workers on the open labor market; France, moreover, could expect rapid monetary returns from the restoration of the old regime in the Caribbean. Supporting the argument of the planters were the once great slave merchants of Le Havre, Nantes, Bordeaux, and elsewhere. The slave trade, they maintained, would return the major ports of France to their past economic prominence.[8] To the persuasion of planters and slave traders was added perhaps even that of Martinique-born Josephine Bonaparte, owner of a plantation in Saint-Domingue.[9] As the First Consul put it, "I believe that Josephine, being born in Martinique, had some influence on that expedition, not directly, but a woman who sleeps with her husband always exerts some influence over him."[10]

Changing conditions in both Europe and the Near East also contributed to Bonaparte's new outlook toward Toussaint and Saint-Domingue. On August 30, 1801, General Menou surrendered the remnants of the French army in Egypt to the British, and for a while the First Consul had to shelve his plans for an Eastern empire. That Bonaparte's hand was stayed in the East appeared reinforced by the preliminary Peace of Amiens, signed on October 1, 1801. Part of that agreement, made in July, was that France would withdraw from Egypt. Obviously Bonaparte would be "twisting the lion's tail" and jeopardizing the peace if he continued to press his Eastern designs; therefore he turned his attention to the New World, where he had already obtained the retrocession of Louisiana on October 1, 1800. Clearly Bonaparte's colonial policy was following the line of least resistance.[11]

England, while opposed to the presence of France in the Near East, readily consented to a French conquest of Saint-Domingue; such a project, according to the French *chargé d'affaires*, also had Jefferson's approval. The support of England and the United States encouraged Bonaparte to take a hard policy toward Toussaint and to develop a Western empire. Ironically, however, the Anglo-American policies boomeranged and contributed to growing tensions between France and the two English-speaking nations.[12]

Great Britain's policy toward Saint-Domingue had made a complete about-face since 1798, when Maitland had offered English support for the colony's independence. By late 1801, with the establishment of "peace" in Europe, England no longer saw any value in Saint-Domingue as an irritant to France and would even aid Bonaparte in the reconquest of the colony.[13] Besides, as one British observer put it, "no one will deny that it was not absolutely necessary for the safety of our colonies, that a black state should not exist in the Western Hemisphere."[14] Yet Perfidious Albion could be hoisted on her own petard if Bonaparte used Saint-Domingue as a base from which to seize the British West Indies or other areas of the New World. Even before the First Consul could organize an offensive against Toussaint, England rushed reinforcements into the British Caribbean, especially to her much prized colony, Jamaica.[15] Saint-Domingue had become a West Indian Malta and added tension to an already unstable peace.[16]

If the policy of any nation was more equivocal than that of England, it was the one the United States developed. President Jefferson wanted to maintain the new Franco-American accord of the Treaty of Mortefontaine (September 30, 1800) and to assuage the fears of Southern slaveholders by curtailing American involvement in Saint-Domingue.[17] On the other hand, there was a steady stream of commerce between Saint-Domingue and the United States estimated at seven times the value of French trade with the colony. Reluctantly Jefferson was willing to sacrifice this prosperity for the other objectives of his policy and might even assist a French invasion of Saint-Domingue. Yet by late July 1801, at the very moment that America's stand on a French invasion of Saint-Domingue was clear, rumors reached Jefferson of the retrocession of Louisiana to France. Now the United States joined England in miscalculation because by encouraging Bonaparte to conquer Saint-Domingue, Jefferson had unknowingly made a French occupation of Louisiana both more attractive and possible.[18]

Another influence that ended Bonaparte's policy of conciliation toward Saint-Domingue was the First Consul's attitude toward Toussaint. No one understood any better than Bonaparte that the black leader was driving in the direction of independence. Both men thought alike, to the extent that they gave priority to the attainment of power; if Toussaint had his Rigaud, Bonaparte had his Duc d'Enghien.[19] Thus, as the black leader swore his loyalty to France and Bonaparte, the First Consul interpreted events in Saint-Domingue for himself. The exile of Roume (September 1801), the defeat of Rigaud, the fall of Spanish Santo Domingo, and the Constitution of 1801 were all unmistakable signs of the path Toussaint was following.[20] The black leader must be removed, wrote the First Consul, to prevent Saint-Domingue from becoming a "new Algiers . . . in the middle of America."[21]

Closely connected with Bonaparte's determination to rid Saint-Domingue of Toussaint was his desire for France to replace the commercial position of the United States in the colony.[22] It was part of Bonaparte's plan to tighten the mercantile system of the French Empire in order to compete with England's economic might. "He perceives," recorded an observer, "that the colonies are a chief source of British wealth; he therefore instantly determines to out colonize her."[23] Colonies, however, thrive on peace rather than on war, and the same observer added that "by no calculation can France derive any benefit to her commerce from them in the days of Bonaparte."[24] Bonaparte nevertheless decided to invade Saint-Domingue; the colony was about to be devastated once again—a devastation from which Haiti still suffers today.

Not until the preliminary Treaty of Amiens, despite the many influences working upon him, was the First Consul able to make serious plans for his Western empire.[25] Although partly couched in obscurity, those plans reveal poor preparation on the part of Bonaparte.

In its broad outline the Western empire of France was to include Louisiana, the Floridas, French Guiana, and the French West Indies. The economic heart of the empire was Saint-Domingue, and the heart of Saint-Domingue was the Negro laborer. Bonaparte certainly had no qualms about the political destruction of Toussaint and his black generals, but there is some evidence that he might have hesitated about returning the liberated Negroes to slavery. One alternative was to allow the blacks of Saint-Domingue to remain freedmen and to import new slaves from Africa.[26] After all, Toussaint's system of forced labor had proved effective, and "the laws and regulations to enforce labour are as rigid as any that can be made."[27] Ultimately Bonaparte decided upon the full restoration and preservation of slavery, not only in Saint-Domingue but in all the French West Indies. Perhaps the First Consul was partly persuaded by the old planter argument that freedom was an infectious disease in a slave society; more certain was Bonaparte's low opinion of the blacks: "How could I grant freedom to Africans, to utterly uncivilized men who did not even know what a colony was, what France was?"[28]

J. Christopher Herold has maintained that the greatest mistake Napoleon made in his Spanish campaign of 1808 was "that while it was safe to despise sovereigns and ministers and even armies, it was fatal to despise the people."[29] The great weakness Napoleon exhibited toward Spain was the same for Saint-Domingue. In fact, he was so contemptuous of the blacks that he believed that a small French army could sweep them aside in a few weeks and easily restore slavery in the colony.[30] The First Consul's misconception about the Negroes was the greatest flaw in his plans for a Western empire.

Although Bonaparte's plans for the French West Indies were clear, the rest of his program for the Americas was not. As late as June 4, 1802, Bonaparte wrote to Minister of Marine Denis Decrès, asking him to map the coast from St. Augustine, Florida, to New Spain and to present him with "a project of organization for this colony."[31] Although Spain's delay in actually transferring Louisiana to France might be some explanation for the premature condition of these plans, the First Consul himself seemed almost casual about the affair, giving Louisiana the appearance of an afterthought. Thus, his sudden decision to sell Louisiana less than ten months after his letter to Decrès is more easily understood.[32]

There is, however, at least one strong indication of the role Louisiana might have played if Bonaparte's program for a Western empire had matured.[33] Before 1793 the bulk of Louisiana's French trade had been with Saint-Domingue; after 1793 Louisiana's trade within the French Empire became more diversified as Bordeaux and Guadeloupe rivaled the position of Saint-Domingue. This diversification of Louisiana's commerce was probably due to the economic devastation of Saint-Domingue and to the Caribbean colony's trade with the United States. As long as France remained at war, American commerce was necessary to prevent the economic collapse of the colony. But by late 1801 Saint-Domingue neared economic recovery and France was at peace. Clearly the importance of the American role began to diminish; moreover, Bonaparte wanted to destroy it, probably with the view that increased trade between Louisiana and Saint-Domingue could compensate for the loss. Thus the First Consul, perhaps with the old mercantile ideal of the self-sustained empire in mind, seemed to be striving to make Louisiana and Saint-Domingue a closely correlated economic unit.[34]

Even though Bonaparte's political and economic designs in the Western Hemisphere lacked clarity, his military plans were quite lucid. Central to his strategy was the reconquest of Saint-Domingue with an expedition of twenty thousand men; from there, once the colony had been quickly subdued, French troops might be redeployed in Louisiana. For supplies, Bonaparte thought the French expedition could depend upon Cuba, Jamaica, and the United States.[35] If these arrangements were insufficient, he planned to have the French soldiers forage for their food European-style; such a policy, according to historian David Chandler, "bred a spirit of self-reliance and creature cunning among the troops . . . and made possible the rapid strategic movements that so bewildered the convoy-minded and depot-bound opponents."[36]

Bonaparte's strategy was well designed for western European conditions, but Saint-Domingue was in the tropical environment of the Caribbean. In the first place, the size of the expedition was too small. As one observer put it, the force was "too big for just a ceremony of taking possession of the island and too small to take up hostilities against it."[37] Bonaparte should have known, if he had listened to his West Indian experts and observed the Saint-Domingue tragedy of the British, that unseasoned white troops had a high casualty rate.[38] If he needed twenty thousand healthy soldiers, he should have sent an invasion force of at least forty thousand men to Saint-Domingue. That Bonaparte did not take the disease factor into account is not surprising, for on his Egyptian campaign he believed that the plague could be manfully ignored.[39]

Equally debilitating to the French expedition was the First Consul's neglect of supply and logistics. To depend largely upon

Jamaica and the United States to provision a French expedition was folly because both viewed the intentions of France in the Caribbean with growing suspicion. Cuba, however, because of the Franco-Spanish alliance, provided many supplies and some troops for the Saint-Domingue expedition, both in inadequate amounts. The case of Saint-Domingue, moreover, was not atypical: in Egypt, Bonaparte's soldiers had suffered severely from the lack of water bottles and had sweltered under their heavy uniforms; during the Polish and East Prussian campaign òf 1806–1807, especially after the Battle of Eylau, the French would endure terrible deprivations because of the lack of supplies; in the Russian campaign of 1812, Napoleon once again would demonstrate his failure to allow for climatic conditions or to supply his troops sufficiently after leaving his base at Smolensk. Thus, the French invasion force in Saint-Domingue, from the time of its arrival to its inglorious departure, had to undergo an acute shortage of provisions and other necessary materials.[40]

The First Consul also neglected the problem of troop reinforcements. Possibly he did not plan to send more troops since the belief among many French officers was that military operations would end in six weeks. This was a gross miscalculation, based perhaps on a disrespect for the fighting ability of the Negro. Once the blacks taught Bonaparte the lesson bitterly learned by the British, he did send some reinforcements to Saint-Domingue—but never enough. Although it was rumored that sixty thousand French "volunteers" were ready to pour into Saint-Domingue, Polish and Swiss conscripts composed a large portion of those troops actually sent. Two Swiss brigades mutinied at Toulon rather than go to the Caribbean hell,[41] prompting one sarcastic observer to write: "Now does it not seem an act of the most wanton despotism to force two brigades on board ships against their will, and at the same time, to mortify sixty thousand gallant fellows, all panting to engage the yellow fever and the Negroes, with the refusal of their services."[42]

With such poor preparations for its important task, the Saint-Domingue expedition was practically doomed before it ever began. If Bonaparte's military reputation had rested upon his invasion of

Saint-Domingue, he would be remembered quite differently today.

To command the French invasion forces, the First Consul selected General Charles Victor Emmanuel Leclerc, his brother-in-law.[43] In secret instructions to Leclerc, Bonaparte ordered that a three-stage program of pacification be conducted in Saint-Domingue. In the first stage the blacks would be promised almost anything so that the expedition might occupy strategic positions peacefully. In the second stage all those whom Leclerc considered dangerous would be deported or declared outlaws if they refused to surrender. In the final stage the invaders were to disarm the population and return the colony to white control. The whole pacification program pointed to the restoration of slavery, a goal Leclerc seemed well aware of, as did many other French officers. In order to make the expedition into a Trojan horse, Bonaparte ordered Toussaint's two sons, Isaac and Placide, to accompany the invaders and to present their father with a conciliatory letter.[44] In the message, dated November 8, 1801, Bonaparte asked: "What can you desire—the freedom of the blacks? You know that in all the countries we have been in, we have given it to the people who had it not."[45] Toussaint would not be fooled.

During October and November 1801 Leclerc assembled his invasion forces at the ports of Brest, Rochefort, Lorient, Le Havre, Nantes, Flushing, and Cadiz. The major portion of the fleet was being prepared at Brest under the direction of Admiral Villaret-Joyeuse. Leclerc's general staff was impressive: General Donatien Rochambeau, a man with much experience in the West Indies, was his second-in-command, and Generals Jean Boudet and Jean Hardy would later prove their outstanding abilities as division commanders. Even Alexandre Pétion and André Rigaud, along with other mulatto exiles, were to be utilized for their knowledge of Saint-Domingue and to organize the *gens de couleur* against the blacks. If there was no fighting, Bonaparte directed, the mulatto leaders were to be banished immediately from the colony.[46] As for Leclerc's soldiers, most were drawn from the Army of the Rhine.[47]

By late October the forces at Brest, Lorient, and Rochefort were prepared to sail, but mishaps soon began to plague the expedition.

One was the news from Guadeloupe that Magloire Pélage, a mulatto, had overthrown Captain-General Lacrosse. Despite Pélage's statements of loyalty to the First Consul, Bonaparte was convinced that Guadeloupe meant to follow the path of Saint-Domingue, and therefore he undertook preparations for a second expedition with General Antoine Richepanse in command. Unfortunately for Leclerc, this meant some distraction of the First Consul's attention from the invasion of Saint-Domingue. Another mishap was the delay caused by Leclerc's pampered and voluptuous wife, Pauline. Finally convinced by Bonaparte that she must accompany her husband, she took weeks to assemble her entourage and wardrobe. Pauline, in fact, was in herself a mishap because Leclerc continually would have to worry about defending his front from the blacks and his home from his generals. Finally, with Leclerc and Pauline on board the flagship *L'Océan*, Admiral Villaret-Joyeuse ordered his Brest fleet to weigh anchor on December 14. If all went according to plan, the entire invasion armada of fifty-four vessels would rendezvous at sea.[48]

While France prepared to invade Saint-Domingue, Toussaint struggled to control his black generals. By mid-October 1801 a large conspiracy had been organized against him. The main leader of the plot was Moyse, Toussaint's second-in-command, who governed North Province. In favor of breaking up the large plantations and destroying the whites, Moyse saw no alternative except a rebellion which would accomplish both aims and overthrow Toussaint. Moyse planned to center the rebellion on the Plaine du Nord and to coordinate it with one under the direction of L'Amourdérance, near Les Cayes in South Province. Those assisting Moyse in North Province were Generals Saintogne, Jean-Baptiste Labon, Bonhomme, and Joseph Flaville.[49]

Promising the black laborers land and claiming that Toussaint would allow the whites to re-enslave them, Moyse built up the anger of many blacks to the kindling point.[50] On the night of October 22 signal fires were set ablaze by conspirators within Le Cap François. Reacting with decision, Henry Christophe, commander of the city, suppressed the rebels and even invited the inhabitants to leave their doors open in order to inspire public confidence. By October 24, even though Christophe had secured Le Cap François, the blacks on the Plaine du Nord vented their fury against the former planters. Cries of "Death to all white men!" rang out across the plains and hundreds of whites were killed; such scenes of horror were only occasional in South Province because Dessalines quickly subdued the L'Amourdérance-led rebels.[51]

Toussaint was deeply wounded by the Moyse rebellion, not only because the plantation and white man were necessary for his plans but also because Moyse, his heir apparent and nephew, was a close friend. Toussaint nonetheless resolved to act swiftly. Ordering Christophe and Dessalines to strike furious blows at the rebels, Toussaint soon began to crush the uprising. Even Moyse, who had quietly remained in the background at Fort Liberté, now perceived the defeat of his plans and joined Toussaint in an attempt to cover his role in the conspiracy. By October 28 the rebellion collapsed with the capture of Flaville, whose treatment was symptomatic of what was to follow.[52] "He is fettered in a cruel manner," a bystander related, "and his cries are heard a long distance. Ingenuity is at work, contriving torments for the poor wretch."[53]

Determined to end challenges to his power, Toussaint decided to conduct a wide purge. He began by arresting Moyse and sending him to Port-de-Paix for court-martial. The most damaging evidence presented against Moyse at the trial was his execution of potential witnesses, the rebel shouts in his favor, and several incriminating testimonies. But the military tribunal, believing Moyse's guilt to be uncertain, acquitted him; not satisfied, Toussaint personally reversed the court's decision. On November 23 a detachment of troops marched Moyse to the square in front of the governor's house. At 11 A.M., after the charges against him had been read, the crack of rifles could be heard as Toussaint's second-in-command slumped to the ground. Toussaint had made an example of his nephew, but the purge itself had hardly begun.[54]

Soon the black leader had two thousand people put to death, as even those remotely associated with Moyse shared his fate.[55] Thomas Lacorunson, an American, uneasily watched the expanding blood bath: "You further observe my barber having been among the number executed, as a fortunate circumstance I discharged him as soon as I did. I conceive now that I must have run a great risk during the time that he shaved me."[56] On the whole, however, the whites approved of Toussaint's actions and their confidence in him reached a new peak. Finally, it seemed, all colors had found a protector in Toussaint Louverture.[57]

Undoubtedly the timing of the Moyse rebellion was disastrous for Toussaint. On December 2, in the midst of his purge, the black leader received news of the signing of the preliminary Treaty of Amiens. He had gambled upon the continued involvement of France in European wars and knew that Bonaparte might now try to destroy him and re-enslave the blacks. Consequently Toussaint decided to fight the First Consul if he must; with one eye on France and the other on Saint-Domingue, he had no easy task.[58]

Toussaint actually had long sensed some type of conflict with France and had attempted to impress the First Consul with the toughness of black soldiers. In a letter sent to Bonaparte on February 12, 1801, he boasted that his infantrymen could outdistance his cavalry and that "more reliance could be placed on them than on ... horses."[59] If Bonaparte had interpreted the black leader's claim to mean that the Negroes were proud and skillful fighters, perhaps he would have permitted the dominion status of Saint-Domingue to stand. Not until his exile on Saint Helena did he finally realize his mistake.[60]

By mid-December 1801 Toussaint seemed to know that his implicit warnings had not altered the First Consul's determination to restore the *ancien régime* in Saint-Domingue. Already rumors of Leclerc's approaching expedition began to reach the colony, and some whites, despite the fact that Toussaint had just saved them from death, gleefully predicted the restoration of French authority. Many blacks, believing that such an event would mean the restoration of slavery, were determined to fight the invaders.[61] Toussaint, in deploying his forces to meet a French attack, suffered the disadvantage of not knowing when or where Bonaparte would strike. Therefore he logically hid supplies in the interior and spread his army out along the coast. He assigned Paul Louverture and Clairvaux to Santo Domingo, Laplume to South Province,

Agé and Dessalines to West Province, and Christophe and Maure-pas to North Province. Wherever the French might land, Tous-saint's strategy was to destroy the resources of the coast and to retreat toward the interior in an effort to exhaust the invaders. The reasoning of the black leader was sound.[62]

When Leclerc reached Samaná Bay on January 29, 1802, he found the Lorient and Rochefort fleets already awaiting his arrival. With twelve thousand men and more on the way, he decided to assault Saint-Domingue immediately rather than to parley with Toussaint. Perhaps this was one of Leclerc's greatest errors, for Toussaint still hoped that his differences with Bonaparte might be resolved without warfare. But Leclerc, who would soon boast that Frenchmen needed only bayonets to rout the blacks, was spoiling for a fight. In tactical plans which Bonaparte had de-vised, the French commander directed Kerversau to land in Santo Domingo, Darbois to disembark in South Province, and Boudet to occupy Port-au-Prince; Leclerc himself, with about seven thou-sand soldiers, planned to seize Le Cap François.[63] He further directed that the Negroes should be won over to the French with glowing proclamations in defense of their freedom. If they could not be won over, Leclerc was quick to add, they were to be destroyed.[64]

On February 2 the sails of twenty-three vessels specked the horizon of Le Cap François; Admiral Villaret-Joyeuse and Gen-eral Leclerc believed that Henry Christophe, commander of the city, would be only too willing to surrender in the face of such military power. Both demanded that Christophe allow the French to occupy the city immediately, and both guaranteed Negro free-dom. Christophe, however, was not deceived and stalled for time, claiming that he could not give up the city without Toussaint's consent. If the French made a hostile move against the port, Chris-tophe warned, they could have it in a pile of ashes.[65]

Toussaint was actually in Le Cap François during the discus-sions between Christophe and Leclerc, but he did not disclose his presence to the French. Probably Toussaint reasoned that he might get a more objective view of French intentions by observing the invaders' transactions with Christophe. Thus, when an American delegation visited Christophe on February 3 to counsel surrender, Christophe told them that he could put no confidence in the French and that they meant to enslave his people. Toussaint had spoken through Christophe: the Negroes must fight or be slaves again.[66]

In the meantime, Leclerc realized that he must seize Le Cap François by force. Leaving a large portion of the fleet before the harbor to draw Christophe's attention, he ordered General Rochambeau to capture Fort Liberté to the east of the city. François Capois, commander of the stronghold, and his black troops bravely resisted, but the French stormed their position and put all the Negroes to the sword. Already the blacks were learning to spell the word *brutality*: R-o-c-h-a-m-b-e-a-u. On February 4 the fleet opened fire on Fort Picolet, one of the forts guarding the harbor of Le Cap François. At the same time Leclerc landed most of his forces at L'Acul, to the west of the city. If the French commander's maneuver succeeded, he and Rochambeau would envelop Christophe's army.[67]

Christophe, true to his vow, ordered his troops to destroy Le Cap François on February 4 and to retreat into the interior. With this command, most of the population rushed to evacuate the city, and there were many scenes of "women and children, passing in all directions, in the most distressed condition, to look for a place of safety."[68] Soon the whole port became a flaming holocaust as Christophe pulled his soldiers back to Haut-du-Cap. When Leclerc entered Le Cap François on February 6, the city was nothing but a charred, crumbling ruins: Tobias Lear estimated that only seventy houses remained undamaged. What had happened to Le Cap François was symbolic of Saint-Domingue's future.[69]

Everywhere the French army seemed to exceed even the fondest expectations of Leclerc himself. In Santo Domingo, Clairvaux and Paul Louverture quickly surrendered to Kerversau.[70] In South Province, Laplume joined the French rather than follow Dessalines' orders to destroy the countryside and to resist the invaders; even Dommage, Dessalines' cousin who commanded Jérémie, took the advice of local planters to capitulate rather than face certain destruction. At Port-au-Prince, second in importance only to Le

Cap François, Boudet's forces broke through Agé's defenses, and the city quickly fell into French hands. By February 12 Leclerc, holding most of South Province and all the important coastal positions, was preparing to launch a series of crushing offensives into the interior.[71]

Toussaint, however, found encouraging signs in his early defeats. One was the resistance of Maurepas at Port-de-Paix. In one offensive after another General Humbert attempted to dislodge the tough Negro commander and his Ninth Regiment. Receiving reinforcements, Humbert finally captured Port-de-Paix, but the city was in ruins and the fighting had cost Humbert four hundred men. The Ninth Regiment, moreover, remained defiantly intact. Another hopeful sign was the terrible Dessalines, black counterpart to Rochambeau. Determined to stop the French and to destroy the whites, Dessalines raced his command all over South and West provinces to block the path of the invaders. Wherever Dessalines went, he usually left a trail of burning plantations and white corpses.[72] "One cannot form an idea of those cannibals," said an irate observer; "they not only murder the white race, without consideration of age or sex, but they also direct their barbarity on some ... who show ... interest for the fate of the whites."[73] Undoubtedly Maurepas and Dessalines helped to dispel much of the defeatism which had gripped the black generals. The French, after all, were only men.

Realizing that the Negroes made much better fighters than he thought possible, Leclerc decided to open negotiations with Toussaint. For this purpose the French commander sent Isaac and Placide, Toussaint's sons, to deliver the one message that Bonaparte was ever to address directly to the black commander-in-chief. Meeting their father at Ennery on February 12, the boys, accompanied by their tutor, Abbé Coisnon, handed the First Consul's letter to Toussaint. Despite Bonaparte's recognition of the black commander's achievements and the guarantees of Negro freedom, Toussaint believed that Leclerc's actions clearly translated the words of the First Consul. Toussaint did send a reply to Leclerc, offering an armistice while they settled their differences. The latter, feeling that Toussaint was close to capitulation, answered immediately: if the black commander-in-chief would just lay down his weapons, he could become lieutenant governor of the colony, but he would have to make his decision within four days or be declared an outlaw.[74]

It was only too clear that both men were stalling for time. Leclerc needed the full strength of his expedition for his planned offensives into the interior. Within four days the remainder of his forces, totaling eight thousand soldiers, landed at Le Cap François. Toussaint, on the other hand, wanted time to regroup his troops. With this aim accomplished, he refused to accept Leclerc's ultimatum and asked his two sons to choose between France and Saint-Domingue. Isaac selected France, believing that Leclerc was sincere in his peace proposals; Placide, actually Toussaint's stepson, tearfully embraced his father and declared for the rebels. On February 17 Leclerc retaliated by proclaiming Toussaint and Christophe outlaws.[75]

On February 18 Leclerc launched his interior offensives. Leaving Humbert and Debelle to face Maurepas, Leclerc ordered his other lieutenants to converge on Gonaives, Toussaint's headquarters. According to Leclerc's plans, Boudet from Port-au-Prince, Desfourneaux from Plaisance, Hardy from Dondon, and Rochambeau from Saint-Raphael would reach their common destination in lightning thrusts.[76] Yet once again Leclerc miscalculated the valor of the blacks, and before the ring could be closed, the French forces had to wade through "fire and bayonets."[77]

Covering Boudet's advance from Port-au-Prince, Jean Jacques Dessalines proved how effective and vicious Negro soldiers could be. As he drew Boudet into the interior, Dessalines put the torch to Léogane and Croix-des-Bouquets and to any plantations within his reach; moreover, he left a trail of murdered white captives to mark his path.[78] "The heaped up bodies," a French general wrote, "still had their last attitudes: they were bent over, their hands outstretched and beseeching; the ice of death had not effaced the looks on their faces."[79] Just when it appeared that Boudet had cornered Dessalines, the black commander slipped away to Saint Marc, destroyed it, and began to double back on Port-au-Prince.[80] Boudet had to race toward the latter city to defend his base of supplies, which he might have lost without the aid of maroon bands. After a stiff battle in which the Negroes suffered severe losses, Dessalines withdrew his forces in good order into the interior.[81]

Meanwhile Debelle pressed Maurepas in North Province. At the Battle of Trois Pavillons, however, the black general defeated Debelle's army; even Leclerc, who did not like to admit that Negroes were killing Frenchmen, confessed that his lieutenant had been defeated. Soon Hardy and Desfourneaux, drawn away temporarily from their drives toward Gonaives, came to the rescue of Debelle and surrounded Maurepas and his Ninth Regiment. Cut off from communications with Toussaint and believing that his position was hopeless, Maurepas not only surrendered to the French but joined Leclerc's expedition along with the entire Ninth Regiment.[82]

Why did Maurepas and his soldiers defect to the French? The answer appears to lie partly in the fact that power was the ultimate aim of Toussaint and his generals. Also, the black soldiers often gave more obedience to their commanders than to any sense of nationhood. Thus the *caudillo* ethic was at least one important reason for the disintegration of the Negro army at such a critical moment.[83]

Rochambeau in the meantime came perilously close to Gonaives, and Toussaint decided to make a stand against him at Ravin-à-Couleuvre, a little over seven miles from Gonaives. Ravin-à-Couleuvre, or Snake Gully, was a natural location for an ambush because it had steep, narrow sides between which Rochambeau would pass with an army of five thousand men. With a force of equal size, Toussaint cleverly concealed his troops in the thickets and wide ruts of the ravine. On February 23 Toussaint surprised Rochambeau, and thousands of men died on both sides. The black commander-in-chief might have defeated the French if anyone had led them except the able Rochambeau.[84] At a crucial moment the Frenchman threw his hat into the ranks of the blacks and shouted, "My comrades, you will not leave your General's hat behind!"[85] They did not, and Toussaint had to break off the action. After ordering the burning of Gonaives, the Negro leader began to re-

ATLANTIC OCEAN

Môle Saint Nicolas
Le Cap François
Gonaives
GONÂVE
Saint Marc
Mirebalais•
•Port-au-Prince
Jérémie
•Tiburon
Léogane
Jacmel•
Santo Domingo
Samaná Bay

INVASION ROUTES OF LECLERC, 1802

treat toward Crête-à-Pierrot, an important supply depot and gateway to the Grands Cahos Mountains. On February 25 Leclerc
entered fire-gutted Gonaives.[86]

In pulling back to Crête-à-Pierrot, Toussaint planned to concentrate his forces in the rugged Cahos Mountains and to make forays
along the coast from time to time in order to harass the French.
This strategy, Toussaint calculated, would weary the enemy and
result in a hopeless deadlock. Such a scheme, if it had been successful, might have led to Leclerc's recall to France and some real
concessions from the First Consul. By late February, Toussaint's
strategy seemed logical because already the French suffered from
a manpower shortage and from the need of more supplies.[87]

By early March the French army was closing in on Crête-à-
Pierrot, the fortress which guarded a main entrance into the
Cahos Mountains. Under the command of Magny, only twelve
hundred Negro soldiers had the undesirable task of holding the
position against twelve thousand advancing Frenchmen. Mean-

while Toussaint ordered Dessalines to relieve Crête-à-Pierrot and to hold it no matter what the cost in lives; Toussaint himself, hoping to lure the French away from the besieged fortress, swung back into North Province to join Christophe and to raise the black laborers against the invaders.[88]

On March 11 Dessalines, who had reached Crête-à-Pierrot, stared at the waves of approaching white soldiers on the plains below. In a desperate gesture to boost morale, he called on all who wished to die free to surround him and promised to explode the powder magazine should the French storm the fortress.[89] Dessalines, however, realized that the position of the Negroes was hopeless unless more reinforcements arrived and unless he could draw the French away from Crête-à-Pierrot. Consequently he broke out of the fortress and called upon Toussaint to hurry to the rescue. Toussaint, bitterly disappointed at having learned of the surrender of Maurepas, hurried southward to prevent another disaster.[90]

For days the blacks at Crête-à-Pierrot, led mainly by Lamartinière, the second-in-command, unflinchingly faced overwhelming odds. In charge after charge, Leclerc's forces had to retreat with serious losses; Boudet alone lost 425 men in one of the assaults. So costly were the French attacks on the fortress that Leclerc decided to undertake siege operations. But the Negroes withstood devastating bombardments and terrible physical deprivations. After one salvo, the blacks defiantly erected a red flag on each corner of the fortress, indicating that no quarter would be given to the French, and during the quiet moments between bombardments and attacks, the blacks could be heard singing the patriotic songs of the French Revolution.[91] Choked with emotion, many French soldiers seemed to be questioning their role in Saint-Domingue: "In spite of the indignation that the Negro atrocities excited, these airs generally produced a painful feeling. Our soldiers looked at each other questionably; they seemed to say: 'Are you right our barbaric enemies? Are not we the only soldiers of the Republic? Have we become servile political instruments?' "[92]

On March 24 Toussaint reached Dessalines' base at Calvarie, not far from Crête-à-Pierrot, but it was too late. Before Toussaint and Dessalines could lift the siege, Lamartinière skillfully broke through French lines with his garrison. Crête-à-Pierrot had fallen.[93]

Even though Leclerc won a major victory at Crête-à-Pierrot, it had been costly: the French had lost two thousand men and the blacks only half that many. The battle, moreover, had proven to be indecisive, for the forces of Toussaint, Dessalines, and Christophe were still in the field.[94] Crête-à-Pierrot had important non-military implications as well. For the first time since the invasion of the French, many blacks appeared to be developing a national sense. While some would continue to follow their leaders blindly, others would "sacrifice particular interests to common independence."[95]

After Crête-à-Pierrot, Toussaint persisted in his struggle against the French army: Charles Bélair would hold the Cahos Mountains while Dessalines, Christophe, and Toussaint himself attempted to regain control of the territory from the Artibonite Valley to Le Cap François. Hit-and-run tactics, known today as guerrilla warfare, constituted the style which the black commander-in-chief planned to employ; pitched battles were to be avoided.[96]

In a short time the Negro armies began to force the French out of areas which Toussaint had designated for reconquest. At Dondon, after ten days of steady fighting, Christophe soundly defeated the forces of General Hardy and drove them back into Le Cap François. Soon the counterattacking blacks recaptured Saint-Michel, Marmelade, Saint-Raphael, and Limbé; Mirebalais and Bayonnais, furthermore, were cut off by Toussaint's advancing forces.[97]

Not only did the French have to battle the Negroes, but the poor preparation for invasion began to cause Leclerc serious concern. Late in March he received three thousand troops of the Batavia Division, but these reinforcements did not offset his loss of seven thousand men by that date. To make matters worse, Leclerc alienated many of the mulattoes by deporting Rigaud for allegedly plotting a separatist movement, and the number of *gens de couleur* joining French ranks noticeably declined. By April 10 Leclerc, because of the dwindling size of his army, decided to order all of the French military to join the ground forces. But even those who could carry rifles faced an acute shortage of supplies: there were no water bottles or medical supplies, and the rotting French uniforms forced one brigade commander to complain that his soldiers were completely naked.[98]

Oddly enough, however, April brought Toussaint's surrender rather than Leclerc's defeat. Early during that month the black commander-in-chief knowingly allowed Christophe to open negotiations with Leclerc; on April 26 he even permitted them to hold an interview at Haut-du-Cap, not far from Le Cap François. At that meeting Christophe agreed to surrender on the conditions that the French guarantee black freedom and that his rank be confirmed in the white army. Leclerc met Christophe's terms, and the Negro general, with his regiment of fifteen hundred regulars, joined the French.[99]

Ralph Korngold, biographer of Toussaint, claimed that "for Christophe to enter into such a private agreement was of course equivalent to treason."[100] Was it treason? Had Christophe capitulated without Toussaint's permission? Although there is no conclusive evidence, there are indications that these questions might be answered in the negative. First of all, Toussaint carried on concurrent negotiations with Leclerc through Boudet while the Christophe-Leclerc talks were in progress; he might have directed his lieutenant to surrender first to be certain of French terms. After all, Toussaint had used Christophe earlier to sound out Leclerc's intentions at the beginning of the invasion. That Toussaint would have allowed Christophe a free hand is also unbelievable. For ten years Toussaint had adroitly dodged political snares by personally directing his rise to power. It would not have been characteristic for him to permit any man, even Christophe, a position from which to betray him.[101]

Following Christophe's surrender, Toussaint came to terms with Leclerc on May 1. According to the agreement, the French commander guaranteed the freedom of the blacks, the acceptance of Negro officers into the French army with no reduction of ranks or functions, and the retirement of Toussaint with his staff to a plantation.[102] On May 6 Toussaint, accompanied by his bodyguard, entered Le Cap François. Amid thunderous salutes and shouts of joy, the black commander experienced his last moments of martial glory. A few days later Toussaint retired to one of his plantations near Gonaives. A great man had stepped down.[103]

Why did Toussaint surrender? Korngold maintained that it was simply a ruse on the part of the Negro leader: "Why not have all of the Negro soldiers join Leclerc's army, wait a few months until the yellow fever had still further decimated . . . the French, then calmly step in, arrest the Captain-General and send him back to France?"[104] C. L. R. James even saw Toussaint's surrender to Leclerc as a Negro victory because the blacks would retain their army. Besides, James added, "at the back of his [Toussaint's] mind he knew that they could never be beaten."[105] While no historian can be positive of the motives which prompted Toussaint's decision, both James and Korngold were probably looking in the wrong direction.

If Toussaint had simply surrendered to await the ravages of yellow fever to destroy the French or to keep the black army intact, he would have committed a stupid error. Once he had turned his officers and army over to Leclerc, what was there to prevent the arrival of more French reinforcements and the eventual annihilation of the black military itself? Besides, why should Toussaint have to surrender to await the deadly work of yellow fever or to keep his army intact? It would have been much safer had he remained in the field, where some control over his army was possible. If one accepts the logic of Korngold and James, Toussaint, by submitting, would have left much of his plans to chance and the decisions of others. This certainly was not characteristic of the black commander.

A different explanation for Toussaint's surrender seems to be more reasonable: he considered the Negro military doomed. It is significant that during April, Toussaint learned of the official signing of the Treaty of Amiens (March 25, 1802). Possibly he realized that with no prospect of war in Europe, France would logically concentrate on Saint-Domingue; even if he defeated Leclerc, others might follow. Toussaint was also quite concerned about the continuous disintegration of the black forces. From the beginning of the invasion, some of his best generals had defected to the French. Even many of Dessalines' Honor Guard, an elite military group, left to join Leclerc's expedition during April. Not only was Toussaint deeply worried about Amiens and the black army, but he himself must have been weary. For ten years he had tirelessly pursued his goals, but by 1802 the burden of power showed signs of sapping his energy. Why not surrender in late April or early May while the French forces were being battered in the field? At least the blacks might gain basic concessions, such as their freedom, which France might not later concede should Bonaparte flood Saint-Domingue with reinforcements.[106]

Even though Toussaint submitted on May 6 and was shortly followed by Dessalines, Negro resistance continued, contrary to the views of several historians.[107] Those who refused to surrender were secondary commanders: Gangé, Alexis Valemo, Janvier Thomas, Noel Guingand, Lafortune, Jean Panier, Scylla, Charles Corrigole, Petit-Noel, and Charles Devoit. The reasons for their continued struggle cannot be easily explained. Yet a growing national spirit, the fear of enslavement, and the desire of the guerrilla leaders to maintain their personal power were all major motives. To say that the blacks of Saint-Domingue were beaten after Toussaint's submission would be like saying that Spain ceased to resist after Dos de Mayo.[108]

Leclerc, after Toussaint's surrender, appeared to be the vanquished rather than the victor. Already his health was beginning to fail, and large numbers of his soldiers died of yellow fever, twelve a day in Le Cap François alone; reinforcements and supply, furthermore, were inadequate. Compounding the grave concern of Leclerc was the constant harassment of the rebel marauders. Unknown to the French commander another severe problem was being created, not by the blacks but by Bonaparte—the immediate restoration of slavery.[109]

NOTES FOR CHAPTER EIGHT

1. General Charles Leclerc to Minister of Marine, Feb. 9, 1802, in *The Times* (London), March 20, 1802; Korngold, *Citizen Toussaint*, 247–48.

2. Charleston *City Gazette*, April 25, 1797; James M. Thompson, *Napoleon Bonaparte* (New York: Oxford Univ. Press, 1952), 100–101; *Le Moniteur*, July 1, 1798; David Chandler, *The Campaigns of Napoleon* (New

York: Macmillan, 1966), 210; Henry Adams, *History of the United States of America during the Administration of Thomas Jefferson,* 2 vols. (New York: A. C. Boni, 1930), I, 353–54.

3. Somerset De Chair, ed., *Napoleon's Memoirs* (New York: Harper, 1948), 332.

4. J. Christopher Herold, *The Age of Napoleon* (New York: American Heritage, 1963), 76; J. Christopher Herold, *Bonaparte in Egypt* (New York: Harper, 1962), 374.

5. The advice of Philippe Roume, the last symbol of French authority in Saint-Domingue, also may have influenced Bonaparte's policy decision. Roume warned against the restoration of slavery in Saint-Domingue and recommended dominion status for the colony under Toussaint's direction. Roume to Minister of Marine, Nov. 22, 1798; Roume to French Government, June 12, 1800, Roume Papers.

6. *The Times* (London), Jan. 3, 1800.

7. Stevens to Pickering, May 24, 1800, Consular Dispatches, Cap-Haitien, vol. 2; Louis Antoine Fauvelet de Bourrienne, *Memoirs of Napoleon,* 4 vols. (New York: Scribners, 1890), II, 93; John Howard, ed., *Letters and Documents of Napoleon,* 1 vol. (New York: Oxford Univ. Press, 1961), I, 360; Great Britain, *State Papers,* X, 147; Korngold, *Citizen Toussaint,* 231.

8. H. A. L. Fisher, *Napoleon,* 2d ed. (New York: Oxford Univ. Press, 1967), 65; O'Jautovoine to Rochambeau, Nov. 13, 1801, Rochambeau Papers; Addington, *Crisis of the Sugar Colonies,* 28–42.

9. Josephine claimed that she warned Napoleon Bonaparte against restoring slavery in Saint-Domingue and removing Toussaint from his position of power. The Martinique biographer Aimé Césaire, however, corroborated Bonaparte's contention that Josephine influenced his change of policy. But the basic reason for the shift, according to Césaire, must be placed upon the First Consul alone. Césaire, *Toussaint Louverture: La Révolution français et le problème colonial* (Paris: Club français du livre, 1960), 244; Josephine Bonaparte, *Memoirs of the Empress Josephine,* 2 vols. (New York: Merrill and Baker, 1903), I, 243–44; Gaspard Gourgaud, *Saint Hélène: Journal inédit de 1815 à 1818,* 2 vols. (Paris: Flammarion, n.d.), I, 402.

10. Gourgaud, *Journal,* I, 402.

11. Georges Lefebvre, *Napoleon,* 2 vols. (New York: Columbia Univ. Press, 1969), I, 112; Howard, *Napoleon,* I, 506; Herold, *Napoleon,* 82.

12. Carl L. Lokke, "Jefferson and the Leclerc Expedition," *American Historical Review* 33 (Jan. 1928), 322–23; *The Times* (London), Jan. 4, 1802; Ragatz, *British Caribbean,* 229; Madison to Lear, Jan. 8, 1802, Consular Dispatches, Cap-Haitien, vol. 4; Louis Pichon to Charles-Maurice Talleyrand, July 22, 1801, France, Ministère des Affaires Étrangères, correspondance politique, États-Unis, vol. 53 (Library of Congress and Archives des Affaires Étrangères). Pichon, the *chargé d'affaires,* affords the historian the best view of Jefferson's policy, for the Frenchman had an important conversation with the President which he reported to Foreign Minister Talley-

rand. Jefferson, according to the report, could be counted on to support and assist a French invasion of Saint-Domingue. Secretary of State Madison's letter of January 8, 1802, to Tobias Lear gives some support to Pichon's claims, as does the actual sequence of events involving United States–French relations until the arrival of Leclerc's invasion force in Saint-Domingue.

13. From all appearances, England's aid was to be restricted to supplying a French invasion of Saint-Domingue from Jamaica. Pichon to Talleyrand, July 22, 1801, correspondance politique, États-Unis, vol. 53; DeConde, *Quasi-War*, 323; Howard, *Napoleon*, I, 506; France, *Correspondance de Napoléon*, VII, 308.

14. *The Times* (London), Jan. 4, 1802.

15. Letter Extract from Jamaica, Dec. 6, 1801, in *ibid.*, Jan. 26, 1802; William Savage to Madison, March 25, 1802, Consular Dispatches, Kingston, Jamaica, vol. 1.

16. The Mediterranean island of Malta was, by the terms of the Treaty of Amiens, supposed to be returned to France. But England, fearing that it would become a base from which Bonaparte might renew his Eastern projects, kept Malta, drawing Britain closer to the renewal of war with France. Lefebvre, *Napoleon*, I, 176–79.

17. Southern opposition to any support of Toussaint was best expressed by a writer in a Charleston newspaper: "Who can defend those who attempted the involvement of the United States in the transactions of St. Domingo?" Charleston *City Gazette*, June 23, 1802.

18. *Ibid.*, Jan. 25, 1802; *Gazette Officielle de Saint-Domingue*, Aug. 21, 1802; George Dangerfield, *Chancellor Robert R. Livingston of New York, 1746–1813* (New York: Harcourt, 1960), 317; Lokke, "Jefferson and Leclerc," 322–25; Madison to Lear, Jan. 8, 1802, Consular Dispatches, Cap-Haitien, vol. 4; DeConde, *Quasi-War*, 323; Bradford Perkins, *The First Rapprochement* (Berkeley: Univ. of California Press, 1967), 160; Pichon to Talleyrand, July 22, 1801, correspondance politique, États-Unis.

19. The Duc d'Enghien, a French nobleman, lived in Ettenheim in the Duchy of Baden, near France. Bonaparte suspected the duke of conspiracy, ordered him kidnapped, gave him a mock trial, and had him shot. Herold, *Napoleon*, 157–58.

20. France, *Correspondance de Napoléon*, VI, 497; VII, 308; Lear to Madison, Sept. 9, 1801, Consular Dispatches, Cap-Haitien, vol. 3; Toussaint to Bonaparte, Feb. 12, 1801, in *The Times* (London), Oct. 21, 1801; Bonaparte to Toussaint, Nov. 8, 1801, in *The Times* (London), March 20, 1802.

21. Howard, *Napoleon*, I, 506.

22. Protest of American Merchants to Tobias Lear, March 10, 1802, in Charleston *City Gazette*, April 22, 1802; Letter Extract from Le Cap François, May 17, 1802, in Boston *Gazette*, June 17, 1802.

23. Charleston *Times*, April 19, 1803.

24. *Ibid.*

25. Bonaparte to Toussaint, Nov. 8, 1801, in *The Times* (London), March 20, 1802.

26. Cole, *Christophe*, 108; Hauterome to Rochambeau, Nov. 15, 1801, Rochambeau Papers; France, *Correspondance de Napoléon*, VII, 503.

27. Lear to Madison, Jan. 17, 1802, Consular Dispatches, Cap-Haitien, vol. 4.

28. Antoine C. Thibaudeau, *Mémoires sur la Consulat, 1799 à 1804, par un ancien conseiller d'état* (Paris: Ponthieu, 1827), 120.

29. *Napoleon*, 230.

30. Thibaudeau, *Mémoires*, 120; France, *Correspondance de Napoléon*, VII, 308.

31. France, *Correspondance de Napoléon*, VII, 485.

32. *Ibid.*; Arthur P. Whitaker, *The Mississippi Question, 1795–1803: A Study in Trade, Politics, and Diplomacy* (New York: Appleton, 1934), 186.

33. The role that the Floridas would have filled was even less certain than that of Louisiana. Bonaparte's failure to get them from Spain probably accounts for their obscurity in his plans. Dangerfield, *Livingston*, 317.

34. Whitaker, *Mississippi Question*, 137; Letter Extract from Le Cap François, May 17, 1802, in Boston *Gazette*, June 17, 1802; *Gazette Officielle de Saint-Domingue*, Aug. 21, 1802.

35. Howard, *Napoleon*, I, 506; Lear to Madison, March 6, 29, 1802, Consular Dispatches, Cap-Haitien, vol. 4; "Mémoire historique," Rochambeau Documents, 39.

36. *Campaigns of Napoleon*, 70.

37. *The Times* (London), March 10, 1802.

38. The "seasoning period" was generally the first six months of a newcomer's stay in the West Indies. During that time the individual often contracted malaria or yellow fever, sometimes referred to as "sickness-of-the-country." If he survived, his immunity to those diseases increased, and he could afterward "hope to enjoy good health." Parham, *My Odyssey*, 39.

39. *The Times* (London), March 20, 1802; Herold, *Napoleon*, 76.

40. Chandler, *Campaigns of Napoleon*, 220, 855–56, 858; Herold, *Egypt*, 79; "Mémoire historique," Rochambeau Documents, 39; Lefebvre, *Napoleon*, I, 264; Felix Markham, *Napoleon* (New York: New American Library, 1963), 182; General Quentin to Rochambeau, Jan. 27, 1803, Rochambeau Papers; France, *Correspondance de Napoléon*, VII, 307–308; Paul Roussier, ed., *Lettres du général Leclerc* (Paris: Société de l'Histoire des colonies françaises, 1937), 82.

41. Letter Extract from Le Cap François, Feb. 20, 1802, in Providence *Gazette and Country Journal*, March 27, 1802; *The Times* (London), Feb. 10, 1803.

42. *The Times* (London), Feb. 10, 1803.

43. Leclerc was 29 years old and had served in Italy and along the Rhine. Sometimes called the "Blond Napoleon" because of his attempts to imitate his brother-in-law, Leclerc had proven himself to be courageous at the Battle

of Rivoli in northern Italy, where he had led a cavalry charge to clear the Osteria Gorge. Yet there was little to recommend him to a command situation on the scale of the Saint-Domingue expedition, except of course his marriage to Pauline, Bonaparte's favorite sister. One of Bonaparte's personal secretaries, Louis Antoine Fauvelet de Bourrienne, even believed that the First Consul wanted to rid himself "of a brother-in-law who had the gift of especially annoying him." Bourrienne, *Memoirs*, II, 92; Chandler, *Campaigns of Napoleon*, 120; Cole, *Christophe*, 78; Korngold, *Citizen Toussaint*, 242.

44. Lear to Madison, March 6, 1802, Consular Dispatches, Cap-Haitien, vol. 4; James, *Black Jacobins*, 292–93; "Mémoire historique," Rochambeau Documents, 33; Bonaparte to Louverture, Nov. 8, 1801, in *The Times* (London), March 20, 1802.

45. *The Times* (London), March 20, 1802.

46. Leclerc to Minister of Marine, Feb. 9, 1802, in *ibid.*; McCloy, *West Indies*, 93; Alexis, *Black Liberator*, 173; Korngold, *Citizen Toussaint*, 243.

47. There is a minor point of historiographic controversy concerning the Army of the Rhine. That is, Felix Markham, Georges Lefebvre, and Ralph Korngold indicated that Bonaparte dumped republican and rebellious soldiers into Saint-Domingue; Hubert Cole, on the contrary, denied that the First Consul ever practiced such a policy. Available evidence, although scanty, seems to uphold the arguments of Markham, Lefebvre, and Korngold; the extent of this practice, however, is unclear. Besides, if some of the troops sent to Saint-Domingue were insubordinate, one wonders whether they became so before or after learning of their destination. Korngold, *Citizen Toussaint*, 234; Lefebvre, *Napoleon*, I, 142–43; Markham, *Napoleon*, 85; Lacroix, *Mémoires*, II, 164; Cole, *Christophe*, 78.

48. Cole, *Christophe*, 79; Howard, *Napoleon*, I, 506; McCloy, *West Indies*, 107; Alexis, *Black Liberator*, 173; *The Times* (London), Feb. 6, 1802.

49. *The Times* (London), Feb. 11, 17, 1802. Lear to Madison, Oct. 22, 30, 1801, Consular Dispatches, Cap-Haitien, vol. 3; *Mirror of the Times and General Advertiser*, Dec. 5, 1801.

50. At Limbé, near Le Cap François, the rebels even showed the black workers chains, claiming that Toussaint had intended to shackle them. *Mirror of the Times and General Advertiser*, Dec. 5, 1801.

51. Lear to John Caldwell, Oct. 28, 1801; Lear to Madison, Oct. 30, 1801; Benjamin Dandridge to Madison, Dec. 15, 1801, Consular Dispatches, Cap-Haitien, vol. 3.

52. Toussaint to Citizens of the United States residing at Le Cap François, Nov. 12, 1801, Consular Dispatches, Cap-Haitien, vol. 3; Cole, *Christophe*, 74; *The Times* (London), Jan. 4, 1802.

53. *The Times* (London), Jan. 4, 1802.

54. *Mirror of the Times and General Advertiser*, Dec. 5, 1801; Letter Extract for Port-de-Paix, Nov. 23, 1801, in Providence *Gazette and Country Journal*, Jan. 18, 1802.

55. *The Times* (London), Feb. 17, 1802; Thomas Lacorunson to Lear, Jan. 10, 1802, Consular Dispatches, Cap-Haitien, vol. 4.

56. Lacorunson to Lear, Jan. 10, 1802, Consular Dispatches, Cap-Haitien, vol. 4.

57. *The Times* (London), Feb. 17, 1802.

58. Lear to Madison, Jan. 17, 1802, Consular Dispatches, Cap-Haitien, vol. 4; Charleston *City Gazette*, Feb. 20, 1802; Chazotte, *Sketches of the Revolution*, 24.

59. Toussaint to Bonaparte, Feb. 12, 1801, in *The Times* (London), Oct. 21, 1801.

60. Gourgaud, *Journal*, I, 402.

61. C. L. R. James maintained that Toussaint made grave mistakes by not declaring the independence of Saint-Domingue and by not informing the blacks of their nearness to re-enslavement. As for the latter, the danger of the approaching expedition to Negro freedom went without saying since many blacks seemed painfully aware of their peril. As for the former, independence would have been tantamount to a declaration of war against France, and Toussaint sought, even after the arrival of Leclerc, a reconciliation between himself and the First Consul. Possibly Toussaint reasoned that the removal of British and American support and peace in Europe made independence an act of suicide. Under the circumstances, what would have prevented an endless flow of troops from France? If Europe was awed by Bonaparte and French arms, why should Toussaint not have been also? To claim, as James did, that independence would have contributed to making Toussaint "invincible" is to see history in terms of inevitability and to fail to appreciate the perspective of the black commander-in-chief. James, *Black Jacobins*, 284–85, 311; Lear to Madison, Jan. 17 and Feb. 12, 1802, Consular Dispatches, Cap-Haitien, vol. 4.

62. Lear to Madison, Jan. 17 and Feb. 12, 1802, Consular Dispatches, Cap-Haitien, vol. 4; New York *Evening Post*, March 16, 1802; Thomas Madiou, *Histoire d'Haiti*, 3 vols., 2d ed. (Port-au-Prince: Département de l'Instruction Publique, 1922–23), II, 129; *The Times* (London), March 15, 1802.

63. The city of Port-au-Prince temporarily changed its name to Port Republicain. To avoid confusion, however, the use of Port-au-Prince will be continued.

64. Leclerc to Minister of Marine, Feb. 9, 1802, in *The Times* (London), March 20, 1802; New York *Evening Post*, March 22, 1802; Stoddard, *San Domingo*, 303–304; Providence *Gazette and Country Journal*, March 20, 1802; Dandridge to Madison, March 5, 1802; Lear to Madison, March 6, 1802, Consular Dispatches, Cap-Haitien, vol. 4.

65. Lear to Madison, Feb. 12, 1802, Consular Dispatches, Cap-Haitien, vol. 4; *The Times* (London), March 19, 1802.

66. Lear to Madison, March 6, 1802, Consular Dispatches, Cap-Haitien, vol. 4.

67. *Ibid.*; Leclerc to Minister of Marine, Feb. 9, 1802, in *The Times* (London), March 20, 1802; Alexis, *Black Liberator*, 177.

68. Lear to Madison, March 6, 1802, Consular Dispatches, Cap-Haitien, vol. 4.

69. *Ibid.*; Letter Extract from Le Cap François, Feb. 20, 1802, in Providence *Gazette and Country Journal*, March 27, 1802.

70. Paul Louverture's surrender was partly due to confusion. His communications with Toussaint, his brother, had been cut by the French. Toussaint, therefore, sent Paul two letters via a courier. The first message, a decoy to be presented to the French for inspection, instructed Paul to surrender. The second and official message, cleverly concealed from sight, ordered Paul to resist. The French, however, killed the courier and forwarded only the decoy message to Paul. Alexis, *Black Liberator*, 180.

71. Chazotte, *Sketches of the Revolution*, 25, 45; *The Times* (London), April 2, 1802; Dandridge to Madison, March 5, 1802, Consular Dispatches, Cap-Haitien, vol. 4.

72. Lear to Madison, March 6, 1802, Consular Dispatches, Cap-Haitien, vol. 4; H. de Poyen, *Histoire militaire de la révolution de Saint-Domingue* (Paris: Berger-Levrault, 1899), 142; Letter Extract from Port Republicain, Feb. 1802, in New York *Evening Post*, April 5, 1802.

73. Letter Extract from Port Republicain, Feb. 1802, in New York *Evening Post*, April 5, 1802.

74. Lear to Madison, March 6, 1802, Consular Dispatches, Cap-Haitien, vol. 4; Bonaparte to Toussaint, Nov. 8, 1801, in *The Times* (London), March 20, 1802; Bourrienne, *Memoirs*, II, 92; Korngold, *Citizen Toussaint*, 266–74.

75. Korngold, *Citizen Toussaint*, 266–74; Lacroix, *Mémoires*, II, 119–26; Letter Extract from Le Cap François, Feb. 20, 1802, in Providence *Gazette and Country Journal*, March 27, 1802; New York *Evening Post*, March 22, 1802.

76. Leclerc to Minister of Marine, Feb. 26, 1802, in *The Times* (London), April 19, 1802.

77. Rey to Brunet, March 4, 1802, Rochambeau Papers.

78. Dandridge to Madison, March 5, 1802, Consular Dispatches, Cap-Haitien, vol. 4; Lacroix, *Mémoires*, II, 153.

79. Lacroix, *Mémoires*, II, 153.

80. Dessalines was particularly brutal, but one should not forget that acts of cruelty were widespread on both sides. Chazotte, *Sketches of the Revolution*, 25; Toussaint Louverture, *Mémoires du Général Toussaint L'Ouverture* (Paris: Pagnerre, 1853), 42.

81. Stoddard, *San Domingo*, 312–13; James, *Black Jacobins*, 309.

82. Lear to Madison, Feb. 28, 1802, Consular Dispatches, Cap-Haitien, vol. 4; Alexis, *Black Liberator*, 187–89; Leclerc to Minister of Marine, Feb. 26, 1802, in *The Times* (London), April 19, 1802.

83. *The Times* (London), April 19, 1802; Leclerc to Citizens of St. Domingo, Feb. 8, 1802, in New York *Evening Post*, March 25, 1802.

84. Leclerc to Minister of Marine, Feb. 26, 1802, in *The Times* (London), April 19, 1802.

85. *Ibid.*, March 26, 1802.

86. Leclerc to Minister of Marine, March 9, 1802, in *ibid.*, May 26, 1802.

87. *Ibid.*, April 19, 1802; Lear to Madison, March 6, 1802, Consular Dispatches, Cap-Haitien, vol. 4; Korngold, *Citizen Toussaint*, 276–77.

88. Toussaint, *Mémoires*, 54; General Hardy to Rochambeau, March 14, 1802, Rochambeau Papers; Lacroix, *Mémoires*, II, 165; Cole, *Christophe*, 97–98; Leclerc to Minister of Marine, March 9, 1802, in *The Times* (London), May 26, 1802.

89. A similar incident occurred during Richepanse's invasion of Guadeloupe in May 1802. The Negroes at Fort Matouba, on Grand-Terre, blew themselves up rather than submit to the French. McCloy, *West Indies*, 110.

90. Alexis, *Black Liberator*, 190, 193; Cole, *Christophe*, 98; Lacroix, *Mémoires*, II, 165.

91. Lacroix, *Mémoires*, II, 161; Michel Descourtilz, *Voyages d'un Naturaliste et Ses Observations*, 3 vols. (Paris: Dufart, 1809), III, 362–65, 371–72.

92. Lacroix, *Mémoires*, II, 164.

93. Alexis, *Black Liberator*, 192.

94. Lacroix, *Mémoires*, II, 161, 172.

95. *Ibid.*, 312.

96. Alexis, *Black Liberator*, 194; General Bertrand Clauzel to Rochambeau, April 10, 1802; Chief of Battalion Cyrien to Rochambeau, April 28, 1802, Rochambeau Papers.

97. Adjutant Gonuing to Rochambeau, April 17, 1802; General Hardy to Rochambeau, April 8, 1802; Repussard to Rochambeau, April 8, 1802, Rochambeau Papers; Korngold, *Citizen Toussaint*, 281; Madiou, *Haiti*, II, 28; Lear to Madison, March 29, 1802, Consular Dispatches, Cap-Haitien, vol. 4.

98. Lear to Madison, March 29, 1802, Consular Dispatches, Cap-Haitien, vol. 4; Lacroix, *Mémoires*, II, 72; Cole, *Christophe*, 96; Chief of Brigade Drouin to Rochambeau, May 22, 1802, Rochambeau Papers; General Order by Leclerc, April 10, 1802, Leclerc Papers; Leclerc to General Dugua, n.d., in *The Times* (London), June 8, 1802.

99. Leclerc to Minister of Marine, May 8, 1802, in *The Times* (London), June 17, 1802; Providence *Gazette and Country Journal*, May 22, 1802; Leclerc to Minister of Marine, n.d., in *Le Moniteur*, June 14, 1802.

100. *Citizen Toussaint*, 288.

101. Charleston *City Gazette*, May 25, 1802; Cole, *Christophe*, 100.

102. Leclerc even promised Toussaint that the only distinction between people would be that of "good" or "bad." Leclerc to Toussaint, n.d., in Providence *Gazette and Country Journal*, June 6, 1802.

103. *Ibid.*; Leclerc to Minister of Marine, n.d., in *Le Moniteur*, June 14,

1802; W. Dodge to Madison, May 6, 1802, Consular Dispatches, Cap-Haitien, vol. 4; Letter Extract from Le Cap François, May 28, 1802, in *Mirror of the Times and General Advertiser*, June 19, 1802; James, *Black Jacobins*, 326–27.

104. *Citizen Toussaint*, 284.

105. *Black Jacobins*, 329.

106. Charleston *City Gazette*, May 25, 1802; Leclerc to Toussaint, n.d., in Providence *Gazette and Country Journal*, June 6, 1802; Titus to Rochambeau, April 9, 1802, Rochambeau Papers.

107. Dessalines, once he joined the French expedition, brutally attempted to suppress the rebels. Leclerc, in fact, could depend on Dessalines more than on any of his own generals to carry out French policy. Dessalines to Leclerc, Oct. 4, 1802; General Quentin to Rochambeau, Sept. 9, 1802; General Martial-Besse to Rochambeau, June 11, 1802, Rochambeau Papers.

108. General Pageot to Rochambeau, Sept. 2, 1802; Gustav Poyer to Rochambeau, July 6, 1802; General Pierre Boyer to Rochambeau, Aug. 12, 1802; Neraud to Rochambeau, Aug. 20, 1802, Rochambeau Papers; Leclerc to Minister of Marine, May 8, 1802, in *The Times* (London), June 17, 1802; Cole, *Christophe*, 115; Herold, *Napoleon*, 145.

109. Commandant Lavalette to Rochambeau, May 11, 1802, Rochambeau Papers; Roussier, *Leclerc*, 165; Toussaint to Citizen Fontaine, May 27, 1802, in *Mirror of the Times and General Advertiser*, July 17, 1802; Letter Extract from Le Cap François, May 28, 1802, in *Mirror of the Times and General Advertiser*, June 19, 1802.

CHAPTER NINE

The French Defeat, 1802-1804

For five months after Toussaint's surrender, teetering Saint-Domingue seemed to gravitate toward French control, but by October 1802 nature, neglect, stupidity, and black resistance combined to pull the "colony" in the direction of the rebels.

Although yellow fever had plagued Leclerc's soldiers almost from the beginning of their invasion, the disease reached epidemic proportions in mid-May. By mid-July over ten thousand French troops were dead, many choking to death on the black vomit caused by excessive temperatures and bodily deterioration. Hospital facilities were inadequate, and even those who did get attention sometimes received nothing more than four oranges a day as treatment for the malady. Reinforcements arrived from time to time, but as of September, Leclerc could count on only eight thousand soldiers to fight the blacks.[1] So thinned were the French ranks that Mary Hassal believed that "if reinforcements do not arrive, it will be impossible to defend the town [Le Cap François]."[2] The stinging aëdes mosquitoes did not discriminate among their victims; beginning with Hardy, 65 percent of Leclerc's general staff and eventually Leclerc himself were killed by the fever.[3] Dejected at the condition of the French army and believing that the climate caused the disease, General Pierre Boyer maintained that "the lowest hills presented obstacles to us proportionate to the inconvenience of the season. . . . Our hospitals were crowded with the sick, and disease daily made new ravages."[4]

With the loss of so many of his soldiers, Leclerc had to depend more and more on Dessalines and Christophe to carry out his policies. The captain-general realized the impossibility of fulfilling

Bonaparte's order to "rid us of these gilded Africans and we shall have nothing more to wish."[5] One "gilded African," however, was marked for destruction—Toussaint Louverture.

No sooner had Toussaint gone into retirement than he began to realize how perilously weak Leclerc's expedition was becoming. Although he probably still believed that he had been correct in surrendering, he must have wondered if the improbable was about to happen. Would France simply lose the colony by default? If so, then power would fall to those blacks in a position of authority. For Toussaint not to have prepared for such an eventuality would have been out of character.[6]

Toussaint sent Tacot, one of his agents, to South Province to encourage the black laborers to resist the French and asked Fontaine, another of his agents close to Leclerc himself, to get information about the French casualty rate and the names of generals who might join him. At the same time Toussaint sent agents to the United States to buy weapons and began to complain to Leclerc about his exclusion from the military. Toussaint realized that despite his use of former soldiers as plantation workers, he needed an active command such as those held by Dessalines and Christophe.[7]

Leclerc was aware of Toussaint's reawakening ambition and became almost neurotic about the necessity of large reinforcements and the exile of Toussaint. One observer felt convinced that "if there should not arrive from France some reinforcements in a very short time, we shall find ourselves in a great deal of trouble, and it is not unlikely that Toussaint will still be Governor of St. Domingo."[8] Leclerc resolved to rid himself immediately of the troublesome black; Dessalines and Christophe supported the captain-general's policy because a re-emerging Toussaint might eclipse or even destroy their power. Another motive in Leclerc's decision to seize Toussaint was the common belief that the former commander had a hidden fortune, a sort of King Solomon's mine in the tropics. Leclerc may have reasoned that Toussaint's supposed wealth would alleviate Bonaparte's financial neglect of his army.[9]

On June 7 Toussaint received a message from General Brunet to meet him at the Georges plantation near Gonaives. There they would discuss, among other matters, the recent ravaging of Toussaint's plantation by French troops. Brunet assured Toussaint that he could feel secure because French integrity would guarantee his safety. Believing that Brunet was an honorable man, Toussaint reached the plantation late at night with practically no escort. Quickly the black leader was arrested, bound, and hustled on board the *Créole* to France. The rest of his family followed in *La Guerrière*.[10] Reaching Brest early in July, he was soon incarcerated in icy Fort de Joux, near the Swiss border. Languishing from the lack of necessities and mistreated brutally by his jailors, Toussaint died on April 7, 1803.[11] He would not, however, be forgotten.[12]

Soon after Toussaint's arrest and deportation, Leclerc discovered that his action, rather than pacifying the Negroes, had caused them to become "enraged at the unfair manner in which Toussaint was sent off to France."[13] Many blacks who might have been pacified took up arms and joined the small guerrilla bands in the mountains. If Bonaparte had properly reinforced the French expedition, Leclerc might have avoided his miscalculation; the First Consul, therefore, must share the captain-general's failure.[14]

It was in this unsettled background caused by Toussaint's deportation that Leclerc attempted to execute Bonaparte's basic plan for pacification—the disarming of the blacks. Theoretically such a plan was sound, but in Leclerc's case it was dangerous because of the small size of his army. He noticed that "the operation of disarmament became long and imperfect because of the impossibility of embracing at one time, with a small number of troops, all the land of the colony."[15] American smugglers, moreover, were selling guns to the rebels, making the task of disarmament next to impossible.[16]

The hidden snares of disarmament, however, were more deadly than the obvious ones. Many blacks saw beyond the tactics to their re-enslavement and joined the growing number of black guerrilla fighters in the mountains of the interior. Even more dangerous was the self-defeating nature of the entire program. By having to depend on Negro leaders and on an army which was 50 percent black, Leclerc unknowingly created a vehicle by which one man —Jean Jacques Dessalines—might once again gain control of the Haitian Revolution. Dessalines could eliminate the rebel leaders under the guise of loyalty to France; then, should the revolution appear headed for success, he could easily gain the leadership of the black resistance. Even Dessalines' black army was in a good position because some of the white inhabitants, following Leclerc's orders, gave these "faithful Negroes" their only weapons. When Dessalines later defected to the rebels, a number of whites discovered that they had both armed their adversary and disarmed themselves.[17]

From June through October efforts were made by Leclerc, Rochambeau, Dessalines, Christophe, Maurepas, and Bélair to destroy the weaponry of the blacks. No one, in fact, went after the rebels with more determination than Leclerc's black lieutenants. Even the Frenchman General Quentin was appalled by the brutality with which Dessalines captured and executed the rebels. Dessalines and the other former rebel leaders were determined to preserve their power by being on the winning side, regardless of who won. For a while Leclerc's program seemed headed for success: Dessalines left the blacks of the Artibonite Valley almost defenseless, and he and Rochambeau forced many laborers to return to their plantations in South and West provinces; in North Province, moreover, General Boyer reported the seizure of seven thousand rifles from the blacks. Yet by mid-August, Leclerc's program had collapsed as a fresh wave of rebel uprisings and attacks swept the colony.[18] As Puquet, the French commandant of Arcahaye, reported in a message to General Rochambeau, "I have the honor of warning you that we are about to be attacked as all of the mountaineers are up in arms."[19]

Why did Leclerc's program fail? As already indicated, the weak condition of the French expedition was partly the cause, but there were other reasons. One was Leclerc's growing ruthlessness, which led him to commit acts of genocide. "Numbers of the Negroes were daily executed," observed Captain Mather, a Yankee shipmaster, "and the scenes of cold blooded massacres which took place were never surpassed in that ill-fated colony."[20] Such treatment, however, only sparked the blacks to that "courage . . . which martyrs of a suppressed sect or opinion show at death."[21] The other reason for the breakdown of Leclerc's disarmament program was Bonaparte's decision to restore slavery immediately in Saint-

Domingue. The First Consul himself thus destroyed any chance France might have had to regain control of the colony.

On April 27, 1802, Bonaparte approved a draft decree which obviously was intended to prepare for the full restoration of slavery in Saint-Domingue and Guadeloupe: the slave trade was re-opened, the decree of 1794 abolishing slavery was nullified, and only those blacks who were either free before the abolition decree or who had rendered service to France would retain their liberty.[22] Bonaparte's policy had the strong support of the French legislature and of an advisory committee which had studied the matter. In mid-May the First Consul sent letters to both Richepanse and Le-clerc directing them to restore slavery at the most propitious moment; by mid-June the two colonial commanders had received their orders.[23]

At first Leclerc, contrary to the views of some historians, seemed to be not the least hesitant about executing Bonaparte's directive. On June 30 he decreed a law governing agriculture. All cultivators absent from their plantations since 1791, according to the ninth article, had to return to their respective habitations. The only exemptions from this law were the "reformed" Negro army officers. Leclerc also decreed that small properties could not be sold and that blacks residing on different plantations could not be married; both of these prohibitions pointed to the revival of the plantation and slavery. By August, however, Leclerc realized that the blacks were fully aware of his program to re-enslave them; spontaneous revolts began to occur in which the mulattoes, sensing that France would restrict them as well as the blacks, increasingly joined forces with the Negro rebels.[24] It was only then that Leclerc earnestly pleaded with Bonaparte to postpone the reinstatement of slavery in Saint-Domingue. He acted too late. The Negro masses were fully aroused and would not lay down their weapons until the French were driven from their land, for they now equated freedom with independence.[25]

Leclerc became desperate as yellow fever continued to ravage his army and as the black rebels literally set the colony in flames. "Scarcely a night passed," observed a tired white, "that plantations, even in the vicinity of the Cape, were not destroyed, and the wretched owners sacrificed to the resentment of the persecuted

Africans."[26] To rescue his deteriorating position, Leclerc applied methodical and ruthless retaliation against the blacks. Yet Negro resistance seemed to increase in proportion to Leclerc's growing brutality.[27]

In late August, Charles Bélair, one of the black lieutenants serving Leclerc, observed the execution of the Seventh Colonial Brigade, an all-Negro unit which had mutinied. Not only did the French sentence the entire brigade to death, but the black mutineers first had to witness the public execution of their wives. Completely disgusted by French behavior, Bélair rebelled and led his Eighth Colonial Regiment to join forces with Sans-Souci, a rebel chief operating in the nearby mountains.[28]

Dessalines, still in the service of the French, saw Bélair's defection as an opportunity to eliminate a potentially dangerous rival. Bélair, Dessalines realized, had the support of many blacks as Toussaint's heir apparent and possessed the necessary qualities to unite the guerrilla bands under his leadership. Marching against Bélair with the support of Christophe, Dessalines captured the new rebel chief and had him executed along with his wife, Sanite. The death of Bélair, however, did not slow the gathering of another violent storm within Saint-Domingue.[29]

During September and early October there were few places left untouched by the fury of rebellion. In South Province thousands of blacks and mulattoes besieged Les Cayes; General Desbureaux, French commander of the city, ordered his soldiers to shoot Negroes on sight and to hang all plantation owners who failed to report disturbances on their estates. When Dommage and Jean Panier, both rebel leaders, were captured and executed, Larose replaced them and the uprising continued. In West Province the revolt threatened most of the French positions, and Commandant Faustin Repussard of Verettes recommended that all rebel crops in the mountains be destroyed; such methods of pacification had little effect on the rebels. In North Province the whites of the Plaine du Nord began to pour into Le Cap François to avoid the attacking blacks.[30] On October 4 Dessalines reported bluntly to Leclerc that "those who tell you that the situation is not so bad are not to be considered your friends."[31] Almost unbelievably many white generals of Leclerc's staff still had gleeful hopes that slavery would soon be restored in Saint-Domingue.[32] Their fantasy, however, was about to be shattered by the reality of three very important defections to the black rebels—Dessalines, Christophe, and Pétion.

Through August and September, Dessalines kept in constant contact with the various rebel bands. Often he left supplies for them to seize and informed them of French troop movements to avoid or ambush. In the meantime Dessalines conspired with Pétion at Haut-du-Cap to desert the French and to take Christophe and Clairveaux with them. The devious Dessalines, however, seemed to value power more than freedom and would not desert Leclerc until he felt assured of the success of the spontaneous black rebellion. By mid-October it became certain that the rebels would win, and Dessalines decided to strike the French immediately.[33]

On the night of October 13 Pétion and Clairveaux mutinied with over three regiments and seized Haut-du-Cap. On the next day they were joined by Christophe and a guerrilla leader, Petit-Noel. The black force of six thousand soldiers seized Fort Liberté and Port-de-Paix and began to march on Le Cap François. Inside the frightened city a feverish and dying Leclerc bravely left his deathbed to face the approaching army of blacks and mulattoes, but he marred his courage with final acts of atrocity.[34] So fearful was he of even the faithful blacks of Le Cap François that he had hundreds of Negro soldiers drowned in the harbor "together with their wives and children; no trial was wanting at this time, their colour condemned them, innocent or guilty, and their corpses floating in the harbour occasioned a pestilence."[35] By October 16 Leclerc's hard-pressed forces had soundly defeated the black and mulatto army, but Le Cap François was the only major city still under French control in North Province.[36]

When Dessalines got the news of Pétion's action, he wasted no time in carrying out his part of the conspiracy. Springing on Saint Marc, he inflicted serious losses on General Quentin and then undertook the conquest of the Artibonite Valley. Soon almost all of West Province, except Port-au-Prince, was in his grasp. By the end of October only Le Cap François, Port-au-Prince, and Les Cayes remained under French rule. Yet Dessalines had another problem which was of equal importance with the fight against

Leclerc—the establishment of his leadership over the black rebels.[37]

While he had been in the service of the French, Dessalines had eliminated his rivals for power. After he joined the rebels, he continued to dispose of those guerrilla leaders who defied him. It was not until the Arcahaye Conference in late November 1802 that Dessalines actually became the recognized leader of the black resistance. At that meeting, moreover, the Negro and mulatto generals supported independence and adopted a red and blue flag as the national banner. The Arcahaye Conference gave a single man control over the Haitian Revolution for the first time since the surrender of Toussaint.[38]

On November 2, at the very moment Dessalines' political strength was solidifying, Colonial Prefect Hector Duare announced to the French army that "your captain-general is no more. He has fallen. An irresistible malady has carried him away."[39] Events following Toussaint's capture had "returned the poisoned chalice to the lips of the French general."[40] Yet the death of Leclerc by no means doomed the French army to certain defeat. Rochambeau, Leclerc's second-in-command, was both brave and capable as a field commander and would soon receive enough troops for a counteroffensive. The struggle would continue for another year.[41]

When Rochambeau took command, the blacks were threatening and harassing the French on all sides. Le Cap François was in danger of collapse as ten thousand rebel soldiers surrounded the city, which was held by two thousand Frenchmen; supplies, moreover, were constantly being threatened because rebel barges would often attack ships at anchor. But by mid-November, Rochambeau received a reinforcement of ten thousand soldiers and launched a counteroffensive.[42] Soon the French commander had recovered Fort Liberté and Port-de-Paix in North Province and Saint Marc in West Province. Brutality and yellow fever, however, prevented Rochambeau from making his offensive a decisive one.[43]

Beginning with the Negroes around Le Cap François, Rochambeau undertook a program of extermination; "freedom-infected" blacks, many believed, would never make good slaves.[44] One eyewitness estimated that the French carried six thousand blacks out to ships in the harbor, bayoneted them, and kicked their bodies into the sea. Around the hull of one ship alone bobbed 240 human buoys. Even Maurepas, a black general faithful to the French, was not spared: he and his entire family were tortured to death on board one of the vessels. At Port-au-Prince, Rochambeau launched a similar program with an almost diabolical ingenuity. There he employed a ship named *The Stifler*, its hold converted into a gas chamber through the use of noxious fumes. Rochambeau included the mulattoes in his program of extermination, driving them more firmly to the side of the blacks.[45]

Rochambeau's brutality, like that of Leclerc, seemed to make the blacks only more determined in their resistance. Many were the scenes such as the one at Port-au-Prince. There the whites placed a gallows in the marketplace and marched a seemingly endless line of prisoners to their deaths, but silhouetted on a nearby hill was another gallows which the blacks had erected to match each black neck with a white one. Clearly the war had become one of racial extermination for both sides. Not all Frenchmen agreed with Rochambeau's policy; some were even sickened by it and may have warned the rebels of French intentions. Rochambeau began to suspect several of his generals of making contacts with the enemy and ordered the arrest of General Nerette for wearing a red bonnet.[46] When the general was brought to trial, he explained that his red bonnet did not mean that he had joined the enemy; instead "he had had a toothache for the past few days and the doctor had ordered him to wear a wool bonnet and that ... he had not paid attention to the color."[47] Even though Nerette was acquitted, the implication of his trial was the same: Rochambeau's policy of extermination not only bolstered black courage but demoralized the white military.

Yellow fever added to the demoralization of the whites. From December 1802 until the end of May 1803 the ravages of that disease showed few signs of diminishing. General Quentin reported on February 6 that his force was either dead or dying and that he himself suffered ill health.[48] The general condition of the enlisted men, furthermore, was clearly terrible, for they were "badly clothed, lodged, and fed; victims of the heat, and of the injustices of the commissioners, who cheat them of their pay. They die by the hundreds daily, like dogs, like flies, they disappear unaccountably."[49]

Despite Rochambeau's declining position, France still had not given up on Saint-Domingue. Bonaparte received the news that slavery had been restored successfully on Guadeloupe by late December 1802 and that a major rebel offensive against Haut-du-Cap and Le Cap François had been smashed by Rochambeau's forces in mid-February. These events may have influenced or at least supported the First Consul's decision to reinforce Rochambeau with fifteen thousand more soldiers. On March 27, 1803, the troops arrived at Le Cap François and were quickly transferred to Port-au-Prince, Rochambeau's new headquarters. By early April the French were in their strongest position since the surrender of Toussaint: Rochambeau probably had more troops than Leclerc's original expedition, a portion of his forces were immunized against yellow fever, and Santo Domingo and most of the key coastal cities were still under French control.[50] With a chance to defeat the rebels, therefore, Rochambeau redoubled his efforts to exterminate the blacks.[51]

On April 7 the French repulsed a serious rebel attack near Les Cayes and shortly afterward introduced a new horror against the retreating blacks. From Cuba the French imported hundreds of killer dogs trained to terrorize Negroes and to rip them apart.[52] Testing his new weapon, Rochambeau ordered several blacks to be stripped of their clothes and released. As soon as the Negroes were liberated, "the dogs were let loose on them; they were almost immediately torn to pieces and their flesh devoured."[53] Bonaparte approved of Rochambeau's vicious behavior and, according to Pellissier, believed that "the situation of Saint-Domingue does not allow a choice of means."[54] The undaunted blacks, however, refused to surrender and continued "to hover around the towns, setting fire to the cane patches and the adjacent buildings."[55]

By early June, French resurgence had reached its high tide: not only was the coast largely in French hands, but there were serious penetrations of the interior. In West Province especially did the French batter the rebels, and much of the Cul-de-Sac and Croix-des-Bouquets returned to white control. But events in Europe soon returned the momentum of victory to the blacks.[56]

On May 18 the Treaty of Amiens was completely shattered with England's declaration of war against France. While the rupture between the two powers meant that Europe would be plunged into twelve more years of war, it also meant that England viewed Dessalines as an expedient ally. Great Britain, therefore, decided to give the blacks naval support and to supply them with arms and ammunition. No official alliance such as the one Maitland had negotiated with Toussaint in 1798 would be made; probably Great Britain wanted to remain as flexible as possible should the black nationalists of Saint-Domingue threaten the British West Indies.[57]

By mid-June, English aggression against the French West Indies was becoming increasingly intense. On the twenty-second of that month the French colony of Saint Lucia surrendered to British forces led by Lieutenant General William Grinfield and Commodore Samuel Hood. Early in July a British fleet began to assault Saint-Domingue with devastating effect: blockades were established around the major ports, and heavy bombardments blasted French positions. At Môle Saint Nicolas, General Lapayse reported that he had twelve hundred casualties and that his position was collapsing. By mid-September the British fleet had played an important role in Rochambeau's retreat from the interior toward the coast and in Dessalines' capture of Jérémie, Jacmel, and Fort Liberté.[58]

In the meantime Dessalines' rebel armies attacked the French with ferocity and vengeance. Hundreds of whites were mercilessly killed and hundreds more fled Saint-Domingue to the other West Indian islands, especially to Cuba. Dessalines was particularily interested in punishing South Province for opening its gates to Leclerc in 1802. Everywhere billows of smoke curled into the air as the blacks destroyed one plantation after another.[59] Peter Chazotte, one of the many whites fleeing toward Jérémie during July, observed the holocaust:

> I reached the top of our highest mountain, on which was the superb coffee estate of the Chevalier de Montagnac. . . . When I reached the spot I sought, I beheld the most awful and desolating

spectacle; no less than ten square leagues of country illuminated by volcanoes. I stood gazing in despair for two hours, upon this beautiful scene, to observe the progress of the conflagration eastward. Its rapidity was such as to make the beholder believe that large and thick trains of gunpowder had previously been . . . laid down, leading from one mansion and outbuildings on each estate to the neighboring ones, as in a large . . . fireworks display.[60]

From June to December the morale of the French army noticeably declined. Military leaders increasingly turned to "every species of extortion; the inhabitants [were] vexed, their houses in requisition."[61] At Jérémie, General Fressinet made a small fortune by charging the refugees exorbitant fees for their evacuation, prompting Chazotte to call him a "gold and silver leech." Everywhere there were signs of disintegration within the French army, but no one personified the degeneration better than Rochambeau himself. Losing touch with military reality, the French commander amused himself with sexual pleasures, military balls, banquets, and the amassing of a personal fortune.[62] Rochambeau even forced his general staff to participate in his orgies of pleasure and escape; his officers had to "fight in the morning, dance in the evening, and then fight again."[63]

With the British and the blacks attacking from two fronts and with supplies slowed to a trickle, Rochambeau decided to concentrate his mauled and hungry army at Le Cap François. On October 8 the French evacuated Port-au-Prince, and most of the city's white inhabitants fled to Cuba. Only ninety-two whites remained to greet the conquering blacks; perhaps they remembered the kind treatment which Toussaint had given the whites a few years earlier. But Dessalines could not see beyond vengeance and promptly had them hanged. At Les Cayes, General Brunet embarked his troops on vessels destined for Le Cap François, but not before he destroyed the military installations of the city and any equipment left behind. Near the end of October only Le Cap François remained under French control.[64]

Within the next few weeks this last white stronghold was in a state of near starvation; Rochambeau estimated that provisions remained for only eight or ten more days. Yet somehow the

French managed to hold out, and on November 18 Rochambeau's soldiers even counterattacked and defeated the advancing blacks. The Negroes, however, were determined to rid themselves of the French and returned to the offensive. On the next day Rochambeau, with Dessalines agreeing to a ten-day truce, began negotiations with Captain John Loring, commander of the blockading British squadron. According to the agreements reached between Rochambeau and Loring, French officers and soldiers in good health could go to Jamaica, but all French planters were to be transported to Cuba. On November 30 twenty ships left Le Cap François with over eighteen thousand refugees on board; eight thousand of them were all that remained of Rochambeau's army. On the same day Dessalines occupied Le Cap François; Saint-Domingue finally belonged to the blacks.[65]

For the French it had been a costly war. By December 1, 1803, only Negrophobe Santo Domingo remained within French control, under the governorship of General Marie-Louise Ferrand. Such a weak foothold was small compensation for the forty thousand or more troops France had lost in Saint-Domingue; the destruction of Leclerc's expedition, moreover, contributed to the inability of France to protect the remainder of the French West Indies.[66] Captain Sorrell, an eyewitness, was one of the first to realize this disastrous result: "France lost there one of the finest armies she ever sent forth, composed of picked veterans, the conquerors of Italy and of German legions. She is now entirely deprived of her influence and her power in the West Indies, as her remaining possessions are left without hope of succour."[67]

After publishing a preliminary declaration of independence on November 29, Dessalines and his generals met at Gonaives. At that meeting the black and mulatto leaders chose the name Haiti to replace that of Saint-Domingue and made Dessalines governor-general for life.[68] On January 1, 1804, the convention members officially proclaimed the independence of Haiti, the second republic of the Western Hemisphere. It was an unsteady independence, for it had been erected upon fifteen years of warfare, economic destruction, and racial annihilation. An able leader was needed for reconstruction, but unfortunately Dessalines was not Toussaint.[69]

NOTES FOR CHAPTER NINE

1. "Mémoire historique," Rochambeau Documents, 26; Bertrand to Rochambeau, June 21, 1802; Pierre Daux to Rochambeau, Aug. 12, 1802; Commandant Lavalette to Rochambeau, May 11, 1802, Rochambeau Papers; Boston *Gazette*, Aug. 5, 1802; *Mirror of the Times and General Advertiser*, Sept. 4, 1802; Roussier, *Leclerc*, 231.

2. Hassal, *Secret History*, 26.

3. Boston *Gazette*, Aug. 5, 1802; *Le Moniteur*, July 7, 1802; Lacroix, *Mémoires*, II, 225.

4. Boyer to Minister of Marine, Nov. 1802, in *Le Moniteur*, Jan. 11, 1803.

5. France, *Correspondance de Napoléon*, VII, 413.

6. Boston *Gazette*, July 1, 1802; *The Times* (London), July 19, 1802.

7. *The Times* (London), Aug. 1, 1802; Boyer to Minister of Marine, Nov. 1802, in *Le Moniteur*, Jan. 11, 1803; Louverture to Rochambeau, n.d.; Commandant Delpech to Rochambeau, May 8, 1802, Rochambeau Papers; Letter Extract from Le Cap François, May 28, 1802, in *Mirror of the Times and General Advertiser*, June 19, 1802.

8. Letter Extract from Le Cap François, May 28, 1802, in *Mirror of the Times and General Advertiser*, June 19, 1802.

9. *Ibid.*, July 17, 1802; Chief of Battalion Margaret to Rochambeau, June 6, 1802, Rochambeau Papers; Roussier, *Leclerc*, 165, 173–74; Chazotte, *Sketches of the Revolution*, 27; *The Times* (London), July 21 and Oct. 18, 1802.

10. Most of Toussaint's family went to Bayonne in southern France, where they were confined. Placide, Toussaint's stepson, was exiled on Belle Île, off the coast of France. Paul Louverture remained in the service of France on Saint-Domingue, but later he was to be killed by a desperate Rochambeau. Korngold, *Citizen Toussaint*, 303; Cole, *Christophe*, 112.

11. Alexis, *Black Liberator*, 214; *Le Moniteur*, July 7, 1802.

12. Even before his death, Toussaint's career was being romanticized. Writing after Toussaint's capture in 1802, William Wordsworth sensed some of the legacy and tragedy of the great black leader:

> *There's not a breathing of the common wind*
> *That will forget thee; thou hast great allies;*
> *Thy friends are exultations, agonies,*
> *And love, and man's unconquerable mind.*

Richard Wilbur, ed., *Wordsworth* (New York: Dell, 1959), 98.

13. Boston *Gazette*, Sept. 20, 1802.

14. *Ibid.*; "Mémoire historique," Rochambeau Documents, 23.

15. Lacroix, *Mémoires*, II, 213.

16. "Mémoire historique," Rochambeau Documents, 37; Roussier, *Leclerc*, 82.

17. Roussier, *Leclerc*, 207, 216–18; Captain Aussenac to Rochambeau, Aug. 11, 1802, Rochambeau Papers; Lacroix, *Mémoires*, II, 213–14; Journal of Proceedings at Le Cap François, between April and Nov. 1802, Given by a French Officer to an Officer of a British Man of War, Nov. 21, 1802, in *The Times* (London), Feb. 1, 1803.

18. Journal of Proceedings, *The Times* (London), Feb. 1, 1803; General Martial-Besse to Rochambeau, July 6, 1802; Commandant Lavalette to Rochambeau, June 18, 1802; General Quentin to Rochambeau, Sept. 9, 1802; General Boyer to Rochambeau, Aug. 12, 1802; Commandant Puquet to Rochambeau, Aug. 16, 1802, Rochambeau Papers.

19. Puquet to Rochambeau, Aug. 16, 1802, Rochambeau Papers.

20. Boston *Gazette*, Aug. 5, 1802.

21. Lacroix, *Mémoires*, II, 223.

22. On those islands England returned to France by the Treaty of Amiens, slavery was maintained in a decree passed by the Legislature Corps on May 20, 1802. Cole, *Christophe*, 115.

23. *Le Moniteur*, May 21, 1802; France, *Correspondance de Napoléon*, VII, 444–47.

24. The blacks discovered French policy in various ways. Many of them were frightened by the boasts of white planters, by Leclerc's decrees, and by information reaching Saint-Domingue from Guadeloupe. Stoddard, *San Domingo*, 333; Lacroix, *Mémoires*, II, 225–27.

25. Lacroix, *Mémoires*, II, 226–27; Law Regarding Agriculture, June 30, 1802, Leclerc Papers; Cole, *Christophe*, 114–15; General Desbureaux to Rochambeau, July 27, 1802, Rochambeau Papers; Roussier, *Leclerc*, 198.

26. Boston *Gazette*, Aug. 5, 1802.

27. *Mirror of the Times and General Advertiser*, Nov. 6, 1802; Roussier, *Leclerc*, 207.

28. Commander Bartet to Rochambeau, Aug. 26, 1802, Rochambeau Papers; Lacroix, *Mémoires*, II, 215–16.

29. Lacroix, *Mémoires*, II, 216, 218; *Mirror of the Times and General Advertiser*, Oct. 4, 1802; Boyer to Minister of Marine, Nov. 1802, in *Le Moniteur*, Jan. 11, 1803.

30. Boyer to Minister of Marine, Nov. 1802, in *Le Moniteur*, Jan. 11, 1803; *Mirror of the Times and General Advertiser*, Nov. 6, 1802; Madiou, *Haiti*, II, 295; Boston *Gazette*, Oct. 21, 1802; General Desbureaux to Rochambeau, Sept. 16, 1802; Brigade Chief Bernard to Rochambeau, Oct. 4, 1802; Commandant Faustin Repussard to Rochambeau, Sept. 27, 1802, Rochambeau Papers.

31. Dessalines to Leclerc, Oct. 4, 1802, Rochambeau Papers.

32. In a letter to Rochambeau, General Quentin wrote that he believed that Bonaparte's order to restore slavery was a well-guarded secret; Quentin, however, indicated that the knowledge of the First Consul's order was common among Leclerc's general staff and that the "honor" of making it public should have been Rochambeau's. This letter helps to disprove the assertion

of C. L. R. James that Leclerc successfully kept the knowledge of the immediate reinstatement of slavery from even Rochambeau, his second-in-command. Of greater importance, Quentin's letter helps to destroy James's important contention that the restoration of slavery in Saint-Domingue was a plan shared only by Bonaparte and Leclerc. The purpose of James was to prove that it might have been possible to unite the Jacobins of France with the black masses. In trying to support his tenuous thesis, James even went so far as to maintain that the soldiers of Leclerc's expedition had no idea that slavery was to be restored and might have joined the blacks had they known.

The weaknesses in James's thesis are apparent. Not only did most of Leclerc's generals know about the restoration of slavery, but many rank-and-file French soldiers probably guessed what was ahead through the loose talk of white planters and Leclerc's decrees; such a prospect was of little concern to them. James, moreover, demonstrated a weak knowledge of the French Revolution. Many of the Jacobins were bourgeois and would have had little attraction for the nonpropertied black masses. Even the *sans-culottes* should not be equated with the blacks, for the former, being a mixture of the propertied and nonpropertied, cannot be identified as a class. James also tended to overlook the fact that the year 1802 was one of reaction in France. His stumbling attempt to connect the Haitian and French revolutions through some sort of common mass movement is a good example of "fact trimming" to fit a particular thesis or ideology. James, *Black Jacobins*, 294, 306, 318; Lacroix, *Mémoires*, II, 225–27; General Quentin to Rochambeau, Oct. 23, 1802, Rochambeau Papers.

33. General Quentin to Rochambeau, Sept. 4, 1802, Rochambeau Papers; Cole, *Christophe*, 121; Journal of Proceedings, Nov. 21, 1802, in *The Times* (London), Feb. 1, 1803.

34. *The Times* (London), Feb. 1, 1803; Cole, *Christophe*, 123.

35. Journal of Proceedings, Nov. 21, 1802, in *The Times* (London), Feb. 1, 1803.

36. Letter from Le Cap François, Oct. 25, 1802, in *The Times* (London), Jan. 12, 1803.

37. Letter from Port-au-Prince, Oct. 23, 1802, in *The Times* (London), Jan. 12, 1803; General Fressinet to Rochambeau, Oct. 31, 1802; Captain David Troy to Rochambeau, Oct. 28, 1802, Rochambeau Papers.

38. General Fressinet to Rochambeau, Jan. 17, 1803, Rochambeau Papers; Cole, *Christophe*, 130–31.

39. Duare to Army and Inhabitants of St. Domingo, Nov. 2, 1802, in *The Times* (London), Jan. 15, 1803.

40. *The Times* (London), Jan. 14, 1803.

41. Pauline accompanied Leclerc's body back to France for a state funeral. At Toulon the dead general was transferred to another ship for a voyage to Marseilles. The vessel was draped in black cloth, and a large awning housed Leclerc's body and coffin. Ironically the black and white colors of the awning

"were appropriately blended." If Leclerc in life had blended blacks and whites as well as Leclerc in death, his role in Saint-Domingue might have been much different. Charleston *Times*, April 1, 1803.

42. With the new troops, Rochambeau's army probably amounted to over 16,000 white regulars and 5,000 colonial volunteers. Rochambeau to Rear Admiral Decrès, Dec. 8, 1802, Rochambeau Papers.

43. Chief of Brigade Gonuing to Rochambeau, Nov. 29, 1802, Rochambeau Papers; *The Times* (London), Jan. 29 and Feb. 17, 1803; Boston *Gazette*, Jan. 17, 1803.

44. While no estimate can be exact, the black population by this time had probably dropped from over 500,000 to about 250,000 or less. "Mémoire historique," Rochambeau Documents, 41; *The Times* (London), June 18, 1804.

45. Cole, *Christophe*, 129–30; Boyer to Minister of Marine, Nov. 1802, in *Le Moniteur*, Jan. 11, 1803; Boston *Gazette*, Dec. 30, 1802.

46. Boston *Gazette*, Dec. 30, 1802; Chief of Brigade Berger to Rochambeau, Dec. 2, 1802; Major LeCarpentier to Rochambeau, Jan. 17, 1803, Rochambeau Papers.

47. LeCarpentier to Rochambeau, Jan. 17, 1803, Rochambeau Papers.

48. Quentin to Rochambeau, Feb. 6, 1803, Rochambeau Papers.

49. Letter from Le Cap François, June 6, 1802, in Boston *Gazette*, July 14, 1803.

50. The role of Saint-Domingue in the sale of Louisiana to the U.S. has been often misinterpreted by historians. Typical are E. Wilson Lyon and Robert Ferrell in their belief that the failure of the Saint-Domingue expedition was one of several important influences on Bonaparte's decision to abandon his Louisiana project. There is, however, no evidence to prove that Bonaparte considered his Saint-Domingue expedition a failure; on the contrary, the First Consul was giving it unprecedented support at the very time he decided to sell Louisiana. Perhaps Bonaparte believed that Rochambeau, if properly supported, could defeat the blacks before the outbreak of war with England.

What, then, was the role of Saint-Domingue in the sale of Louisiana to the U.S.? One must be conservative in any estimate, but certainly the long duration of the war in Saint-Domingue tied up troops that might otherwise have been redeployed in Louisiana. To the blacks of Saint-Domingue, commented a writer in the New York *Evening Post*, "are we indebted for the obstacle which delayed the colonization of Louisiana, until the auspicious moment, when a rupture between England and France gave a new turn to the projects of the latter." E. Wilson Lyon, *The Man Who Sold Louisiana: The Career of Barbé-Marbois* (Norman: Univ. of Oklahoma Press, 1942), 118; Robert Ferrell, *American Diplomacy* (New York: Norton, 1969), 119; New York *Evening Post*, July 5, 1803; Pellissier to Rochambeau, May 15, 1803, Rochambeau Papers.

51. Chief of Battalion Arnauld to Rochambeau, Dec. 29, 1802, Rocham-

beau Papers; Charleston *Times*, April 23, 1803; Letter Extract from Le Cap François, March 3, 1803, in Providence *Gazette and Country Journal*, March 26, 1803.

52. Boston *Gazette*, May 5, 1803; Letter Extract from Le Cap François, April 7, 1803, in *Mirror of the Times and General Advertiser*, May 11, 1803.

53. Letter Extract from Le Cap François, April 17, 1803, in *Mirror of the Times and General Advertiser*, May 11, 1803.

54. Pellissier to Rochambeau, May 15, 1803, Rochambeau Papers.

55. Letter Extract from Le Cap François, April 7, 1803, in *Mirror of the Times and General Advertiser*, May 11, 1803.

56. Boston *Gazette*, Nov. 24, 1803; General Fressinet to Rochambeau, June 7, 1803, Rochambeau Papers.

57. Chief of Brigade Valdomy to Rochambeau, June 8, 1803, Rochambeau Papers; Chazotte, *Sketches of the Revolution*, 30-31, 35-36.

58. Chazotte, *Sketches of the Revolution*, 35; Charleston *Times*, July 22, 1803; *Mirror of the Times and General Advertiser*, July 20, 1803; General Lapayse to Rochambeau, July 3, 1803; Chief of Battalion Corvinus to Rochambeau, Sept. 11, 1803; Chief of Brigade Valdomy to Rochambeau, Sept. 21, 1803; General Pageot to Rochambeau, Oct. 21, 1803, Rochambeau Papers.

59. Lajonquiere to Rochambeau, Sept. 28, 1803, Rochambeau Papers; Jean Pierre Esnard to Antoine Barbot, April 30, 1827, Barbot-Chartrand Papers; "Mémoire historique," Rochambeau Documents, 41; James Leyburn, *The Haitian People* (New Haven: Yale Univ. Press, 1941), 31; *The Times* (London), Oct. 1, 25, 1803; Chazotte, *Sketches of the Revolution*, 32-33.

60. *Sketches of the Revolution*, 32-33.

61. Boston *Gazette*, July 14, 1803.

62. *Ibid.*; Chazotte, *Sketches of the Revolution*, 31; Grand Judge Ludot to Rochambeau, July 31, 1803, Rochambeau Papers.

63. Boston *Gazette*, July 14, 1803.

64. *Ibid.*, Nov. 24 and Dec. 26, 1803; *The Times* (London), Jan. 5, 12, 1804.

65. *The Times* (London), Jan. 5, 27, 1804; W. Dodge to Madison, Nov. 25, 1803, Consular Dispatches, Cap-Haitien, vol. 4; Captain J. W. Loring to Rochambeau, Nov. 19, 1803, Rochambeau Papers; McCloy, *West Indies*, 101.

66. McCloy, *West Indies*, 100-101; Lacroix, *Mémoires*, II, 341-42; *The Times* (London), Jan. 27, 1804.

67. *The Times* (London), Jan. 27, 1804.

68. The Indian word *haiti* means "mountainous" and was the aboriginal name of the island known as Hispaniola to the Spanish. Perhaps Dessalines and his lieutenants selected the new name to help blot out the colonial past of their new nation.

69. *The Times* (London), Feb. 6, 1804; Cole, *Christophe*, 140.

CHAPTER TEN

Conclusions and Legacy of Revolution

Social and racial struggle appears as the most salient feature of the labyrinthine course of the Haitian Revolution. From the early eighteenth century, tensions gathered in Saint-Domingue between bureaucrat and *grand blanc*, *grand blanc* and *petit blanc*, white and mulatto, mulatto and black, black and white. Beginning in 1789, each group played a role upon the stage of revolution. From 1789 to 1791 the whites created explosive conditions with their intracaste struggle, and from 1790 to 1799 the mulattoes sought elevation to white status while ignoring a similar drive in the blacks. The chief beneficiaries of this strife were the Negroes, because both whites and mulattoes forced them onto a course of freedom and independence which otherwise might have been beyond their awareness and ability to achieve. Therefore, the important influences of the French Revolution, key personalities, and foreign intervention should be considered subsidiary to social and racial conflict, the major theme of the Haitian Revolution.

Had the French Revolution not caused disintegration within France and the spread of dangerous ideology, the upheaval in Saint-Domingue might never have occurred. This partly explains why social revolution struck in the French West Indies and not elsewhere in the Caribbean from 1789 to 1804. The French Revolution, of course, was merely a detonator, since the real ingredients of explosion were the racial and class tensions within Saint-Domingue.

Even the roles of key leaders during the Haitian Revolution can be best explained in terms of their relation to the social strife in Saint-Domingue. Léger Félicité Sonthonax, the feared Jacobin, could never have achieved personal power had whites and mulattoes not been at loggerheads and had he not offered freedom to the blacks. Yet the very conditions which led to Sonthonax's rise contributed to his downfall because he could neither bring an end to anarchy nor guarantee the permanence of Negro freedom. He was replaced by the next great personality—Toussaint Louverture. This great black leader proceeded to defeat the British, destroy mulatto power, rebuild Saint-Domingue, and carry the colony to the threshold of independence. None of his accomplishments, however, might have been realized had he not anchored them to social strife. Clearly both the mulattoes and the British invasion represented a return to the *ancien régime* for the blacks, making it easier for Toussaint to gather forces to oppose them. Even the drive for independence can be explained in terms of social struggle, since it seemed the only way to ensure Negro freedom. When Toussaint was unable to take this final step, it fell to the furious Jean Jacques Dessalines to complete the revolution. This is not to say that the great leaders of the revolution could not guide the upheaval to some extent, but they succeeded only to the degree that they were attuned to social demands.

Foreign intervention also was closely attuned to the social struggle. England felt that with the aid of French planters and the internal problems of France, Saint-Domingue would be an easy conquest. As soon as possible England would have imposed the *ancien régime* on the colony to protect the Anglo-Caribbean, especially Jamaica. Spain invaded at about the same time, partly to prevent social disorder from reaching Santo Domingo. And Bonapartist France invaded Saint-Domingue to suppress the new status of the blacks and return them to slavery; such narrowmindedness was Bonaparte's single solution to the task of regaining the former prosperity of France in the colony. Only the United States, among the foreign powers, had a different role, since it was primarily interested in Saint-Domingue as a trade base and supported Toussaint as a means of hurting France during the Quasi-War. But eventually the United States turned its back on Saint-Domingue to appease Bonaparte and Southern slaveholders—a policy shift influenced by social conditions in the colony. Foreign intervention— at least in the cases of France, Spain, and England—also helped to increase social strife by causing political uncertainty and great physical destruction. Saint-Domingue, in fact, was something of an eighteenth-century Vietnam.

Few wars have been so completely destructive as was the Haitian Revolution. Many of the planters fled, the population fell from about 500,000 people to about 250,000 or less, the labor supply was dislocated, and sugar production practically ceased. Of the many plantations which had dotted the once prosperous countryside, only a small number remained intact.[1] "The few which are still worked," wrote a British agent, "are cultivated by women, children and old men; and all the sugar works and distilleries, except for a few instances, have been destroyed."[2] The important task of restoring this ruined land rested upon Dessalines.

At first Dessalines, like Toussaint, seemed to realize the value of white technology in the reconstruction of Haiti. On November 29, 1803, he invited "redeemed planters" to return, but he warned that those persisting in their traditional habits would only "meet with chains and deportation."[3] Dessalines even apologized for the killing of innocent whites by the rampaging blacks. A large number of planters returned to Haiti in the belief that the new ruler would continue Toussaint's policies toward the whites.[4]

Dessalines, however, was a product of the revolution and found his desire to reconstruct Haiti overwhelmed by his hatred of the whites. On January 1, 1804, with the declaration of Haitian independence, he announced that "the bones of the dead [blacks] would not rest until their blood was avenged."[5] Extermination, he believed, was the only way to rid Haiti of the white man.[6]

Beginning in March 1804, Dessalines killed every white he could find. At Jérémie, Chazotte witnessed a band of blacks executing four hundred whites in front of Dessalines' headquarters. At Port-au-Prince and at Le Cap François the scenes of genocide were repeated, despite the opposition of Christophe at the latter city.[7] One particularly heartbreaking episode involved the slaughter of a father and his daughters:

> Two amiable girls . . . hung to the neck of their father when the Negroes seized him. They wept and entreated the monsters to spare him; but he was torn rudely from their arms. The young-

est, attempting to follow him, received a blow on the head with a musket which laid her lifeless on the ground. The eldest, frantic with terror, clung to her father, when a ruthless Negro pierced her with his bayonet, and she fell dead at his feet. The hapless father gave thanks to God that his unfortunate children had perished before him, and had not been exposed to lingering sufferings and a more dreadful fate.[8]

If white destruction was a logical consequence of the Haitian Revolution, so was mulatto-black tension. "The people of colour, particularly the women," noted an observer, "experienced the most cruel treatment."[9] Dessalines did attempt to decrease racial strain by simply recognizing all inhabitants as blacks, but his effort was in vain as rivalry between the castes increased. Basic to the problem was the superiority that the mulattoes, now known as the *élite*, attached to their white ancestry and French heritage. All through Haitian history of the nineteenth and twentieth centuries this chronic problem continued to erupt. Under Faustin Soulouque (1847–59) a general massacre of the mulattoes was ordered; in 1883 Louis-Félicité Lysius Saloman did nothing to stop the blacks from attacking the mulatto district of Port-au-Prince; and the *gens de couleur* of Haiti continued to suffer oppression as recently as the brutal regime of François "Papa Doc" Duvalier.[10]

Another logical consequence of the revolution was the growth of militarism and dictatorship. After twelve years of steady conflict, the black army had established such a grip on Haiti that independence did not alter the basic power structure. Soldiers still mechanically followed their commanders, and commanders greedily followed their selfish ambitions. Anticipating Bonaparte, Dessalines attempted to bring political stabilization by having himself crowned Emperor Jacques I on October 8, 1804. Because he failed to name a successor, his assassination on October 17, 1806, plunged Haiti into a civil war between Christophe in the north and Pétion in the south. Others have attempted Dessalines' formula, but all have failed: Christophe was crowned Henri I in June 1811 and established a nobility, and Faustin Soulouque became Emperor Faustin I in 1849. Undeniably, therefore, the revolution did much to impose a political pendulum of *caudillo-turmoil-caudillo* on Haiti. If the present regime of Jean-Claude

Duvalier collapses, Haitian politics will probably swing into another period of turmoil.[11]

Even though recent Haitian politicians cannot be accused of intellectualizing the revolution, they have indulged in the cult of hero worship, a practice Katherine Dunham observed during her thirty years in Haiti. Dumarsais Estimé (1946–50) identified with Toussaint; especially did he share the black liberator's humanistic outlook. Paul Eugène Magloire (1950–56) identified with Christophe; both were sensuous, dignified, materialistic, and power hungry. But Papa Doc Duvalier (1957–71) made Dessalines his culture hero. He declared October 17, the anniversary of Dessalines' death, a national holiday and ordered an eternal flame installed on the tomb of the first ruler of Haiti at Pont Rouge. Of greater importance to Duvalier were the influences of Dessalines' antipathy toward whites and political insecurity. Both men feared a white world that might devour them: Dessalines faced the uncertainties of French policy and Duvalier faced the vicissitudes of United States policy. Thus when Duvalier embarked upon a program of white persecution and isolationism, he acted in the tradition of the Dessalines regime. Even Papa Doc's police state relied heavily upon the examples of Dessalines' rule. Dessalines distrusted the army and sought to weaken it with an armed peasant militia; Duvalier likewise distrusted the army and enfeebled it with his gestapo-type *Ton-Ton Macoute*.[12]

Not only domestic disorders but also strained foreign relations contributed to the growth of militarism and dictatorship in Haiti. France refused to recognize the new republic until 1825, and the United States, because of Southern opposition, did not do so until 1862. Jamaica, moreover, continued to fear black independence, and Governor Edward Eyre deported Haitians for alleged disturbances in 1865. Thus Haitian dictators, with justification, believed that the white world in general and France in particular might engulf their small state. A strong military, they rationalized, was the only way to prevent such a catastrophe, but a strong military also meant the depletion of Haiti's labor force, making reconstruction more difficult.[13]

The most troubled foreign relationship of Haiti, however, has been with her next-door neighbor, the Dominican Republic. During the revolution this poor relationship began when white-dominated Spanish Santo Domingo vehemently opposed the black invaders of Saint-Domingue. In 1802 the French conquered Spanish Santo Domingo and continued to hold it for seven years. In 1809 the colonists overthrew the rule of France and re-established their control, only to be once again subdued by invading Haitians in 1822. Not until 1844 did the Dominican Republic finally overthrow black rule and achieve independence. For the remainder of the nineteenth century and even to the present day, the legacy of the revolution has continued to rage: in 1937 Rafael Trujillo of the Dominican Republic slaughtered at least twelve thousand Haitian migrant workers in order to keep the country "white," and in 1963 Haitian-Dominican relations were strained to the point of war.[14]

Born into a world of constant upheaval, Haiti has staggered through more than one and a half centuries since independence. Much of the tone of Haiti's national experience was set in the decade following the revolution: plantations were subdivided into small plots, workers drifted into the hills to live at a subsistence level, and coffee became the most important export crop.[15] Surprisingly, Haiti, the poorest of the Latin American nations, has been able to maintain national integrity, except for the interlude of American occupation from 1915 to 1934. The legacy of the revolution, however, was not confined to Haiti.[16]

One area of influence was the Spanish American struggle for independence from 1808 to 1826. In February 1816 Simón Bolívar, driven into exile by the Spanish, visited Alexandre Pétion in southern Haiti.[17] In return for Pétion's material support, Bolívar promised to free the slaves of Venezuela and other areas that he might conquer. Although Bolívar could not immediately abolish slavery in northern South America, he was able to begin a program of gradual emancipation. Bolívar was also impressed by the idea of Haiti's lifelong presidency, which had begun with Toussaint, and duplicated the institution in the Bolivian Constitution of 1826.[18]

Bolívar was also apprehensive about Haiti, the land of socio-economic upheaval and black freedom. As a member of the conservative creole class, he had no desire to expose South America to the violent Haitian influence.[19] The blacks, he believed, were a "tremendous monster who has devoured the island of Santo Domingo."[20] To prevent the contamination of social turbulence from Haiti, Bolívar refused to recognize Haitian independence and would not invite the black nation to the Panama Congress of 1826; the fear of creating another Haiti, moreover, entered into his decision not to invade Cuba.[21]

Much of proslavery Cuba wholeheartedly endorsed Bolívar's reservations about the Haitian Revolution. After the economic collapse of Saint-Domingue, Cuba replaced the former French colony as the "Pearl of the Antilles"; many of those sharing in the Cuban bonanza were the former planters of Saint-Domingue who had migrated with their slaves and technology. These refugees kept the Cuban planters in a constant turmoil with stories of Negro atrocities. Their tales became real when José Antonio Aponte, a black woodcarver, was captured in 1810 for attempting a Cuban-wide rebellion; Aponte's followers had killed several planters and Aponte himself had been in touch with the successful rebels of Haiti.[22]

The rapid growth of slavery further frightened slaveholding Cuba. From 1792 to 1845 the Cuban slave population grew from a little over 44,000 to 350,000. With this fantastic expansion, the Cuban institution of slavery became increasingly oppressive and the slave masters became increasingly fearful. Such fear drove the creole-dominated slave masters to oppose joining the struggle for Spanish American independence because it might ignite a Negro revolution in Cuba.[23] Alarm over a Haitian-type rebellion even continued to haunt the slaveholders after the Spanish American conflicts ended: by mid-century, planters organized the Junta Cubana and in their tracts followed the tradition of calling up the horrors of Saint-Domingue.[24]

Ironically, the Haitian Revolution also supported the views of Cuban abolitionists. In 1822 Father Félix Varela y Morales indicated that, with the revolutionaries of Haiti so near, slavery jeopardized Cuban safety. Morales and orators like him probably played a large role in tormenting the planters into realizing their delicate position; many supporters of human bondage soon came to fear the increasing number of slaves and began to approve of the abolition of the African slave trade. Even as late as the 1870s Emilio Castelar, known as "Golden Beak," continued to use examples from the Haitian Revolution to support antislavery. When Cuban slavery was finally abolished in 1886, the lingering spirit of the first successful quest for black freedom in the Western Hemisphere had played its part.[25]

In the United States, as in Cuba, the Haitian Revolution alarmed proslavery advocates. Many Southerners realized that once slaves got "a taste for freedom ... they will not easily be made to abandon the enterprise."[26] Many Southern states feared that the French might dump their "infected" slaves in the South. In October 1802 Georgetown, South Carolina, called out local militia to prevent a French frigate from unloading slaves from Saint-Domingue. Two years later the planters of Pointe Coupée, Louisiana, believed that their slaves had been "infected" with Haitian ideology and braced for a rebellion which never occurred, but the planters demanded that Governor William Claiborne use any inhumane means to punish the culprits. Despite such measures, slaves from Saint-Domingue continued to arrive in Louisiana, causing the plantation masters to become increasingly brutal in their regulation of slavery.[27] Claiborne himself admitted that when it came to Haitian blacks "no effectual stop can at present be put to their introduction."[28]

Since there was no way to guarantee that slaves from Saint-Domingue were not reaching the South, the fear of a general slave rebellion gained currency among Southern whites. From the Garwin conspiracy of 1793 in South Carolina and Virginia to the Denmark Vesey insurrection in 1822, there seemed to be direct connections between growing slave unrest and the Haitian Revolution.[29] As a result, "many Americans came increasingly to feel that slavery was a closed subject, entirely unsuitable for frank discussion."[30]

No better example of this growing American attitude can be cited than South Carolina in the 1820s and 1830s. As planters from Saint-Domingue settled in the Charleston area, they made the whites in the low country increasingly aware of the dangers their slaves presented. When the Denmark Vesey rebellion was uncovered in June 1822, the Carolina planters were horrified, for the

Haitian Revolution seemed ready for a replay upon a Southern stage. Planter fears were confirmed with the information that Vesey had communicated with Haitian blacks and even expected a Haitian invasion to support the slaves of South Carolina. The fear of a Negro revolution hardly subsided in low-country South Carolina for the remainder of the decade. Consequently, historian William H. Freehling is correct in his analysis that tidewater planters viewed the Nullification Crisis of 1832 as a federal threat to the security of their slaves; they even recalled the meddling of France in Saint-Domingue before the Haitian Revolution as a parallel to their own experience.[31]

Ironically, as in Cuba, the Haitian Revolution supported American abolitionism as well as the defense of slavery. In 1792 a request by Saint-Domingue refugees to land their slaves in Pennsylvania led not only to a refusal by the legislature but also to the outright abolition of slavery within the state. In the 1830s William Lloyd Garrison used the Haitian Revolution to elucidate his argument that the safety of Southern slavery depended upon Northern bayonets; this assumption led him to conclude that the foundations of slavery rested upon free and slave states alike. By the mid-nineteenth century Wendell Phillips, another leading abolitionist, was drawing upon the example of Toussaint to demonstrate that Negroes were not inferior beings and were quite capable of freedom. Later, during the Civil War, Phillips made effective use of his lecture on Toussaint to gain blacks a place in the Union army. The slaves of the South, furthermore, despite the lack of conclusive evidence, must have felt encouraged by the abolition of slavery in Haiti.[32]

The influence of the Haitian Revolution upon abolitionists elsewhere in the Western Hemisphere is not as clear as in Cuba and the United States. The revolution, however, hurt the English abolition movement during the decade of the 1790s; white Jamaicans especially were in the throes of hysteria regarding the safety of their slaves and attempted to muzzle criticism of their society. From 1803 to 1833, with the economic decline of the British West Indies, English abolitionists successfully and gradually emancipated the blacks of the Anglo-Caribbean. The memory of Saint-Domingue, reinforced by uprisings in Barbados (1816) and

Jamaica (1831), probably played an important part in the cautious attitude of British abolition.[33]

France, on the other hand, moved even more slowly than Great Britain. One reason was Napoleon's desire to reconquer Haiti and re-establish slavery there. But English diplomatic pressure and French abolitionists sided in stopping the slave trade of France in 1818. From that date until 1848, the memory of the Haitian Revolution and a revolt in Martinique in 1822 probably contributed to the slow, hard struggle which Victor Schoelcher and his followers had in freeing the slaves in the French West Indies.[34]

After the abolition of slavery in the Western Hemisphere, the Haitian Revolution continued to have a lingering influence upon whites, especially upon advocates of racism. During Reconstruction in the American South, defenders of white superiority feared a Negro uprising, a Haitian Revolution in Dixie. To them, Haiti exemplified Negro rule at its worst, a rule based upon white destruction. This fear led many white Southerners to join the Ku Klux Klan and other secret societies dedicated to the suppression of blacks and the establishment of home rule. Whenever a Klansman confiscated a weapon from a black or dispersed a Negro band armed for its self-defense, the specter of a black rebellion was reinforced.[35]

The fear of a race war outlived Reconstruction. Such a dread was present in the 1920s, when acts of violence, a new Klan, and certain intellectuals manifested a national white racism. One of those intellectuals was T. Lothrop Stoddard, a graduate of Harvard and author of a study of the Haitian Revolution (published in 1914). In his *Rising Tide of Color* (1920), Stoddard avidly defended white supremacy and saw race war as a distinct possibility; he found support for both assertions in the Haitian Revolution.[36] In his own words, the Haitian Revolution "was the first real shock between the ideals of white supremacy and race-equality; a prologue to the mighty drama of our own day. It ... shows what real race war means."[37]

Several Negro thinkers were as interested as Stoddard in the Haitian Revolution. This was true of both Frederick Douglass and Benjamin Brawley. Douglass, a former slave and a reformer, was the American ambassador to Haiti from 1889 to 1891. Douglass obviously took pride in the Haitian Revolution as the first example of Negro freedom in the Western Hemisphere. Consequently, he was placed in an embarrassing position when he received instructions from his home government to aid Admiral Bancroft Gherardi in negotiations for Môle Saint Nicolas, an important Haitian deep-water port. In a dilemma, Douglass obeyed his instructions, but felt an uneasiness about the future of Haitian independence.[38] He reminded the Benjamin Harrison administration that the experience of the Haitian Revolution would cause the black republic to stand up to American aggression, for the Negro masses "would burn their towns and freely shed their blood over their ashes to prevent such a consummation."[39]

In the 1920s historian Benjamin Brawley agreed with Douglass that the Haitian Revolution was a Negro accomplishment; he especially reminded his readers how much the United States owed the Louisiana Purchase to the independence of Haiti. He also looked with pride toward Toussaint as one of the great black leaders of the nineteenth century. Brawley was obviously incensed over the American occupation of Haiti and identified that nation's plight with the plight of Negroes within the United States. With the end of American occupation of Haiti in 1934, however, black moderates ceased serious consideration of the Haitian Revolution. This was natural, because once Haiti no longer personified white oppression of blacks, the revolution itself became increasingly irrelevant to the Negro reform movement.[40]

If Negro moderates occasionally glanced at the Haitian Revolution, black radicals gave it a hard stare. From 1914 to 1926 Marcus Garvey, founder of the Universal Negro Improvement Association and editor of *Negro World*, was particularly active in black separatism and unity. Although Garvey, a Jamaican, looked primarily to Africa for a solution to the modern Negro's problems, he did appropriate elements of the Haitian Revolution for his ideology. He considered Toussaint an example of Negro superiority, even surpassing the most brilliant white leaders: Cromwell, Washington, and Napoleon. In Garvey's racist ideology Toussaint was not a Haitian leading Haitians; instead he was a late-eighteenth-century world leader of blacks. This is significant because Garvey saw himself playing the same role in the twentieth century. He probably identified with Toussaint and considered the Haitian, like himself, a black Moses.[41]

Since the late 1930s there has emerged a group of Negro racist intellectuals best described as proponents of Black Marxism. According to their theories, the proletariat is black and the capitalists are white; Black Marxism, in other words, combines racial strife with economic determinism and class struggle. Although Black Marxists glorify Africa as an orthodox Marxist might glorify the classless society, they have found much in the Haitian Revolution suitable to their ideology. Such is the case of C. L. R. James, a Trotskyite and politician from Trinidad. In his *Black Jacobins* (1938), James identified former slaves with the proletariat and whites with capitalists; his assertions, however, became inconsistent with Black Marxism when he combined the Jacobins of France with the former slaves of Haiti as allies in a common class struggle. Perhaps this inconsistency was the result of a conflict within James to be a Negro racist and West Indian nationalist on the one hand and a traditional Marxist on the other.[42]

More consistent to Black Marxism is Aimé Césaire, a Martinique poet and politician. Césaire has extolled the virtues of Africa and may have been the one to originate the term Negritude, a term which emphasizes Negro brotherhood around an African center-piece. It is significant that Césaire wrote a biography of Toussaint which was published in 1960. In it he attempted to portray Toussaint as more African than Haitian. Thus Césaire subtly appropriated part of the Haitian Revolution to support his ideology.[43]

One of the most interesting Black Marxists was W. E. B. DuBois. During most of his career DuBois, a leader of the National Association for the Advancement of Colored People, advocated Negro equality and attacked white racism. He became increasingly radical and by the 1940s was a Black Marxist. As a result, DuBois viewed the Haitian Revolution as an example of the Negro proletariat overthrowing the economic foundations upon which slavery was based; moreover, he saw Toussaint as a precursor in the West of the black sultans of Arabia who had treated Negroes well.[44]

Since the 1950s the Haitian Revolution has steadily lost prominence in the thinking of black radicals. African imagery crowds much of their thought, and if they give consideration to any Caribbean revolution, it is to the Castro revolution of 1959. This is seen in the career of the black separatist LeRoi Jones. Shortly after Castro seized control of Cuba, he invited Jones and other black radicals to view his island nation. Jones was obviously impressed by what he saw and was convinced that an oppressed people could rise. By Jones's own admission, his visit had turned his thoughts to a Negro revolution in the United States. It might also be argued that the freshness of the Castro revolution and the remoteness of the Haitian Revolution made the latter obscure in radical thinking. In any case, neither Negro extremists nor moderates now have much to say about that upheaval.[45]

This, then, was the Haitian Revolution. Physically it left Haiti a ravaged land with dictators continually passing on and off the stage of politics. No one can deny that the influence of the revolution was widespread, especially on the opposing views of slavery. Its greatest monument, however, was the hope of freedom which it gave to perhaps thousands of slaves in many areas of the Western Hemisphere.

NOTES FOR CHAPTER TEN

1. "Mémoire historique," Rochambeau Documents, 41; Boston *Gazette*, Nov. 24, 1803; *The Times* (London), June 18, 1804.

2. *The Times* (London), June 18, 1804.

3. *Ibid.*, Feb. 6, 1804.

4. *Ibid.*; Chazotte, *Sketches of the Revolution*, 37.

5. Dessalines to Haitian People, Jan. 1, 1804, in *The Times* (London), April 28, 1804.

6. Chazotte, *Sketches of the Revolution*, 39.

7. *Ibid.*, 50; *The Times* (London), June 13, 1804; Cole, *Christophe*, 142–43.

8. Hassal, *Secret History*, 145–46.

9. *The Times* (London), Feb. 1, 1804.

10. John E. Fagg, *Cuba, Haiti, and the Dominican Republic* (Englewood Cliffs, N. J.: Prentice-Hall, 1965), 136; Cole, *Christophe*, 145; Rayford Logan, *Haiti and the Dominican Republic* (New York: Oxford Univ. Press, 1968), 22, 95–96, 109.

11. Logan, *Haiti and the Dominican Republic*, 95–96; Cole, *Christophe*, 145, 148, 153, 190–91.

12. Katherine Dunham, *Island Possessed* (Garden City, N. Y.: Double-day, 1969), 161–62, 170–71.

13. Arvel Erickson, "Empire or Anarchy: The Jamaica Rebellion of 1865," *Journal of Negro History*, 44 (Apr. 1959), 116; William S. Jenkins, *Pro-Slavery Thought in the Old South* (Chapel Hill: Univ. of North Carolina Press, 1935), 64; *The Times* (London), June 18, 1804; Logan, *Haiti and the Dominican Republic*, 95, 99–103.

14. Logan, *Haiti and the Dominican Republic*, 101; John B. Martin, *Overtaken by Events: The Dominican Crisis from the Fall of Trujillo to the Civil War* (Garden City, N. Y.: Doubleday, 1966), 16, 417–18, 422; Fagg, *Cuba, Haiti, and the Dominican Republic*, 133.

15. Maturin Ballou, touring Haiti in the mid-19th century, deplored the chaotic condition of the masses. He compared those living in the interior with the inhabitants of Tierra del Fuego; some of the black peasants, he maintained, even continued the practice of cannibalism. Maturin Ballou, *Equatorial America: A Description of a Visit to St. Thomas, Martinique, Barbadoes, and the Principal Capitals of South America* (Boston: Houghton, 1900), 5.

16. Parry and Sherlock, *West Indies*, 169; Logan, *Haiti and the Dominican Republic*, 97–98.

17. After the assassination of Dessalines in 1806, Christophe ruled the area north of the Artibonite River, known as the State of Haiti, and Pétion ruled the area to the south, known as the Republic of Haiti.

18. John V. Lombardi, *The Decline and Abolition of Negro Slavery in Venezuela, 1820–1854* (Westport, Conn.: Greenwood, 1971), 13, 41; Harold Bierck, "The Struggle for Abolition in Gran Colombia," *Hispanic American Historical Review* 33 (Aug. 1953), 365, 386; Harold Bierck, ed., *Selected Writings of Bolívar*, 2 vols. (New York: Colonial Press, 1951), I, 222–23; II, 599.

19. Bierck, *Bolívar*, I, 308; II, 483, 546.

20. *Ibid.*, II, 562.

21. *Ibid.*, 499; Logan, *Haiti and the Dominican Republic*, 100.

22. Gwendolyn M. Hall, *Social Control in Plantation Societies: A Comparison of St. Domingue and Cuba* (Baltimore: Johns Hopkins Press, 1971), 126; "Mémoire historique," Rochambeau Documents, 91; Billy Moulton to Arthur and Andrew Company, Jan. 10, 1805, Parker Family Papers (Essex Institute); Hugh Thomas, *Cuba: The Pursuit of Freedom* (New York: Harper, 1971), 90.

23. In 1825 Secretary of State Henry Clay supported the planters of Cuba and warned Colombia and Mexico not to invade the colony. Another Negro revolution, Clay believed, might spread to the American South; moreover, it might complicate the designs of the U.S. to annex Cuba. Thomas, *Cuba*, 104.

24. Parry and Sherlock, *West Indies*, 224; Arthur Corwin, *Spain and the*

Abolition of Slavery in Cuba, 1817–1886 (Austin: Univ. of Texas Press, 1967), 12, 51, 70, 89, 220.

25. Corwin, *Abolition of Slavery in Cuba*, 81–82, 250.

26. *Mirror of the Times and General Advertiser*, Nov. 6, 1802.

27. Letter Extract from Georgetown, S. C., Oct. 7, 1802, in Boston *Gazette*, Nov. 1, 1802; U.S., Dept. of State, *The Territorial Papers of the United States*, ed. Clarence Carter, 27 vols. (Government Printing Office, 1934–), IX, 326; Donnan, *Documents*, IV, 663.

28. Donnan, *Documents*, IV, 663.

29. Gram to Vanderhorts, Aug. 16, 1793, San Domingo File; Boston *Gazette*, Oct. 9, 1800; Herbert Aptheker, *American Negro Slave Revolts* (New York: International Publishers, 1943), 96; John Lofton, *Insurrection in South Carolina: The Turbulent World of Denmark Vesey* (Yellow Springs, Ohio: Antioch Press, 1964), 143; Dwight Dumond, *Antislavery: The Crusade for Freedom in America* (Ann Arbor: Univ. of Michigan Press, 1961), 112–13; Robert McColley, *Slavery and Jeffersonian Virginia* (Urbana: Univ. of Illinois Press, 1964), 49.

30. Winthrop Jordan, *White over Black: American Attitudes Toward the Negro, 1550–1812* (Chapel Hill: Univ. of North Carolina Press, 1968), 384.

31. *Prelude to Civil War: The Nullification Controversy in South Carolina* (New York: Harper, 1965), 16, 55, 60, 112, 114.

32. Oscar Sherwin, *Prophet of Liberty: The Life and Times of Wendell Phillips* (New York: Bookman Associates, 1958), 419; Ralph Korngold, *Two Friends of Man: The Story of William Lloyd Garrison and Wendell Phillips, and their Relationship with Abraham Lincoln* (Boston: Little, 1950), 315–16; Arthur Zilversmit, *The First Emancipation: The Abolition of Slavery in the North* (Chicago: Univ. of Chicago Press, 1967), 202–203; Louis Filler, *The Crusade Against Slavery, 1830–1860* (New York: Harper, 1960), 140; Truman Nelson, ed., *Documents of Upheaval* (New York: Hill, 1966), 43–44.

33. Orlando Patterson, *The Sociology of Slavery: An Analysis of the Origins, Development and Structure of Negro Slave Society in Jamaica* (Rutherford, N. J.: Fairleigh Dickinson Univ. Press, 1969), 277, 279; Alec Waugh, *A Family of Islands* (Garden City, N. Y.: Doubleday, 1964), 242–46; Burn, *British West Indies*, 114–19; Parry and Sherlock, *West Indies*, 180–86.

34. Parry and Sherlock, *West Indies*, 186–87; Roberts, *French West Indies*, 245.

35. Allen W. Trelease, *White Terror: The Ku Klux Klan Conspiracy and Southern Reconstruction* (New York: Harper, 1971), 8, 31, 38–39, 73, 93.

36. *The Rising Tide of Color Against White World Supremacy* (New York: Scribners, 1920), 100–101, 227n.

37. *Ibid.*, 227n.

38. Myra Himelhoch, "Frederick Douglass and Haiti's Môle St. Nicolas,"

Journal of Negro History 56 (July 1971), 174–75, 178–79; Frederick Douglass, *Life and Times of Frederick Douglass* (New York: Macmillan, 1962), 596, 601–602, 606, 613–14.

39. Douglass, *Life and Times*, 613.

40. Brawley, *A Social History of the American Negro*, 2d ed. (New York: Macmillan, 1971), 84, 114–15, 330, 341, 366.

41. Edmund David Cronon, *Black Moses: The Story of Marcus Garvey and the Universal Negro Improvement Association* (Madison: Univ. of Wisconsin Press, 1955), 46–47, 177; Amy Jacques Garvey, *Garvey and Garveyism* (New York: Macmillan, 1970), vii–xv.

42. Ivar Oxaal, *Black Intellectuals Come to Power: The Rise of Creole Nationalism in Trinidad and Tobago* (Cambridge, Mass.: Schenkman, 1968), 74–77; James, *Black Jacobins*, 85–86, 120, 128, 283–84.

43. James, *Black Jacobins*, 399–402; Césaire, *Toussaint, passim*; Shelby T. McCloy, *The Negro in France* (Lexington: Univ. of Kentucky Press, 1961), 181.

44. *The World and Africa* (New York: Viking, 1947), 65–66, 195; *The Autobiography of W. E. B. DuBois* (New York: International Publishers, 1968), 352.

45. Jones, *Home: Social Essays* (New York: Morrow, 1966), 61.

Bibliography

O f the various subjects with which historians frequently occupy themselves, the study of revolutions has been a favorite. Although the American, French, Russian,
and Mexican revolutions have received the attention of many scholars,
the Haitian Revolution has remained in relative obscurity, despite the
efforts of an occasional historian. Even those who have made a study
of that upheaval often viewed much of the conflict ideologically, varying from T. Lothrop Stoddard's white racism to C. L. R. James's
Marxism. Thus one purpose of this book has been to bring the Haitian
Revolution into clearer historical perspective.

To do this, it was necessary to concentrate on many non-French
sources. Among them are the many accounts, mainly written by
Yankee seamen, which can be found in American newspapers of the
late eighteenth and early nineteenth centuries. While not always accurate or unemotional, these virtually untapped reservoirs of information
are generally the most objective accounts of the Haitian Revolution.
American consul reports are also good sources: especially did Edward
Stevens, American consul general in Saint-Domingue, write letters of
keen observation and detachment. Another good non-French supply
of information is the journal which Lieutenant Howard, a member of
the British forces in Saint-Domingue, recorded. Howard has left little
doubt that the fighting ability of the Negro has been underrated in
most previous assessments of the Haitian Revolution. Two other narratives of specialized value are Samuel Perkins' *Reminiscences* and
Mary Hassal's *Secret History*. The former gives the historian an insight
into Toussaint's complex character, and the latter allows him to glimpse
the brutality and destruction of the last years of the revolution.

The many French sources, some practically unused until now, were
not neglected in this study. Among them are the important papers of
Etienne Laveaux, Léger Félicité Sonthonax, Philippe Roume, Donatien
Rochambeau, and Charles Victor Emmanuel Leclerc, to name a few.
As an untapped collection, the Rochambeau Papers are of great use

because they bring the period after Leclerc's death (November 1802) into clearer focus than do other primary materials.

Several French travel accounts, especially those picturing Saint-Domingue before the revolution, are also important primary resources. Moreau de Saint-Méry's *La Partie française* and Baron de Wimpffen's *Voyage to Saint-Domingo* are the best of the prerevolution accounts. *My Odyssey*, an anonymous narrative by a white creole refugee, is essential for a study of the early phases of the revolution. Especially revealing are the author's statements about Jean François and about French attitudes toward the black rebels.

Many secondary works were used to complement the primary sources in this study. For the period before the revolution, Pierre Vaissière's *Saint-Domingue* (1909) stands as the foremost work. No historian has equaled Vaissière's careful research of Saint-Domingue before 1789, but one does have to guard against his occasional bias in favor of the white planters. An interesting synthesis of basically secondary works on Saint-Domingue before the revolution is Gwendolyn Hall's *Social Control in Plantation Societies* (1971). Her work, however, lacks depth in primary research.

The revolution itself has drawn the attention of several historians and biographers. In addition to the fact that the monographs of James and Stoddard are marred with extreme bias, lack of scholarship has blemished other works, especially biographies. Ann Griffiths' *Black Patriot and Martyr* (1970) is the most recent of a succession of such works on Toussaint Louverture. She viewed Toussaint as a super-hero and generally excused his Machiavellian and egocentric traits. The Toussaint of her biography battled for black freedom and was invincible both on the battlefield and at the conference table. Griffiths also used quotations, even precise dialogues, without footnoting them; one would be interested in seeing her sources. In fact, the research in this biography is weak. A better study is Ralph Korngold's *Citizen Toussaint* (1944), a thoughtful but not always scholarly biography. Korngold viewed Toussaint as the main and most forceful black leader in the Haitian Revolution; moreover, he brought to light some of Toussaint's personality characteristics, such as his religious nature, and did not excuse the black leader's slaughter of mulattoes after the "War of the Knives." But Korngold's assertions that Toussaint planned the revolution in 1791 and that he saw the goal of independence in 1796 detract from the value of the study. Stephen Alexis' *Black Liberator* (1949) is useful in analyzing Toussaint's rise to political power, his military achievements, and his paradoxical character. Alexis' study stands above Aimé Césaire's *Toussaint* (1960) because the latter, although temperate on most matters, is not well researched. The definitive biography of Toussaint Louverture is yet to be written.

Biographies about Toussaint's lieutenants are sparse and of low quality. One exception is Hubert Cole's *Christophe* (1967), which is well documented. Tracing Christophe's political career from 1791 to 1820, Cole portrayed Christophe as disciplinarian, reformer, and white aspirant; perhaps Cole's greatest weakness is his failure to see the revolutionary aspects of Toussaint's programs. Nonetheless, this is at present the best biography about a black or mulatto leader of the revolution.

For the impact of the revolution upon other countries and colonies of the Western Hemisphere, there are a number of beneficial studies. Hall's *Social Control in Plantation Societies* (1971) contains valuable information about the fear Cuban planters experienced because of slavery; such social paranoia was ignited by the Haitian upheaval. Hugh Thomas' *Cuba* (1971) is even more important for tracing the socioeconomic impact of the revolution upon the island colony. William Freehling's *Prelude to the Civil War* (1965) and Allen Trelease's *White Terror* (1971) are significant in determining the influence of the revolution upon the United States. There was, according to Freehling, a close connection between the explosion in Haiti and the Denmark Vesey conspiracy in South Carolina. Trelease has shown that the fear of a Haitian Revolution in the South shaped Southern white attitudes even after the Civil War.

Of the recent books dealing with the influence of the revolution upon Haiti, two are extremely important: James Leyburn's *Haitian People* (1941) and Katherine Dunham's *Island Possessed* (1969). Leyburn's work gives a good view of the overall impact of the revolution upon Haiti from 1804 to 1941; Dunham's work is essential for the period after 1941. Of particular interest is her observation that the last three Haitian "presidents" identified with and acted in the tradition of certain key figures of the revolution.

PRIMARY SOURCES

Manuscripts

Barbot-Chartrand Papers. South Carolina Historical Society, Charleston.

A collection of limited use but one which contains several important references concerning the economic havoc of the Haitian Revolution.

Matbon de la Cour, "Sur la Traite et l'Esclavage des Nègres." Library of Congress, Washington, D.C., and Bibliothèque de l'Académie, Lyons, France.

This document deals primarily with the treatment of the slaves in Saint-Domingue on the eve of the Haitian Revolution. The oppression of the blacks is a persistent theme.

France, Ministère des Affaires Étrangères, correspondance politique, États-Unis. Library of Congress, Washington, D.C., and Les Archives des Affaires Étrangères, Paris.

A few letters in the collection relate to Jefferson's policy toward Saint-Domingue, especially the letter from Pichon to Talleyrand dated July 22, 1801.

France, Ministère de la Guerre, Mémoire historique, "Saint-Domingue, 1791–1803." Library of Congress, Washington, D.C., and Les Archives du Ministère de la Guerre, Paris.

This brief version of the Haitian Revolution reported by the French military presents a good view of the low regard many whites had of Negro accomplishments in Saint-Domingue.

Edmond C. Genêt Papers. Library of Congress, Washington, D.C.

Genêt, who came to the United States in 1793 as a French diplomat, wrote and received several important letters concerning the early phases of upheaval in Saint-Domingue. Royalism, often associated with the white planters, is discussed in several of the writings.

Great Britain, Public Record Office, Colonial Office 137/50, Jamaica Correspondence. Library of Congress, Washington, D.C., and Public Record Office, London.

In detecting the reasons for the British invasion of Saint-Domingue and in understanding Toussaint's relationship with England after 1798, the Jamaica Correspondence is a necessity.

Great Britain, Public Record Office, Colonial Office 245/1, San Domingo Correspondence. Library of Congress, Washington, D.C., and Public Record Office, London.

Although a small collection of letters, this file of correspondence contains valuable information regarding the British failure to defeat Toussaint.

Lieutenant Howard, "Journal of the Army of Occupation in Haiti from February 8, 1796, to January, 1798." 3 vols. Boston Public Library, Boston.

Howard, a keen observer with a high respect for the black rebels, recorded one of the best accounts of the entire British invasion (1793–1798), emphasizing especially the last two years.

Rufus King Papers. Henry E. Huntington Library, San Marino, Calif.

Serving as an American diplomat to England during the Haitian Revolution, King wrote several significant letters dealing with American-British relations in regard to Saint-Domingue. One letter, written on March 7, 1799, from Timothy Pickering to Edward Stevens, is especially useful in determining the economic role of the United States in Toussaint's rising black state.

Etienne Laveaux Papers. Library of Congress, Washington, D.C., and Bibliothèque Nationale, Paris.

In tracing the political rise of Toussaint and the period from 1793 to 1797, the Laveaux Papers are indispensable.

Charles Victor E. Leclerc Papers. Univ. of Florida Research Library, Gainesville.

While neither indexed nor a total compilation of Leclerc's papers, this material proved useful in assessing the early months of Napoleon's invasion of Saint-Domingue.

Manigalt Papers. South Carolina Historical Society, Charleston.

Although providing the researcher with information concerning the plight of the white caste in Saint-Domingue, the Manigalt Papers do not generally focus on the Haitian Revolution.

DuBois Martin Papers. Maryland Historical Society, Baltimore.

These documents have a limited use in a study of the Haitian Revolution, but they do contain several good descriptions of the economic dislocation which Saint-Domingue suffered after 1791.

Maynadier-Gibson Papers. Maryland Historical Society, Baltimore.

This collection has a few letters of importance which deal with the economic devastation and migrations of the Haitian Revolution.

Miscellaneous Papers. Maryland Historical Society, Baltimore.

In determining the shifting economic conditions of Saint-Domingue, these papers are of some value.

Miscellaneous Papers. South Carolina Historical Society, Charleston.

There are scattered references throughout this collection about the socioeconomic destruction of the white caste in Saint-Domingue.

Sir George Nugent Papers. Institute of Jamaica, Kingston, Jamaica.

Nugent, a former governor of Jamaica, maintained correspondence with Toussaint and various British agents. Covering the period from 1793 to 1806, the collection is especially significant for its inclusion of letters which Nugent wrote to Edward Corbet, a British envoy in Saint-Domingue during the last months of the French invasion.

Parker Family Papers. Essex Institute, Salem, Mass.

Of limited value for a study of the Haitian Revolution, the Parker Papers contain some pertinent information regarding Saint-Domingue's commercial relations with New England before and immediately after 1791. The utility of the collection could be increased with a better index.

Donatien Rochambeau Documents. Univ. of Florida Research Library, Gainesville.

Composed of several official French publications and of an important anonymous memoir, the Rochambeau Documents are significant and cover the Haitian Revolution expansively.

Donatien Rochambeau Papers. Univ. of Florida Research Library, Gainesville.

These papers, many of them field dispatches, are the most important single collection for the period after Leclerc's death and perhaps for the whole period of the French invasion, 1802–1804. The papers are well organized and indexed.

Philippe Roume Papers. Library of Congress, Washington, D.C.

This is a very important compilation of letters and dispatches, which Roume probably left in the United States, the land of his temporary exile. In tracing Toussaint's rise to power after 1797, these writings are a necessity.

San Domingo File. South Carolina Archives, Columbia.

A collection which contains important information about the early phases of the Haitian Revolution and about South Carolina's reaction to that upheaval.

Léger Félicité Sonthonax Correspondence. Library of Congress, Washington, D.C., and Bibliothèque Nationale, Paris.

This collection of letters is of the utmost importance for the period of 1796 through 1797, the twilight years of Sonthonax's political career in Saint-Domingue.

Spain, Sección de Estado, Legajos 3,895 and 3,897. Library of Congress, Washington, D.C., and Archivo Histórico Nacional, Madrid. These files contain mostly diplomatic dispatches between the Spanish embassy in Philadelphia with officials of Spain in Santo Domingo. These collections are useful in understanding the Toussaint-Rigaud struggle and the Negro invasion of Santo Domingo.

Silas Talbot Papers. Marine Historical Association, Mystic Seaport, Conn.

Talbot served as a commander in the United States Navy off the coast of Saint-Domingue, and his accounts are particularly valuable for the period from 1799 through 1800.

U.S., Dept. of State, Consular Dispatches, Cap-Haitien. 17 vols., 1797–1906. National Archives, Washington, D.C.

The first four volumes pertain to the Haitian Revolution and are important for the years 1797–1801. Edward Stevens, who wrote many of the dispatches, was a close friend of Toussaint and had access to information not commonly available to many other observers.

U.S., Dept. of State, Consular Dispatches, Kingston, Jamaica. 40 vols., 1797–1906. National Archives, Washington, D.C.

Only the first volume pertains to the Haitian Revolution, and its use is restricted mainly to the relationship between Jamaica and Saint-Domingue.

U.S., Dept. of State, Consular Dispatches, Les Cayes, Haiti. 4 vols., 1797–1906. National Archives, Washington, D.C.

Only the first few messages of the first volume contain any important information about the Haitian Revolution in general or in South Province specifically.

U.S., Dept. of State, Consular Dispatches, St. Pierre, Martinique. 11 vols., 1790–1906. National Archives, Washington, D.C.

Volume 1 alone contains a small number of messages for the period of 1790–1804; all subsequent volumes cover events after 1804. These few dispatches, however, reveal the general turmoil of the French Caribbean.

U.S., Dept. of State, Diplomatic Dispatches, France. 128 vols., 1789–1906. National Archives, Washington, D.C.

In the first eight volumes scattered references to Saint-Domingue can be found. The chief value of those references is that they demonstrate the various diplomatic problems surrounding the Haitian Revolution.

Newspapers

Bahama Gazette (Nassau), 1789–1804.
Baltimore *Daily Repository*, 1791–1793.
Baltimore *Federal Gazette*, 1796–1804.
Baltimore *Federal Intelligencer*, 1794–1795.
Baltimore *Intelligencer*, 1798–1799.
Boston *Gazette*, 1789–1802.
Boston *Independent Chronicle*, 1789–1804.
Boston *Price-Current*, 1795–1798.
Bulletin Officiel de Saint-Domingue (Le Cap François), 1791–1804.
Charleston *City Gazette*, 1789–1804.
Charleston *Times*, 1800–1804.
Cornwall Chronicle (Montego Bay, Jamaica), 1796–1798.
Le Courier de L'Amérique (Philadelphia), 1792–1793.
Courrier Français (Philadelphia), 1794–1798.
Courrier de la France et des Colonies (Philadelphia), 1795–1798.
Courrier Politique (Philadelphia), 1793–1794.
L'Étoile Américaine (Philadelphia), 1794.
Gazette Nationale, ou Le Moniteur Universel (Paris), 1789–1804.
Gazette Officielle de Saint-Domingue (Le Cap François), 1789–1804.
Journal des Révolutions (New York), 1793.
Maryland Journal and Baltimore Advertiser, 1789–1797.
Minerva and Mercantile Evening Advertiser (New York), 1796–1797.
Mirror of the Times and General Advertiser (Wilmington, Del.), 1799–1804.
Moniteur de la Louisiane (New Orleans), 1794–1804.
Newport *Mercury*, 1789–1804.
New York *Daily Gazette*, 1789–1795.
New York *Evening Post*, 1794–1795, 1801–1804.
Le Patriote françois (Paris), 1789–1804.
Philadelphia *Aurora*, 1794–1804.
Philadelphia *General Advertiser*, 1790–1794.
Providence *Gazette and Country Journal*, 1789–1804.
St. George's *Chronicle and Grenada Gazette*, 1798–1799.
Salem *Gazette*, 1790–1804.
State Gazette of South Carolina (Charleston), 1789–1793.
The Times (London), 1789–1804.

Ships' Logs

Herald, "Journal of a West Indies Cruise, April 24, 1799 to May 9, 1799." Essex Institute, Salem, Mass.

Industry, "West Indies, December 10, 1801, to May 22, 1802." Phillips Library in the Peabody Museum, Salem, Mass.

Matilda, "West Indies, November 12, 1796, to May 29, 1797." Marine Historical Association, Mystic Seaport, Conn.

Retrieve, "Newburyport to the West Indies, May 13, 1796, to February 8, 1797." Phillips Library in the Peabody Museum, Salem, Mass.

Public Documents

France, Convention Nationale, *Précis de la justification de Joseph-Paul-Augustin Cambefort, Colonel du Régiment du Cap, et des autres Militaires déportés de Saint-Domingue, Rigoureusement demontrée par les seules Pieces deposées au Comité Colonial de la Convention Nationale.* Paris: N. H. Nyon, 1793.

France, *Lettre du Comité Colonial de France, au Comité Colonial de Saint-Domingue.* Paris: n.n., 1788.

France, Ministère de Finance, *État Détaillé des Liquidations par la Commission chargée de répartir l'Indemnité attribuée aux ancien Colons de Saint-Domingue, en exécution de la loi du 30 avril, 1826, et conformément aux dispositions de l'Ordonnance du mai suivant.* Paris: De L'Imprimerie Royale, 1831.

France, Ministère de la Guerre, *Correspondance de Napoléon 1er.* 32 vols. Paris: Henri Plom, 1858–70.

France, *Recueil des Actes du Comité de Salut Public: Collection de Documents Inédits sur L'Histoire de France.* 30 vols. Paris: Imprimerie Nationale, 1894–99.

Great Britain, *A Collection of State Papers Relative to the War Against France Now Carrying on by Great Britain.* John Debrett, ed. 10 vols. London: n.n., 1794–1801.

Great Britain, War Office, *Bulletins of the Campaign, 1793–1815.* 20 vols. London: A. Strahan, 1794–1816.

Guadeloupe, *Rapport fait a L'Assemblée coloniale de la Guadeloupe.* Paris: Postillon, 1790.

North Province, Assemblée Provinciale du Nord, *Adresse des membres de L'Assemblée Provinciale du Nord de Saint-Domingue à L'Assemblée Nationale.* Paris: Imprimerie Nationale, 1790.

Pennsylvania, *The Pennsylvania Archives.* Series 9. 10 vols. Philadelphia: J. Severns, 1852–56.

Santo Domingo, Assemblée Générale, *A Particular Account of the Insurrection of the Negroes in St. Domingo, begun in August, 1791.* London: J. Sewell, 1792.

U.S., *State Papers and Publick Documents of the United States.* Boston: Thomas Wait, 1819.

U.S., Congress. *Annals of Congress, 1789–1824.* 42 vols. Washington, D.C.: Gales and Seaton, 1834–56.

U.S., Dept. of Navy, *Naval Documents related to the Quasi-War between the United States and France.* 7 vols. Washington, D.C.: Government Printing Office, 1935–38.

U.S., Dept. of State. *The Territorial Papers of the United States.* Clarence Carter, ed. 27 vols. Washington, D.C.: Government Printing Office, 1934–.

Published Journals, Memoirs, Diaries,
and Other Primary Sources

Almanach de Saint-Domingue. Port-au-Prince: De L'Imprimerie de Mozard, 1790.

Anderson, Frank, ed., *The Constitutions and Other Select Documents Illustrative of the History of France, 1789–1907.* 2d ed. New York: Russell and Russell, 1908.

Ballou, Maturin, *Equatorial America: A Description of a Visit to St. Thomas, Martinique, Barbadoes, and the Principal Capitals of South America.* Boston: Houghton, 1900.

Bierck, Harold, ed., *Selected Writings of Bolívar.* 2 vols. New York: Colonial Press, 1951.

Bonaparte, Josephine, *Memoirs of the Empress Josephine.* 2 vols. New York: Merrill and Baker, 1903.

Bossu, Jean-Bernard, *Travels in North America, 1751–1762.* Seymour Feiler, trans. and ed. Norman: Univ. of Oklahoma Press, 1962.

Bourrienne, Louis Antoine Fauvelet de, *Memoirs of Napoleon Bonaparte.* 4 vols. New York: Scribners, 1890.

Brawley, Benjamin, *A Social History of the American Negro.* 2d ed. New York: Macmillan, 1971.

Brissot de Warville, Jacques Pierre, *J. P. Brissot: Mémoires.* 2 vols. Paris: A. Picard et Fils, 1911.

————, *Oration upon the Necessity of Establishing at Paris, A Society to Promote the Abolition of the Trade and Slavery of the Negroes.* Philadelphia: Francis Bailey, 1788.

Caulaincourt, Armand de, *With Napoleon in Russia.* New York: Morrow, 1935.

Chazotte, Peter S., *Historical Sketches of the Revolution, and the Foreign and Civil War in the Island of St. Domingo, with a Narrative of the Entire Massacre of the White Population of the Island: Eyewitness Report.* New York: William Applegate, 1840.

Clarkson, Thomas, *The History of the Rise, Progress, and Accomplishment of the Abolition of the African Slave-Trade by the British Parliament.* Philadelphia: Brown and Merritt, 1808.

Cocherel, Robert de, Marquis de Nicolas, *Réclamations de Marquis de Nicolas, Robert de Cocherel, Relative au travail du Comité des Douze sur le mode de convocation des Assemblées des Colonies.* Paris: n.n., 1790.

Conscience, André, *André Conscience à La Convention Nationale sur les derniers événements de Saint-Domingue.* Paris: n.n., 1794.

Considérations politique sur les Esclaves. Paris: Chez Baudouin, n.d.

Corbett, Julian, ed., *Private Papers of George, Second Earl of Spencer: First Lord of the Admiralty.* London: Naval Records Society, 1913.

Correspondance secrète des Députés de Saint-Domingue avec les Comités de cette île. Paris: n.n., 1790.

De Chair, Somerset, ed., *Napoleon's Memoirs.* New York: Harper, 1948.

Descourtilz, Michel E., *Voyages d'un Naturaliste et Ses Observations.* 3 vols. Paris: Dufart, 1809.

Discours sur les Troubles de Saint-Domingue. Paris: L'Imprimerie du Patriote françois, 1789.

Dissertation sur La Nécessité de L'Ouverture des Ports de Saint-Domingue à toutes Les Nations. Paris: Chez Desenne, 1794.

Donnan, Elizabeth, ed., *Documents Illustrative of the History of the Slave Trade to America.* 4 vols. New York: Octagon Books, 1965.

Douglass, Frederick, *Life and Times of Frederick Douglass.* New York: Macmillan, 1962.

DuBois, W. E. B., *The Autobiography of W. E. B. DuBois.* New York: International Publishers, 1968.

————, *The World and Africa.* New York: Viking, 1947.

Dunham, Katherine, *Island Possessed.* Garden City, N. Y.: Doubleday, 1969.

Essai sur L'Administration des Colonies Françoises. Paris: Chez Monory, 1788.

Ford, Worthington C., ed., *The Writings of John Quincy Adams.* 7 vols. New York: Macmillan, 1913–17.

Garran de Coulon, Jean Philippe, *Rapport sur les troubles de Saint-Domingue, fait au nom de la Commission des Colonies, des Co-*

mités de Salut Public, de Législation et de Marint réunis. 6 vols. Paris: De L'Imprimerie Nationale, 1799.

Gourgaud, Gaspard, *Saint Hélène: Journal inédit de 1815 à 1818.* 2 vols. Paris: Flammarion, n.d.

Grégoire, Abbé Henri-Baptiste, *Mémoires de Grégoire, ancien évêque de Blois, député à l'Assemblée Constituante.* 2 vols. Paris: A. Dupont, 1837.

Gros, M., *Récit historique sur les qui se succédes dans les camps de la Grande-Rivière, du Dondon, de Ste.-Suzanne et autres, depuis le 26 Octobre jusqu'au 24 Decembre de la même année.* Baltimore: S. and J. Adams, 1793.

Harlow, Vincent, and Frederick Madden, eds., *British Colonial Developments, 1774–1834: Select Documents.* Oxford: Clarendon, 1953.

Hassal, Mary, *Secret History of the Horrors of St. Domingo in a Series of Letters Written by a Lady at Cape François to Colonel Burr, Late Vice-President of the United States.* Philadelphia: Bradford and Inskeep, 1808.

Herold, J. Christopher, ed., *The Mind of Napoleon: A Selection from his Written and Spoken Words.* New York: Columbia Univ. Press, 1955.

Howard, John E., ed., *Letters and Documents of Napoleon.* 1 vol. New York: Oxford Univ. Press, 1961.

Jones, LeRoi, *Home: Social Essays.* New York: Morrow, 1966.

Lacroix, François Joseph Pamphile, *Mémoires pour servir à l'historique de la révolution de Saint-Domingue.* 2 vols. Paris: Pillet Aine, 1820.

Laurent, Gerard, ed., *Toussaint Louverture à travers sa correspondance, 1794–1798.* Madrid: Gerard Laurent, 1953.

"Letters of Toussaint L'Ouverture and of Edward Stevens, 1798–1800," *American Historical Review* 16 (Oct. 1910), 64–101.

"Letters Written in 1799 by Steven Higginson," *American Historical Association Annual Report,* 1896, I (1897), 824–30.

Lodge, Henry Cabot, ed., *The Works of Alexander Hamilton.* 12 vols. New York: Putnam's, 1904.

Louverture, Toussaint, *Mémoires du Général Toussaint L'Ouverture.* Paris: Pagnerre, 1853.

McKitrick, Eric L., ed., *Slavery Defended: The Views of the Old South.* Englewood Cliffs, N. J.: Prentice-Hall, 1963.

Maurel, Blanche, ed., *Cahiers de doléances de la colonie de Saint-Domingue.* Paris: Libraire Ernest Leroux, 1933.

Moreau de Saint-Méry, Medéric-Louis-Élie, *Description topographique, physique, civile, politique, et historique de la Partie française de l'île de Saint-Domingue.* 2 vols. Philadelphia: Chez l'auteur, 1798.

———, *A Topographical and Political Description of the Spanish Part of Saint-Domingue.* 2 vols. Philadelphia: Chez l'auteur, 1796.

Morison, Samuel Eliot, trans. and ed., *Journals and Other Documents in the Life and Voyages of Christopher Columbus.* New York: Dial (Heritage), 1963.

Nelson, Truman, ed., *Documents of Upheaval.* New York: Hill, 1966.

Parham, Althéa de Puech, trans. and ed., *My Odyssey: Experiences of a Young Refugee from Two Revolutions, By a Creole of Saint-Domingue.* Baton Rouge: Louisiana State Univ. Press, 1959.

Perin, René, *L'incendie du Cap; ou, Le règne de Toussaint Louverture.* Paris: Marchand, 1802.

Perkins, Samuel G., *Reminiscences of the Insurrection in St. Domingo.* Cambridge, Mass.: Harvard Univ. Press, 1886.

Perroud, Claude, ed., *J. P. Brissot, Correspondance et Papiers.* 2 vols. Paris: Alphonse Picard et fils, 1912.

Pétition des Citoyens de couleur des Colonies. Paris: n.n., 1796.

Réflexions sur le sort des Noirs dans nos Colonies. Paris: De L'Imprimerie Nationale, 1789.

Roberts, J. M., and R. C. Cobb, eds., *French Revolution Documents.* 1 vol. New York: Barnes and Noble, 1966–.

Roussier, Paul, ed., *Lettres du général Leclerc.* Paris: Société de l'Histoire des colonies françaises, 1937.

Sparks, Jared, ed., *The Writings of George Washington.* 12 vols. Boston: Russell, Shattuck and Williams, 1834–37.

Stanislaus, François Alexandre, Baron de Wimpffen, *A Voyage to Saint-Domingo, In the Years 1788, 1789, and 1790.* J. Wright, trans. London: T. Codell and W. Davies, 1797.

Steward, John H., ed., *A Documentary Survey of the French Revolution.* New York: Macmillan, 1951.

Stoddard, T. Lothrop, *The Rising Tide of Color Against White World Supremacy.* New York: Scribners, 1920.

Syrett, Harold, ed., *The Papers of Alexander Hamilton.* 13 vols. New York: Columbia Univ. Press, 1961–67.

Thibaudeau, Antoine Claire, *Mémoires sur le Consulat, 1799 à 1804, par un ancien conseiller d'état.* Paris: Ponthieu, 1827.

Tousard, Louis, *Lt. colonel du Régiment du Cap, à la Convention Nationale.* Paris: N. H. Nyon, 1793.

Wilber, Richard, ed., *Wordsworth.* New York: Dell, 1959.

SECONDARY SOURCES

Books

Adams, Henry, *History of the United States of America during the Administration of Thomas Jefferson*. 2 vols. New York: A. and C. Boni, 1930.

Addington, Henry, *The Crisis of the Sugar Colonies, or an Inquiry into the Probable Effects of the French Expedition on the West Indies*. London: J. Hatchard, 1802.

Alexis, Stephen, *Black Liberator: The Life of Toussaint Louverture*. William Sterling, trans. New York: Macmillan, 1949.

Aptheker, Herbert, *American Negro Slave Revolts*. New York: International Publishers, 1943.

Arciniegas, Germán, *Latin America: A Cultural History*. Joan MacLean, trans. New York: Knopf, 1966.

Burn, William Laurence, *The British West Indies*. London: Hutchinson House, 1951.

Cancelalada, Juan López, *La Vida de J. J. Dessalines*. Mexico City: Ontiveros, 1809.

Cannon, Richard, *Historical Record of the Fifty-Sixth or the West Essex Regiment of Foot*. London: Parker, Turnwell, and Parker, 1844.

————, *Historical Record of the Seventeenth Regiment or the Leicestershire Regiment of Foot*. London: Parker, Turnwell, and Parker, 1848.

————, *Historical Record of the Thirteenth Regiment or Light Dragoons*. London: John W. Parker, 1842.

Césaire, Aimé, *Toussaint Louverture: La Révolution française et le problème colonial*. Paris: Le Club français du livre, 1960.

Chandler, David, *The Campaigns of Napoleon*. New York: Macmillan, 1966.

Clarkson, Thomas, *An Essay on the Impolicy of the African Slave Trade*. Philadelphia: Francis Bailey, 1788.

Cole, Hubert, *Christophe, King of Haiti*. New York: Viking, 1967.

Corwin, Arthur, *Spain and the Abolition of Slavery in Cuba, 1817–1886*. Austin: Univ. of Texas Press, 1967.

Coupland, Reginald, *The British Anti-Slavery Movement*. 2d ed. New York: Barnes and Noble, 1964.

Cronon, Edmund D., *Black Moses: The Story of Marcus Garvey and the Universal Negro Improvement Association*. Madison: Univ. of Wisconsin Press, 1955.

Crouse, Nellis, *The French Struggle for the West Indies, 1665–1713*. New York: Octagon Books, 1966.

Curtin, Philip D., *The Atlantic Slave Trade: A Census*. Madison: Univ. of Wisconsin Press, 1969.

Dangerfield, George, *Chancellor Robert R. Livingston of New York, 1746–1813*. New York: Harcourt, 1960.

Davidson, Basil, *History of West Africa to the Nineteenth Century*. Garden City, N.Y.: Anchor Books, 1966.

Davis, David B., *The Problem of Slavery in Western Culture*. Ithaca, N.Y.: Cornell Univ. Press, 1966.

Davis, H. P., *Black Democracy*. New York: Dial, 1928.

DeConde, Alexander, *The Quasi-War: The Politics and Diplomacy of the Undeclared War with France, 1797–1801*. New York: Scribners, 1966.

Dumond, Dwight L., *Antislavery: The Crusade for Freedom in America*. Ann Arbor: Univ. of Michigan Press, 1961.

Edwards, Bryan, *History, Civil and Commercial of the British Colonies in the West Indies*. 4 vols. Philadelphia: James Humphreys, 1806.

————, *An Historical Survey of the French Colony in the Island of San Domingo*. London: John Stockdale, 1797.

Elkins, Stanley, *Slavery: A Problem in American Institutional and Intellectual Life*. Chicago: Univ. of Chicago Press, 1959.

Ellery, Eloise, *Brissot de Warville: A Study in the History of the French Revolution*. Boston: Houghton, 1915.

Fagg, John, *Cuba, Haiti, and the Dominican Republic*. Englewood Cliffs, N. J.: Prentice-Hall, 1965.

Ferrell, Robert, *American Diplomacy*. New York: Norton, 1969.

Filler, Louis, *The Crusade Against Slavery, 1830–1860*. New York: Harper, 1960.

Fisher, H. A. L., *Napoleon*. 2d ed. New York: Oxford Univ. Press, 1967.

Foner, Philip S., *A History of Cuba*. 2 vols. New York: International Publishers, 1962.

Fortescue, J. W., *The British Army, 1793–1802*. London: Macmillan, 1905.

————, *A History of the British Army*. 13 vols. London: Macmillan, 1899–1930.

Freehling, William H., *Prelude to Civil War: The Nullification Controversy in South Carolina*. New York: Harper, 1965.

Garrett, Mitchell B., *The French Colonial Question, 1789–1791.* Ann Arbor: George Wahr Publishers, 1916.

Garvey, Amy Jacques, *Garvey and Garveyism.* New York: Macmillan, 1970.

Gershoy, Leo, *The French Revolution and Napoleon.* New York: Appleton, 1933.

Gibson, Charles, *Spain in America.* New York: Harper, 1966.

Greenidge, Charles W. W., *Slavery.* New York: Macmillan, 1958.

Griffiths, Ann, *Black Patriot and Martyr: Toussaint of Haiti.* New York: Julian Messner, 1970.

Griggs, Earl, and Clifford Prator, eds., *Henry Christophe and Thomas Clarkson: A Correspondence.* Berkeley: Univ. of California Press, 1952.

Hall, Gwendolyn, *Social Control in Plantation Societies: A Comparison of St. Domingue and Cuba.* Baltimore: Johns Hopkins Press, 1971.

Harlow, Vincent, *The Founding of the Second British Empire, 1763–1793.* 2 vols. London: Longmans, 1964.

Herold, J. Christopher, *The Age of Napoleon.* New York: American Heritage, 1963.

————, *Bonaparte in Egypt.* New York: Harper, 1962.

Herskovits, Melville J., *Life in a Haitian Valley.* New York: Octagon Books, 1964.

Hollander, Barnett, *Slavery in America: Its Legal History.* New York: Barnes and Noble, 1964.

Holtman, Robert, *The Napoleonic Revolution.* Philadelphia: Lippincott, 1967.

James, C. L. R., *The Black Jacobins.* 2d ed. New York: Vintage Books, 1963.

Jeffreys, Thomas, *The Natural and Civil History of the French Dominions in North and South America.* London: Charing-Gros, 1760.

Jenkins, William, *Pro-Slavery Thought in the Old South.* Chapel Hill: Univ. of North Carolina Press, 1935.

Jordan, Winthrop, *White over Black: American Attitudes toward the Negro, 1550–1812.* Chapel Hill: Univ. of North Carolina Press, 1968.

Klein, Herbert, *Slavery in the Americas: A Comparative Study of Virginia and Cuba.* Chicago: Univ. of Chicago Press, 1967.

Knight, Franklin, *Slave Society in Cuba during the Nineteenth Century.* Madison: Univ. of Wisconsin Press, 1970.

Korngold, Ralph, *Citizen Toussaint*. 2d ed. New York: Hill, 1965.

————, *Two Friends of Man: The Story of William Lloyd Garrison and Wendell Phillips, and their Relationship with Abraham Lincoln*. Boston: Little, 1950.

Lefebvre, Georges, *The French Revolution*. 2 vols. New York: Columbia Univ. Press, 1962.

————, *Napoleon*. 2 vols. New York: Columbia Univ. Press, 1969.

————, *The Thermidorians and the Directory*. New York: Random, 1964.

Leyburn, James G., *The Haitian People*. New Haven: Yale Univ. Press, 1941.

Lofton, John, *Insurrection in South Carolina: The Turbulent World of Denmark Vesey*. Yellow Springs, Ohio: Antioch Press, 1964.

Logan, Rayford W., *The Diplomatic Relations of the United States with Haiti, 1776–1891*. Chapel Hill: Univ. of North Carolina Press, 1941.

————, *Haiti and the Dominican Republic*. New York: Oxford Univ. Press, 1968.

Lokke, Carl L., *France and the Colonial Question, 1763–1801*. New York: Columbia Univ. Press, 1932.

Lombardi, John V., *The Decline and Abolition of Negro Slavery in Venezuela, 1820–1854*. Westport, Conn.: Greenwood, 1971.

Ludwig, Emil, *Napoleon*. New York: Horace Liveright, 1926.

Lyon, E. Wilson, *Bonaparte's Proposed Louisiana Expedition*. Chicago: Univ. of Chicago Press, 1932.

————, *The Man Who Sold Louisiana: The Career of Barbé-Marbois*. Norman: Univ. of Oklahoma Press, 1942.

McCloy, Shelby T., *The Negro in France*. Lexington: Univ. of Kentucky Press, 1961.

————, *The Negro in the French West Indies*. Lexington: Univ. of Kentucky Press, 1966.

McColley, Robert, *Slavery and Jeffersonian Virginia*. Urbana: Univ. of Illinois Press, 1964.

Madiou, Thomas, *Histoire d'Haiti*. 3 vols. 2d ed. Port-au-Prince: Département de l'Instruction Publique, 1922–23.

Mannix, Daniel, and Malcolm Cowley, *Black Cargoes: A History of the Atlantic Slave Trade, 1518–1865*. New York: Viking, 1962.

Markham, Felix, *Napoleon*. New York: New American Library, 1963.

Martin, John B., *Overtaken by Events: The Dominican Crisis from the Fall of Trujillo to the Civil War*. Garden City, N. Y.: Double-day, 1966.

Mathiez, Albert, *The French Revolution*. Catherine Phillips, trans. New York: Knopf, 1928.

Montague, Ludwell Lee, *Haiti and the United States, 1714–1938*. Durham, N.C.: Duke Univ. Press, 1940.

Morison, Samuel Eliot, *Admiral of the Ocean Sea: A Life of Christopher Columbus*. Boston: Little, 1942.

———, Henry S. Commager, and William E. Leuchtenburg. *The Growth of the American Republic*. 2 vols. 6th ed. New York: Oxford Univ. Press, 1969.

Oxaal, Ivar, *Black Intellectual Come to Power: The Rise of Creole Nationalism in Trinidad and Tobago*. Cambridge, Mass.: Schenkman, 1968.

Pares, Richard, *War and Trade in the West Indies, 1739–1763*. Oxford: Clarendon, 1936.

Parkes, Henry, *A History of Mexico*. Boston: Houghton, 1966.

Parry, J. H., and P. M. Sherlock, *A Short History of the West Indies*. London: Macmillan, 1956.

Patterson, Orlando, *The Sociology of Slavery: An Analysis of the Origins, Development and Structure of Negro Slave Society in Jamaica*. Rutherford, N. J.: Fairleigh Dickinson Univ. Press, 1969.

Perkins, Bradford, *The First Rapprochement*. Berkeley: Univ. of California Press, 1967.

Poyen, H. de, *Histoire militaire de la révolution de Saint-Domingue*. Paris: Berger-Levrault, 1899.

Quarles, Benjamin, *The Negro in the American Revolution*. Chapel Hill: Univ. of North Carolina Press, 1961.

Ragatz, Lowell J., *The Fall of the Planter Class in the British Caribbean, 1763–1833*. 2d ed. New York: Octagon Books, 1963.

Roberts, W. Adolphe, *The French in the West Indies*. Indianapolis: Bobbs-Merrill, 1942.

Robertson, William S., *France and Latin American Independence*. Baltimore: Johns Hopkins Press, 1939.

Rodman, Selden, *Haiti: The Black Republic*. New York: Devin-Adair, 1961.

Rose, J. Holland, *William Pitt and the Great War*. London: G. Bell and Sons, 1911.

Rudé, George, *Revolutionary Europe, 1783–1815*. New York: Harper, 1964.

Saintoyant, J., *La Colonisation Française pendant La Période Napoléonienne, 1799–1815.* Paris: La Renaissance du Livre, 1931.

Sherrard, Owen W., *Freedom from Fear: The Slave and His Emancipation.* New York: St. Martin's Press, 1959.

Sherwin, Oscar, *Prophet of Liberty: The Life and Times of Wendell Phillips.* New York: Bookman Associates, 1958.

Sloan, William M., *The Life of Napoleon Bonaparte.* 4 vols. New York: Century, 1909.

Stoddard, T. Lothrop, *The French Revolution in San Domingo.* Boston: Houghton, 1914.

Sydenham, M. J., *The French Revolution.* New York: Capricorn Books, 1966.

Tannenbaum, Frank, *Slave and Citizen: The Negro in the Americas.* New York: Knopf, 1947.

Thomas, Hugh, *Cuba: The Pursuit of Freedom.* New York: Harper, 1971.

Thompson, James M., *The French Revolution.* New York: Oxford Univ. Press, 1945.

———, *Napoleon Bonaparte.* New York: Oxford Univ. Press, 1952.

———, *Robespierre.* 2 vols. New York: Appleton, 1936.

Trelease, Allen W., *White Terror: The Ku Klux Klan Conspiracy and Southern Reconstruction.* New York: Harper, 1971.

Trevelyan, George Macaulay, *British History in the Nineteenth Century, 1791–1901.* London: Longmans, 1931.

Vaissière, Pierre de, *Saint-Domingue: La société et la vie créole sous L'Ancien Régime (1629–1789).* Paris: Perrin et Cie, 1909.

Vastey, Baron de, *An Essay on the Causes of the Revolution and Civil Wars of Hayti.* London: Western Luminary Office, 1823.

Waddell, David A. G., *The West Indies and the Guianas.* Englewood Cliffs, N. J.: Prentice-Hall, 1967.

Warwick, Charles, *Mirabeau and the French Revolution.* Philadelphia: Lippincott, 1905.

Waugh, Alec, *A Family of Islands.* Garden City, N. Y.: Doubleday, 1964.

Waxman, Percy, *The Black Napoleon.* New York: Harcourt, 1931.

West, Robert, and John Augelli, *Middle America: Its Lands and Peoples.* Englewood Cliffs, N. J.: Prentice-Hall, 1966.

Whitaker, Arthur P., *The Mississippi Question, 1795–1803: A Study in Trade, Politics, and Diplomacy.* New York: Appleton, 1934.

Zilversmit, Arthur, *The First Emancipation: The Abolition of Slavery in the North.* Chicago: Univ. of Chicago Press, 1967.

Articles

Bierck, Harold, "The Struggle for Abolition in Gran Colombia," *Hispanic American Historical Review* 33 (Aug. 1953), 365–86.

Brown, George W., "Haiti and the United States," *Journal of Negro History* 7 (April 1923), 134–52.

Corbitt, Duvon C., "Immigration in Cuba," *Hispanic American Historical Review* 22 (May 1942), 280–308.

Curtin, Philip D., "The Declaration of the Rights of Man in Saint-Domingue, 1788–1791," *Hispanic American Historic Review* 30 (May 1950), 157–75.

Davis, David B., "The Emergence of Immediatism in British and American Anti-Slavery Thought," *Mississippi Valley Historical Review* 49 (Sept. 1962), 209–30.

Debien, G., "Le Marronnage aux Antilles Françaises au XVIIIe Siècle," *Caribbean Studies* 6 (Oct. 1966), 3–43.

Erickson, Arvel, "Empire or Anarchy: The Jamaica Rebellion of 1865," *Journal of Negro History* 44 (April 1959), 99–122.

Goveia, Elsa V., "The West Indian Slave Laws of the Eighteenth Century," *Revista de ciencias sociales* 4 (March 1960), 75–105.

Himelhoch, Myra, "Frederick Douglass and Haiti's Môle St. Nicolas," *Journal of Negro History* 56 (July 1971), 161–80.

Jordan, Winthrop, "American Chiaroscuro: The Status and Definition of Mulattoes in the British Colonies," *William and Mary Quarterly*, 3d ser., 19 (April 1962), 183–200.

Lokke, Carl L., "Jefferson and the Leclerc Expedition," *American Historical Review* 33 (Jan. 1928), 322–28.

———, "The Leclerc Instructions," *Journal of Negro History* 10 (Jan. 1925), 80–98.

———, "Malouet and the St. Domingue Mulatto Question in 1793," *Journal of Negro History* 24 (Oct. 1939), 381–89.

———, "A Plot to Abduct Toussaint Louverture's Children," *Journal of Negro History* 21 (Jan. 1936), 47–51.

Lombardi, John, "Manumission, *Manumisos*, and *Aprendizaje* in Republican Venezuela," *Hispanic American Historical Review* 49 (Nov. 1963), 656–78.

Lowenthal, David, "Colonial Experiments in French Guiana," *Hispanic American Historical Review* 32 (Feb. 1952), 22–42.

Padgett, James A., "Diplomats to Haiti and their Diplomacy," *Journal of Negro History* 21 (July 1940), 265–330.

Pitman, Frank W., "Slavery on British West Indian Plantations in the Eighteenth Century," *Journal of Negro History* 11 (Oct. 1926), 610–17.

Schaeffer, Wendell, "The Delayed Cession of Spanish Santo Domingo to France, 1795–1801," *Hispanic American Historical Review* 29 (Feb. 1949), 46–68.

Index

Abergavenny, H. M. S., 101
Acquaire, M., 11
Agé, Adj. Gen., 117, 151
Ailhaud, Jean-Antoine, 65, 67
Alexis, Stephen, 205
Amiens, Treaty of, 141, 143, 150, 160, 180
Amis des Noirs, 21, 26–27 n.96, 29–32, 35, 37–40, 43 n.7, 65, 71, 82
Aponte, José Antonio, 194
Aradas, 13–14. *See also* Saint-Domingue
Arcy, Gouy d', 29
Arrault (agent of Toussaint), 115
Assembly of Notables (France), 28
Austria, 77

Ballou, Maturin, 201 n.15
Baptiste, John, 47, 49
Barbados, 196
Barbé-Marbois, François, 33
Barnave, Antoine Pierre Joseph Marie, 31–32, 35
Basle, Treaty of, 86, 116
Bastille, fall of, 30
Bâtiment d'État (ship), 114
Beaudierre, Ferrand de, 31
Beauharnais, Marquis de, 133
Beauvais, Louis, 51, 61 n.27
Becker, Gen., 120
Bélair, Charles, 58, 87, 158, 175
Bélair, Sanite, 175
Belley, Mars, 82
Biassou, 41, 56–58, 68, 79, 83, 125 n.94

Bickford (ship captain), 49
Black Jacobins (James), 199
Black Liberator (Alexis), 205
Black Patriot and Martyr (Griffiths), 205
Blake, Gen., 59
Blanchelande, Gov. (Saint-Domingue), 37–38, 51, 59, 65–66
Bolívar, Simón, 193–94
Bonaparte, Josephine, 141, 162 n.9
Bonaparte, Napoleon: decision of, to invade Saint-Domingue, 140–43; and the Directory's West Indian policy, 140; Egyptian failure of, 140; Latin American dictators and, 135 n.13; preparations by, to invade Saint-Domingue, 143–48; racial attitudes of, 144; and relationship with Toussaint, 115, 118, 140, 145; restoration of slavery by, 143–44, 184 n.32, 173–74; summary of the Saint-Domingue campaign of, 189; Toussaint compared with, 142–43
Bonaparte, Pauline, 148, 164–65 n.43, 185 n.41
Borgella, Bernard, 118
Bossu, Jean-Bernard, 10
Boudet, Gen. Jean, 147, 151, 153–54
Boukmann (black leader), 25 n.67, 47, 49
Bowyer, Maj. Gen., 92
Boyer, Gen. Pierre, 170, 173
Brawley, Benjamin, 197–98
Bréda plantation, 57–58, 131

Brienne, Loménie de, 28
Brisbane, Lt. Col. Thomas, 84–85
Brissot de Warville, Jacques Pierre, 21, 54, 82
Brunet, Gen., 171
buccaneers, 4–5
Bunel, Joseph, 132

Cambefort, Joseph-Paul, 66
Casalola (Spanish officer), 81
Castelar, Emilio, 195
Castro, Fidel, 200
Cathcart, Hugh, 114
Central Assembly (Saint-Domingue), 118–19, 134
Césaire, Aimé, 162 n.9, 199, 206
César, Philippe, 115
Chandler, David, 145
Chanlatte, Gen. Antoine, 116
Charming Sally (ship), 40
Chavannes, Marc, 36–37
Chevalerie, Bacon de la, 33
Chouans (France), 77
Christophe, Henry, 96 n.45, 112, 130–31, 133, 136 n.24, 148–49, 151–52, 158–59, 170, 175–76, 191, 201 n.17
Christophe: King of Haiti (Cole), 206
Churchill, Maj., 101–102
Citizen Toussaint (Korngold), 205
Claiborne, Gov. William (Louisiana), 195
Clairfontaine (*grand blanc* agent), 77
Clapham Sect, 20
Clarkson, Thomas, 19–20, 36
Clay, Henry, 201 n.23
Clement plantation, 47
Club Massiac, 31
Cocherel, Robert de, Marquis de Nicolas, 32
Code Noir (1685), 12, 15–16, 31
Colbert, Jean-Baptiste, 7
Cole, Hubert, 129, 136 n.24, 206

Colonial Assembly (Le Cap François), 52, 56–57, 66
Colonial Committee (France), 31
Colonial Committee (Saint-Domingue), 28, 30–31
Colons Américains, 29–30
Columbus, Christopher, 3, 4
Committee for the Abolition of the Slave Trade (England), 20
Committee of Public Safety (France), 69, 82
Congolese, 13–14. See also Saint-Domingue
Connecticut, U. S. S., 114
conquistadores, 4
Constitution of 1801 (Saint-Domingue), 118–20, 131, 134, 143
Constitution of 1826 (Bolivia), 193
Constitution of the Year VIII (France), 115, 125 n.80
Constitution of the Year III (France), 89, 125 n.80
Corrigole, Charles, 161
Council of Elders (France), 90
Council of Five Hundred (France), 89
Cour, Matbon de la, 17
Coutard (planter), 51, 55
Cowley, Malcolm, 14
Créole (ship), 172
Crête-à-Pierrot, siege of, 156–58
Cuba, 194–95
Cuba: The Pursuit of Freedom (Thomas), 206

Damask, Comte, 44 n.23
Darbois, Gen., 151
Davidson, Basil, 14, 42
Davidson (ship captain), 40
Debelle (French officer), 155
Decker (ship captain), 68
Declaration of the Rights of Man and the Citizen, 30–31, 41
Decrès, Denis, 144
Delaire, James, 41, 123 n.53

Desbureaux, Gen., 175
Desfourneaux, Gen., 98, 154
Desparbes, Gov. (Saint-Domingue),
  65–68
Dessalines, Jean Jacques, 58, 79, 87,
  112–16, 133–34, 149, 151–55, 157–
  58, 160, 169 n.107, 170, 172–73,
  175–76, 180–82, 189–92, 201 n.17
Dessources, Col., 102
Directory (France), 103–104, 106,
  109, 114–15, 125 n.88, 140
dokpwe, 14
Dominica, 46 n.67
Dominican Republic, 192–93
Douglass, Frederick, 197–98
Duare, Hector, 177
Duchillau, Le Comte, 8
Dudonait (black commander), 86
Dufay (agent of the National Con-
  vention), 82
Duluc (grand blanc agent), 77
Dundas, Henry, 76–77, 91
Dunham, Katherine, 192, 206
Duperier, Chevalier, 17, 48
Duvalier, François "Papa Doc," 191
Duvalier, Jean-Claude, 192

Edmundson, William, 19
Edwards, Bryan, 7
Effingham, Lord Gov. (Jamaica),
  52
Eggar (ship captain), 71
18 Fructidor, 90
élite, 191
Elkins, Stanley, 16
émigrés, 105–106, 131
Estates-General, 28–29
Estimé, Dumarsais, 192
Exclusive, theory of, 7–8
Eyre, Gov. Edward (Jamaica), 192

fermage, 130–31, 136 n.24
Ferrand, Gen. Marie-Louise, 182
First Coalition, 77

Flaville, Joseph, 87, 148–49
Flaville plantation, 47
Forbes, Gen. Gordon, 91–92
Forfait, Pierre, 115
Fort Bombardé, 92
Fort Borough, 100
Fort Dauphin, massacre of whites
  at, 82
Fort de Joux (France), 172
Fort Escahobe, 100
Fort Liberté, 107
Fortescue, John, 99 n.92
François, Jean, 41, 47, 56–58, 68, 79,
  82–83, 85–86, 125 n.24, 205
Freehling, William, 196, 206
Fressinet, Gen., 181

Gagnon (French officer), 68
Galbaud, Gen., 69–70
Galifauit plantation, 50
Gangé (black commander), 161
García y Moreno, Capt.-Gen. Joa-
  quín, 37, 79, 117–18, 125 n.94
Garden, Alexander, 54
Garvey, Marcus, 198
Garwin conspiracy, 195
General Greene, U. S. S., 114
Georges plantation, 171
Gherardi, Adm. Bancroft, 198
Gilles (black commander), 47, 49
Grant, Lt. Col. James, 92, 123 n.57
Great Britain: and Bonaparte's in-
  vasion of Saint-Domingue, 141–42;
  Dessalines and, 180; Haitian inde-
  pendence movement and, 119; in-
  vasion of Saint-Domingue by, 53;
  response to the Saint-Domingue
  slave rebellion by, 122–23; sum-
  mary of role in Saint-Domingue
  of, 189; treaty with Toussaint by,
  122–23 n.44
Grégoire, Abbé Henri, 39, 41, 81
Greyhound (ship), 59
Grinfield, Lt. Gen. William, 180

Guadeloupe, 6, 8, 39, 46 n.67, 77, 148, 174
Guingand, Noel, 161

Haitian People (Leyburn), 206
Hall, Gwendolyn, 205–206
Hamilton, Alexander, 95 n.21, 119, 126 n.102
Harcourt, Lord, 103
Harrison, Benjamin, 198
Hassal, Mary, 127, 170, 204
Hawkesbury, Lord Charles, 94–95 n.14
Heads of Regulations, 110
Hédouville, Théodore: mission of, 103, 139; and negotiations with Maitland, 103–104; return to France of, 108–109; Rigaud and, 106–107; and struggle with Toussaint, 105
Herold, J. Christopher, 144
Herskovits, Melville, 14
Histoire des deux Indies (Raynal), 20
History of the French Revolution (Lefebvre), 42
Hood, Com. Samuel, 180
Howard, Lt., 10, 18, 99 n.92, 100, 204
Huin (Toussaint's agent), 101, 103–104

Instructions of March 28 (1790), 28, 32, 36–37
Intermediate Commission (Saint-Domingue), 66
Island Possessed (Dunham), 206

Jacobin Club of Angers (France), 38
Jamaica, 12, 86, 105–106, 110, 142, 163 n.13, 182, 189, 192, 196
James, C. L. R., 10, 91, 95–96 n.22, 120 n.3, 136 n.24, 160, 166 n.61, 184–85 n.32, 199, 204

Jaucourt, Chevalier de, 20
Jefferson, Thomas, 120, 132, 162–63 n.12
Johnson, Samuel, 20
Jones, LeRoi, 200
Jumecourt, Humus de, 51, 55
Junta Cubana, 194

Kerversau, Gen., 116, 151
Korngold, Ralph, 96 n.39, 121 n.18, 159–60, 165 n.47, 205
Ku Klux Klan, 197

Labon, Jean-Baptiste, 148
Lacorunson, Thomas, 149
Lacrosse, Capt.-Gen., 148
La Diligente (ship), 114
Lafortune (black commander), 161
La Luzerne, Minister of Marine, 31
Lamartinière (black commander), 157–58
L'Amourdérance (black commander), 148–49
Laplume (black commander), 112, 150
Laporte-Lalanne, Jean-Baptiste, 6
La Roque (French officer), 57
Lartigne (Toussaint's mistress), 128
Latour plantation, 51
Laveaux, Gen. Etienne, 67, 73, 78–80, 83, 87–89, 91, 96–97 n.46, 130, 136 n.24, 204
Lear, Tobias, 128, 134, 152, 163 n.12
Leclerc, Gen. Charles Victor Emmanuel, 147, 150–54, 157–61, 164–65 n.43, 168 n.102, 169 n.107, 170–73, 176–77, 180, 185–86 n.41, 204
Leclerc, Pauline, 148
Lee, Charles, 123 n.55
Lee, Henry, 122 n.39
Lefebvre, Georges, 42, 165 n.47
Legislative Assembly (France), 62 n.44

Le Jeune case (1788), 16
Léogane Assembly (Saint-Domingue), 40
Léopard (ship), 35
Leveille, Barthélemy, 112
Leyburn, James, 206
Libertad, Bayon de, 131
López, Francisco Solano, 135 n.13
Loring, Capt. John, 182
Louis XIV (France), 5, 12
Louis XVI (France), 28, 41–42
Louverture, Isaac (son of Toussaint), 90, 147, 153
Louverture, Paul (brother of Toussaint), 118, 150, 152, 167 n.70, 183 n.10
Louverture, Placide (son of Toussaint), 90, 147, 153, 183 n.10
Louverture, Toussaint: campaigns of, against the British, 91–93, 100–105; character sketch of, 127–29; and the Constitution of 1801, 119–20; defection of, to the French, 82–83; deportation and death of, 171–72; guerrilla strategy of, 156, 158; joined the slave rebellion, 57–58; joined the Spanish, 68; and Leclerc conferences, 151–54; Moyse rebellion and, 148–50; and Napoleon Bonaparte compared, 142–43; Negro views of, 198–99; Paul Magloire's identification with, 192; reconstruction program of, 131–35; revolutionary role of, 189; Rigaud's defeat by, 106–16; Spanish Santo Domingo invaded by, 118; struggle of, with Sonthonax, 88–91; surrender of, to the French, 159–61; as a symbol for abolitionists, 196; and treaty with Great Britain, 104–105; U. S. policy of, 108–10; Villatte and, 87–88
Lyon, E. Wilson, 186 n.50

Macandal, François, 18
Macaya (black commander), 71, 74 n. 39
Magloire, Paul, 192
Magny (black commander), 156
Mainguy (*grand blanc* planter), 25 n.72
Maitland, Gen. Thomas, 93, 101, 103–107, 123–24 n.57, 141–42
Malta, 142, 163 n.16
Mannix, Daniel, 14
March Decree (1790), 32–33
maréchausée, 13
Markham, Felix, 165 n.47
maroons, 18
Martin, Augustin Du Bois, 9
Martinique, 6, 8, 35–36, 39, 44 n.23, 46 n.67, 77, 99 n.92
Mather (ship captain), 173
Mathieu, Gen., 140
Mauduit, Col. Antoine, 33–35, 37–38
Maurepas, Gen., 151, 153, 155, 157, 178
May Decree (1791), 39–40, 52, 54–55
Mayer, Jacob, 108
Meharon (Toussaint's agent to the National Convention), 87
Menou, Gen. Jacques-Abdallah, 141
Michel, Pierre, 112
Middle Passage, 14
Millet, Thomas, 34–35
Mills, Jean Baptiste, 82
Mirbeck (commissioner to Saint-Domingue), 55, 58, 60
Moline, Louis Nicolas, 112
Montalambert, Baron de, 78
Montarand, Couet de, 16
Montbrun, Gen., 78, 80
Montesquieu, Charles de Secondat, 19
Moreau de Saint-Méry, Medéric-Louis-Élie, 15, 17–18, 205
Mortefontaine, Treaty of, 119, 142
Mountain Blues, 52

Moyse, Gen., 58, 79, 87, 107, 118, 122 n.36, 148–50
Mulatto Question, 29, 31, 38

National Assembly (France), 29–33, 35–36, 38–40, 54–55, 62 n.44
National Association for the Advancement of Colored People (NAACP), 199
National Convention (France), 65–66, 69, 80–83, 87, 97–98 n.64
Nau, Jean David, 5
Negritude, 199
Nelson, Adm. Horatio, 139
Nerette, Gen., 178
Newton, John, 19
Newton, Thomas, 53
Nightengale (agent of Maitland), 101
Noé, Comte de, 57–58
Noé plantation, 47–48
Nullification Crisis (South Carolina), 196

Ogeron, Bertrand d', 4–5
Ogé, Vincent, 30, 36–38, 40, 71
"Old Sambo," guerrilla tactic of, 50–51

Panier, Jean, 161
Parker, Adm. Sir Hyde, 114
Paulinaire (rebel leader of Dominica), 46 n.67
Paul, Pierre, 112
Pebarte, Jean, 9
Pélage, Magloire, 148
Perkins, Samuel, 6, 17, 204
Perroud, Henri, 87
Perry, Raymond, 114
Pétion, Alexandre, 113, 147, 176, 193
Petit-Noel (black commander), 161, 176
Petrie (French consul at Charleston, S. C.), 36

Peynier, Gov. (Saint-Domingue), 29, 32, 35, 37
Phillips, Wendell, 196
Pickering, Timothy, 108, 123 n.53
Pinchinat, Pierre, 51, 61 n.27
Pinchon, Louis, 162 n.12
Pinckney, Gov. Charles (South Carolina), 53
Pitt, William, the Younger, 20, 58, 76–77, 91, 95 n.14
Polverel, Etienne, 65, 67, 69, 78, 97–98 n.64
Porter, Elias, 59
Prelude to the Civil War (Freehling), 206
Provincial Assembly of the North (Saint-Domingue), 36–37

Quasi-War, 119, 132, 189
Quentin, Gen., 173, 176, 178, 184–85 n.32

Raimond, Julien, 27 n.96, 30, 90, 98 n.64
Ravin-à-Couleuvre, Battle of, 155
Rawbell (Jacobin deputy), 39
Renaud (mulatto commander), 92
Repussard, Faustin, 175
Richepanse, Gen. Antoine, 148, 168 n.89
Rigaud, André, 51, 61 n.27, 72, 85–86, 88, 90–92, 98 n.77, 102–104, 106–16, 123–24 n.57, 143, 147
Riggs (ship captain), 112
Robespierre, Maximilien, 39, 82, 98 n.64
Rochambeau, Gen. Donatien, 147, 152, 155, 177–79, 181, 183 n.10, 186 n.42, 204
Roume, Philippe, 55, 58, 60, 98 n.64, 109, 116–18, 133, 143, 162 n.5, 204
Rousseau, Jean Jacques, 19
Rudé, George, 30
Ryswick, Treaty of, 5

Saint-Domingue: British trade interest in, 8; buccaneering in, 4–5; colonial administration in, 5–6; economic prosperity in, 6–7; French trade interest in, 6; geographic description of, 3–4; slave culture in, 14–15; slave resistance in, 18–21; social structure in, 9–19, 24 n.51 and n.59; Spanish trade interest in, 7–8; treatment of slaves in, 15–18, 25 n.72; U.S. trade interest in, 7–8
St. John (member of Commons), 93
Saint-Léger (French commissioner), 55, 58, 60
Saint Marc Colonial Assembly (Saint-Domingue), 33–35
Saint-Michel plantation, 57
Sally (ship), 68
Saloman, Louis-Félicité Lysius, 191
Santa Anna, Antonio López de, 135 n.13
Schoelcher, Victor, 197
Scylla (black commander), 161
"seasoning period," 14, 164
Sharp, Granville, 20
Simcoe, Lt. Gen. John, 92–93
slave rebellion, causes of, 40–42
Social Control in Plantation Societies (Hall), 205–206
Somerset case (1772), 20
Sonthonax, Léger Félicité: British and Spanish struggle with, 78–79; dictatorial authority established by, 66–68; Galbaud and, 69–71; recall in 1794 of, 80; reconstruction program of, 129–31; return to Saint-Domingue in 1796 by, 88; revolutionary importance of, 188–89; slave freedom and, 72; Toussaint's expulsion of, 88–91; treatment of whites by, 67
Soulouque, Faustin, 191
Spain, 53, 68, 77–83
Spencer, Second Earl of, 76

Stanislaus, François Alexandre, Baron de Wimpffen, 3–4, 15, 205
Stevens, Edward, 108, 111, 204
Stoddard, T. Lothrop, 18, 120 n.1, 131, 133, 197, 204
"Swiss, The," 51–52, 63 n.71

Talleyrand, Charles-Maurice de, 162–63 n.12
Tennis Court Oath (France), 29
Third Estate (France), 29
Thomas, Hugh, 206
Thompson, J. M., 139
Tobago, 77
Ton-Ton Macoute, 192
Touzard, Col. Louis, 49, 51
Trelease, Allen, 206
Trujillo, Rafael, 193
Turpin plantation, 47

United States: and Bonaparte's invasion of Saint-Domingue, 141–42, 162–63 n.12; and economic relations with Saint-Domingue, 130–32, 144–45; reaction to the slave rebellion by, 53–54; summary of role in Saint-Domingue, 189; treaty with Toussaint, 122–23 n.44, 123 n.53, 132; withdrawal of support from Toussaint, 119–20
Universal Negro Improvement Association, 198

Vaissière, Pierre de, 16–17, 205
Valabrègue (Toussaint's mistress), 128
Valemo, Alexis, 161
Varela y Morales, Félix, 194
Vaudreuil, Marquis de, 6
Vendée (France), 77
Vesey, Denmark, 195–96, 206
Villaret-Joyeuse, Adm., 147, 151
Villatte (mulatto commander), 83, 86–88

Vincent, Col., 91, 115, 130–31, 136 n.24

voodoo, 15, 18, 47, 128

War of Knives, 112–16

Wesley, John, 19

Whyte, Gen. John, 78, 81

Wickham (ship captain), 83

Wilberforce, William, 19–20

Williamson, Gen. Adam, 78

Windham, William, 77

Wood, James, 53

Wordsworth, William, 183 n.12

Zuzards, 63 n.71

The Haitian Revolution has been set on the Linotype in eleven-point Granjon. The display type used is Garamont, set by hand.

The book was designed by Jim Billingsley, composed and printed by Heritage Printers, Charlotte, North Carolina. The paper, bearing the watermark of the S. D. Warren Company, has been developed for an effective life of at least 300 years.

THE UNIVERSITY OF TENNESSEE PRESS : KNOXVILLE